NORTH CAROLINA
STATE BOARD OF COMMUNITY COLLEGES
LIBRARIES
CAPE FEAR COMMUNITY COLLEGE

Subject to Negotiation

Feminist Issues: Practice, Politics, Theory
ALISON BOOTH AND ANN LANE, EDITORS

Subject to Negotiation

READING FEMINIST CRITICISM AND
AMERICAN WOMEN'S FICTIONS

Elaine Neil Orr

University Press of Virginia
Charlottesville and London

The University Press of Virginia
© 1997 by the Rector and Visitors
of the University of Virginia
All rights reserved

Printed in the United States of America

First published 1997

∞ The paper used in this publication meets the minimum requirements
of the American National Standard for Information Sciences—
Permanence of Paper for Printed Library Materials, ANSI Z39.48-1984.

Library of Congress Cataloging-in-Publication Data
Orr, Elaine Neil.
    Subject to negotiation : reading feminist criticism and American women's fictions / Elaine Neil Orr.
        p. cm.—(Feminist issues (Charlottesville, Va.))
    Includes bibliographical references and index.
    ISBN 0-8139-1715-8 (cloth : alk. paper)
    1. American fiction—Women authors—History and criticism—Theory, etc. 2. Feminism and literature—United States. 3. Women and literature—United States. 4. Feminist literary criticism.
I. Title. II. Series.
PS374.W6077 1997
813.009'9287—dc21   96-44391
                                                                               CIP

For my parents,
who are at the heart of my feminism.

Contents

Preface   *ix*

Acknowledgments   *xv*

1
Negotiated Homelands:
The States of Feminist Reading   *1*

2
Negotiation Our Text:
The Search for Accommodations in Edith Wharton's
The House of Mirth   *27*

3
Our Confounded Identities:
Negotiating Audience in Zora Neale Hurston's
Their Eyes Were Watching God   *46*

4
The Character of Her Writing:
Eudora Welty's *The Optimist's Daughter* and the
Stories of Feminist Criticism   *67*

5
Sifting through Bags and Bones:
Practical Negotiations in Toni Morrison's
Song of Solomon   *85*

Contents

6
Negotiated Motherhood:
Contradictory Leanings in Marge Piercy's
Woman on the Edge of Time   105

Epilogue
Riparian Corridors and Other Progressive Middles:
New Directions for Feminist Criticism?   127

Notes   131

Index   145

Preface

Every form of criticism, like every form of discourse, is a social practice that can only be comprehended satisfactorily in terms of its effects.
—Giles Gunn

I FIRST BECAME INTERESTED in this project as a way of addressing what I felt were common realities for many junior feminist academics, primarily women, in the 1980s. We were, I thought, negotiating not only the traditional (white) male establishment but the power relations and theoretical challenges within feminism.[1] In our personal lives, many of us were choosing to have children and found our feminist mentors no more accommodating of this *diversion* than our male professors were. In the classroom, we were trying to strike a balance between students' apprehensions about feminism and our belief that feminist analysis would improve our lives. In an increasingly competitive job market, we were still expected to exercise feminist solidarity in the department, the college, the state. Within feminist theory and criticism, descriptions of ethnic and class difference made it increasingly difficult to write about *women* (since *woman* could hardly be defined).

Feminist intellectuals, I thought, should fashion a critical fiction that brought this lived reality to light. My experience suggested that feminist practitioners who live somewhere between obscurity and a tenure track job could ill afford to celebrate the models of marginality and subversion. Instead, we needed a critical model that emphasized coalition and difference in the light of the feminist ideals of inclusion and experimentation. To put this another way, I hoped for a theoretical framework that did not pull all figurative and literal grounds out from under us, one that allowed some space for us to work out the "insider/outsider" challenges of the day.

Nowhere did I feel this need more keenly than within feminist criticism. A brief chronicle of the stages of feminist criticism demonstrates our arrival in a period of complex and contentious pluralism. In the first stage of feminist criticism—beginning in the 1960s and extending into the 1970s—American academic feminists, building on the success of female consciousness-raising groups, focused on women's experience as an essential component of feminist theory in general and feminist literary criticism in particular. This first stage of feminist criticism sought to recuperate women as writers and to insert women as critics and professionals into university English departments; in other words, to achieve equality. Separate female canons were established and male writers were often critiqued for their images of women.

Second-wave feminist criticism of the early to late 1980s, influenced in part by the rise of *theory* in academe, repudiated the appeal to direct experience. While it often strove to identify the difference in women's writing, and thus effect a further subversion of masculinism, it also sought the *high* standards of dispassionate analysis. Thus a separate female or feminine enunciation and an ethics of feminist subversion provided a framework for the first and second stages in our field's development.

Since the late 1980s, the field has simultaneously become more heterogeneous and more established. In third stage feminist criticism, more critics are contesting to tell their stories and yet the coveted places in feminist scholarship (whether tenure track jobs or places on panels) are carefully regulated. Self-consciousness about ethnicity, for example, is a necessary posture in feminist criticism. Naive appeals to unmarked racial *experience*, on the other hand, are almost certain to be rejected.[2] But a third sort of option began emerging in the late 1980s, what I would call a negotiation of self-consciousness and experience. This practice—one shared by feminist writers as differently situated as Jane Tompkins, bell hooks, Gloria Anzaldúa, and Elizabeth Meese[3]—is exercised where critics write with an awareness of their construction in language and yet invest in personal narrative because it gives a somewhat reliable accounting of where they have been.

From these beginnings, my interest in this book has always been in the feminist subject's exercise of choice within limits, her (or his) productive use of the materials at hand in the light of a political commitment. My project addresses a tantalizing special paradox in feminist work: canny movement *within* limits as well as *expansion* of territory through crossings of antagonistic fields. This is, fundamentally, what I mean by negotiation. Like Nancy K. Miller, quoted in the book's epigraph, I have imagined feminist practitioners as nowhere at home but instead as always in the process of assembling a life and a landscape. But an unexamined edge to this critical image lies in the feminist writer's inescapable need for temporary housing, for some *accommodations*. If "negotiations between scenes of power" is at the heart of feminist difference, then feminist difference is acquired through the hinged gestures of concession and demand, resistance and cooperation, not through the purer political tactics of resistance or subversion alone.

Yet another edge to this perspective on feminist difference is that it exposes feminist collaborations in *othering*. In order to move between identities and locations, feminist practitioners act as if some "other" terms and identities are stable and predictable. Miller and I, for example, imagine someone on the mainland (male theorists?) and someone on the island (women outside the academy?). The way through this conundrum is not to refuse all identifications but to remember that the storytellers change and to prefer feminist fictions that allow slippage between one and the other, insider and outsider. In another feminist critic's telling, Nancy K. Miller may be on the mainland and I with her. What I hope to show in this book is that this conundrum provides the trouble and the wealth that keep feminist criticism politically and imaginatively viable. Like the feminist academic worker I imagined in my first paragraph, feminist criticism necessarily operates between scenes of power; it is therefore implicated in relations of power (it creates and uses others and selves); nonetheless it can expand the limits of literary investigation and produce shifts in power relations where it recognizes its own internal negotiations, its own necessary interest in dominant and subordinate locales, subjects, and languages.

To move beyond merely oppositional and concessional models of negotiation, *to use negotiation for feminist reading* requires that I define *negotiation* as precisely as possible. For my purposes, negotiation is first of all a name for the subject's construction of a self—and a politics and a text—through artful movements among discreet and even competing loyalties and laws. Negotiation also names a social practice between subjects who create noisy coalitions in order to make some moral progress in a socially uneven world. Finally, negotiation is an interpretive community's acceptance of impure grounds as a location out of which to evolve a more progressive politics.

In chapter 1, I demonstrate the emergence of *negotiation* in recent feminist theory and criticism (primarily American), recommending some related meanings that circulate around it. My theory of negotiation is exactly the opposite of a traditional legal view based in the image of two agonistic players, either of whom could take all of the winnings. This view, critically outlined by feminist lawyer Carrie Menkel-Meadow, derives from a "limited-pie" model of goods and an individualist model of human agency. The purpose of such negotiations is to meet, settle, and have done with it.[4] I prefer to think of negotiation as a rubric for life compositions that sustain difficult connections—between feminism and the academy, motherhood and writing, white identity and black theory—as a way of evolving a new sense of self and community. Negotiation creates changes of mind through non-ironic appeals to more than one *side*.

My model assumes Judith Butler's argument that "the culturally enmired subject negotiates its constructions, even when those constructions are the very predicates of its own identity."[5] While no position is free or pure, canny movement between unequal positions and utopian outposts may yield a difference in thought, in practice, in identity and knowledge. Feminist negotiations are undertaken in order to provide a certain play—a space for maneuvers of unequal forces—within the cultural worlds that women inhabit.[6] This definition implies a contiguous rather than a containing view of culture. Without dismissing the injustices of history, such a view reevaluates history from the position of those who are neither authorities nor authority's subject but somehow both. This view underlies the optimism in my project since it presumes that systems can be changed from within and between and that the agents of positive change are not necessarily pure and uncompromising.

My project as a whole shares in the effort of many feminist writers to move away from totalizing views of reality, language, and politics. Much like Laurie Finke, I ask "not only how science or literature might be changed by feminism but also how we might appropriate aspects of dominant discourses [for] . . . feminist theory."[7] I am assisted in my thinking by the inventive work of cross-disciplinary theorists such as Gloria Anzaldúa, Michel de Certeau, Ross Chambers, and Donna Haraway, all of whom prefer the impure, even go-between character of hybrid identities over pure genealogies. My maneuver is to graft theories of hybridity with feminist enunciations of negotiation in order to read the go-between subjectivities of American women's fiction and criticism. In Gloria Anzaldúa, Edith Wharton, and Wharton's heroine Lily Bart, for example, we find personal and political investment in both sides of a cultural contest: Mexican and American, housekeeping and writing, critical thinking and friendly encouragement. These generic, thematic, and discursive negotiations are manifested, I argue, through each subject's simultaneous commitment to this-world realities and other, better-world horizons.

Chapters 2 through 6 of this book suggest rather than demonstrate authoritatively a criticism of negotiation. They should be viewed as local applications of a negotiating criticism, not as essential components of a closed or finished argument. In composing this book, I have regarded contemporary American feminist criticism and American women's twentieth-century fiction as constituting analogous scenes of writing and power. By "American," I mean performed in North America, often with international accents. When I speak of *women's* fiction, I really mean *feminist*, though in the sense that I am evolving of a negotiating feminism. In each location—feminist criticism and women's feminist fiction—publishing writers work between and among competing social and discursive fields to enlarge the circle of agency. I choose to work out of women's fiction (just as I work out of feminist criticism) not to further encode *women's writing* but to assist in the production of a more complex American literature and a more heterogeneous feminist identity. The fictive texts I examine foreground mixed genealogies and progress within limits; thus they temper a separatist feminist identity at the same time that they open feminist criticism to negotiation. Methodologically, I negotiate gynocriticism and postmodernism, women's writing and the writing of women, by focusing on female-authored texts that conceive nontotalizing models for sexual/textual discussion. In this regard, I convey my belief that for now we need to negotiate identity politics and postmodern theory. The fictions I study move us in such a direction.

My technique for recognizing and explicating novels that are appropriately parsed by a theory of negotiation is less scientific than occasional. I did not read *x* number of novels and create a tropological menu of negotiations before I began writing. Nonetheless I do in chapter 1 locate narrative and rhetorical tropes that invite a feminist negotiating criticism. The critical peregrinations of each chapter advance and complicate my initial definitions.

Though the dangers in this project are many, I hope to contribute to a conversation that others will enliven and problematize, as indeed they already have: consider Michael Awkward's 1995 book, *Negotiating Difference*.[8] I am aware that in bringing negotiation to the center of feminist practice I assume a subject position which claims at least a modicum of agency and freedom. Some readers have cautioned that I may be defining negotiation too diffusely, thus privileging a term that I simultaneously allow too free a rein. Writing about recent efforts to codify Queer Theory, Lauren Berlant and Michael Warner remind us that readers do look for answers. In their words, "When a new thing emerges, people want to know how it is going to solve problems. When it is called theory, it is expected to produce a program."[9]

My aim is to suggest a "moving" and negotiating theoretical orientation for feminist literary criticism. Since I use Zora Neale Hurston and Toni Morrison in this study, it is clear that I view African-American literature as a likely space for critical negotiations. But I also wonder if more traditional fiction studies might be enhanced by negotiating criticisms. For example, Henry James's prose, it seems to me, would offer fecund territory for working out a negotiating logic. Such an operation would deepen an investigation of the generic qualities of negotiation and offer a new perspective for considering the gendering of the concept. The possibilities for negotiation are limitless and yet always, it seems to me, specific. Every negotiating practice will require clear definitions as well as specific statements of purpose, such as I hope to make clear in the next chapter.

Acknowledgments

I wish first to acknowledge and thank all of those feminist critics who go before me and make this book possible. I hope it is understood that even when I disagree with other critics' interpretations, I do so out of deep respect for their work.

For important encouragement during the early stages of this project—when I could not yet say what I meant by *negotiation*—I would like to thank Robert Detweiler, Anne Mellor, Karla Holloway, Elizabeth Meese, Laura Severin, Steve Katz, and Corinne Dale, as well as the National Endowment for the Humanities, which offered me a summer's support at UCLA in Anne Mellor's "Romanticism and Gender" Seminar. Among the warm and informative scholars I encountered there, I wish to thank Sharon Bassett, Renee Cox, Mitzi Meyers, and Chris Straayer. I also owe a special thanks to Carrie Menkel-Meadow at UCLA for talking with me about feminist legal negotiation.

My deepest debt is to Dale Bauer for tireless critical response during the years that I worked on *Subject to Negotiation*. Her enthusiasm was literally life sustaining. In addition, I am forever indebted to other readers along the way: to Lucinda MacKethan for commenting on drafts of chapters and always telling me to believe in myself; to Marianne Hirsch for meeting with me during her stay at the National Humanities Center, Research Triangle Park, and providing many comments in the margins as well as enlightening conversation. For salient response during the last revisions of the manuscript, I thank Andrea Atkin, who held me to the same standards of clarity and good argumentation that she holds her undergraduates.

I cannot say enough by way of thanks to my editor, Cathie Brettschneider, for her enthusiasm about this project. She would not let go of this book and negotiated its completion. My readers at the University Press of Virginia commented in extremely useful ways on the manuscript; I am grateful for their determination that I make this book the best possible. Adrienne Mayor provided valuable assistance as a trenchant copyeditor.

Acknowledgments

At North Carolina State University, I was supported by two research grants awarded through the College of Humanities and Social Sciences as well as by a research stipend administered by the Provost's Office. In particular, I would like to thank Michael Reynolds, CHASS Dean for Research, for his advocacy of my scholarship and his advice throughout my years as an assistant professor. I can say without hesitation that I could not have written this book without institutional support. I urge North Carolina State University to continue to fund young scholars, especially in the Humanities.

In addition to those named already, I would like to thank Jeff Richards, David Herman, and Robert Lane for supportive readings of grant proposals.

For technical support, I am grateful to David Covington, who put together the computer I needed (even though it was weird) and Elizabeth Lawrence, who typed and edited these chapters during various stages of the writing.

I have been sustained intellectually, politically, and emotionally by friends and colleagues old and new. I extend an affectionate thanks to Robanna Knott, Deborah Hooker, Maria Pramaggiori, Jim Morrison, Jon Thompson, Eyal Amiran, Sharon Setzer, Judy Small, Christine Pierce, Walt Wolfram, Janice Odom, and Lynn Rhodes.

Finally, there is the reference librarian at the Cameron Village Public Library in Raleigh, North Carolina, who excavated her attic to find her personal, first-edition copy of *Woman on the Edge of Time*. Thanks too to the generous-spirited reference librarians at North Carolina State University who tracked down numerous references over the phone.

I am grateful to my students at North Carolina State University for keeping me focused on the classroom, a space I love and cannot do without and for challenging me to be as good as my word.

For good humor in abundance and for the best company in town, I extend hearty thanks to my son, Joel Orr. For steadfastness and equipoise, I am grateful to my husband, Andy Orr. My sweet family, Anne and Lloyd Neil, Becky, Bob, Neil, and Anne Albritton, keep me company even when I stubbornly refuse to be sociable. My thanks to all of them for loving me through this project.

I dedicate this book to my mother and father because they taught me to think broadly and to follow through.

An early and different version of chapter 2 appeared in *Modern Language Quarterly* ("Contractual Law, Relational Whisper: A Reading of Edith

Acknowledgments

Wharton's *The House of Mirth*," *MLQ* 52.1 (1991); an earlier version of chapter 6 appeared in *Journal of Narrative Technique* ("Mothering as Good Fiction: Instances from Marge Piercy's *Woman on the Edge of Time*," *JNT* 23 (1993). My thanks to the editors and review readers of both journals, especially Paul Bruss, for critical encouragement during early stages of this project. Their faith in my writing made all the difference.

> *We have acquired the freedom to move between the island and the mainland: we can leave and return, and we do. Indeed the definition of feminist difference historically has been bound up with this movement between identities and locations; with the negotiations between scenes of power.*
>
> —Nancy K. Miller

> *Whether she turns the inside out or the outside in, she is, like the two sides of a coin, the same impure, both-in-one insider/outsider.*
>
> —Trinh T. Minh-Ha

> *I'm between.*
>
> —Susan Rubin Suleiman

Subject to Negotiation

1

Negotiated Homelands
The States of Feminist Reading

We feminists have come to the same conclusion by a different route: after the euphoric mirage of sisterhood as sameness and unity, we have learned that deep differences among women can make solidarity complicated. . . . But . . . we may learn to cherish difference as a source of enrichment. . . . Not that appreciation of diversity can wish away real conflicts. But it can at least suggest ways of arguing that negotiate the "either/or" impasse, by not insisting on simply winning out over the opposite point of view.
—Jerry Aline Flieger

My principal aim is not to separate but to connect, and I am interested in this for the main philosophical and methodological reason that cultural forms are hybrid, mixed, impure, and the time has come in cultural analysis to reconnect their analysis with their actuality.
—Edward Said

Although the film [The Color Purple] is a patriarchal text, its black viewers found ways to empower themselves through their negotiated reception of it.
—Jacqueline Bobo

CAN FEMINIST PRACTITIONERS negotiate without becoming the negotiated term, without being compromised? Is it possible, for example, for feminist readers to give and take with other critical schools while resisting the structures that make *woman* the object of exchange? And if a clear demarcation between *negotiating* and *being negotiated* is not possible, must feminist criticism remain otherwise confined to an oppositional politics and discourse?

Within feminist interpretation, negotiation suffers a peculiar eclipsing. Frequently deployed, it is nonetheless strangely ignored as an interpretive model. Where the metaphors of dominance, containment, and subversion

Negotiated Homelands

meet manifold unfoldings, negotiation meets silence. It is often hinted at, especially in those metacritical moments when scholars reflect on their writing, but in ominous ways. Elaine Showalter, for example, wonders what will become "the distinguishing idiom or role of the black or feminist critic. . . . *Can we make the compromises* necessary for acceptance by the mainstream, and still work for a criticism of our own?" (emphasis added).[1] The subtext of Showalter's sentence—negotiations with mainstream and/or white or masculinist criticism—is ruefully acknowledged, but the assumption seems to be that such practices will only compromise the black and feminist critic, not that multiple crossings may yield the difference that makes a criticism "our own."

I aim to contribute in this book to a progressive shift in feminist discourse: from a criticism of subversions—the dominant mode of American feminist criticism from Judith Fetterley's *The Resisting Reader* to Alicia Ostriker's poetics of theft—to a criticism of negotiations, a form of work that emerges where feminist readers and intellectuals argue for productive relations at the crossroads of difference and opposition.[2] Noting this shift in other critics' work, I redress a lacuna in feminist interpretation by enunciating a negotiating poetics. In this interest, I offer three critical fictions: first of all, that feminist readers are positioned as negotiating subjects between and among the demanding sites of feminism and a number of other theoretical schools; second, that the writers I study occupy culturally liminal positions and must negotiate their aesthetic visions against their actual world limits;[3] third, that these writers represent their own negotiations of authority and history through their characters' canny oscillations between and across contested political and historical lines. My fictions reorganize the plot of feminist criticism by imagining that the metaphors of *subversion* and *separatism* are subsets of *negotiation*. In my narrative, what comes first is the situation of insider/outsider and crossed loyalties. Thus separatism may be a strategy of negotiation, much like the bus boycotts led by Martin Luther King during the civil rights movement of the 1960s. Such a tactic may operate to subvert the status quo. But only momentarily. The point is to get back on the bus and to choose one's seating here and elsewhere. Thus my negotiating fictions are not meant to replace separatist and subversive feminist modes of reading but to recast them within a larger frame.

Now more than ever, negotiating theories and practices are necessary tools for a feminist politics of reading. Coming from different directions and borders, feminist critics speak less of *female*, or *black*, or *lesbian* identity and instead coin phrases such as "oscillating identities," "multiple angles of vision," "crosshatched subjectivity." These new metaphors signify an increasing disenchantment with what Gloria Anzaldúa calls "the counter-stance" and what Elizabeth Meese calls "Feminist Literary Criticism as institutional discourse."[4] They also register what Adrienne Rich has called a "wild patience," a faith in feminist women's ability to transform language and culture through daily negotiations between "scenes of power."[5] But these multiple names within and around feminist discourse also threaten to fragment feminist conversation or to deflect feminist argument through discursive imprecision. As Jerry Aline Flieger cautions: "We feminists are perhaps more divided than ever—by issues of race and sexuality, by questions of strategy, by theoretical issues around difference and equality, by disagreements concerning the efficacy of theory to help us get where we're going."[6] This book seeks to identify and define negotiating modalities in feminist criticism in order to think with some precision about proliferating choices among feminist practitioners. Tracing the contours of a negotiating criticism, my proposal is not simply that feminist critics need to negotiate. Instead I argue that discursive negotiations already construct feminist rhetoric as well as feminist reason and feminist ethics. A critical fiction of negotiation will affirm a likeness in feminist interpretive work—our thinking between contentious locations which we do not "give up" or "give up on"—and provide some grounds for commonality in our methods if not in our histories and identities. In other words, *what* we negotiate may differ but negotiating operations in our written work provide a feminist epistemological connection.

To trace the motifs of a negotiating mode of criticism, I turn to American women's fiction. It should not surprise us to find a strong negotiating sensibility in American women writers of the twentieth century. What comes as a surprise is how silent feminist critics have been about this sensibility. Negotiating the demands of white middle-class mores and black historical experiences has always shaped the inscription of African-American women's texts. Some white female authors early in the twentieth century turned briefly to the stark poetics of the heroine's death, but even in Edith Wharton's *The House of Mirth*, this drama is achieved through formal and thematic negotiations. Simultaneously accommodating cultural context and making a bid for feminist revision, the writers in my study are in many ways more moderate than their male counterparts: consider Zora Neale Hurston and Richard Wright. But Hurston's politics is too accommodating only if one imagines oneself on one or the other side of the black/white divide. The key to understanding the poetics and politics of many American women's texts, I argue, is to occupy the insider/outsider, "both/and" location of the go-between subject who knows that her survival—and her progeny's—depends on the negotiation of opposing positions. What may appear in one light as a timid or underdeveloped feminism may, in this light, reappear as a more complex, more advanced feminist method.

Indeed, the novels I read in the following chapters dramatize the go-between thinking of hybrid subjects. In other words, they feature protagonists who are systematically positioned on more than one side of the fiction's sexual/textual politics. For example, Laurel McKelva in Eudora Welty's *The Optimist's Daughter* sides sympathetically with her father (the patriarch) as well as with her mother (a character whose identity is always ancillary). Janie, in Hurston's *Their Eyes Were Watching God*, exercises the masculine prerogative of finding herself through sexual exploits but is also the victim of domestic violence. Lily Bart, Wharton's heroine in *The House of Mirth*, expresses a morally mixed desire to establish a relatively free life. Like many feminist academics, she wants financial security (which depends on male support) at the same time that she wants to shift male/female relations from the axis of sex and exchange to the axis of friendship and loyalty.

But who is helped by Lily's insistence on "accommodations?" That may be the crucial question in naming and advancing a feminist negotiating criticism. Whose utopian visions are brought closer to reality in our negotiations of self and text? This book is written in the interest of that question and on behalf of the negotiating character of feminist criticism.

Deploying Negotiation in Feminist Criticism

The patriarchal bias in literary criticism led feminist critics of the 1970s and 1980s to prefer an oppositional poetics. For many, the possibility of *women's voice* seemed to reside in textual subversions and cultural separations.[7] Until recently, the metaphor of negotiation received little positive attention, perhaps because theories of cultural hegemony (whether male or white or heterosexual) have been so persuasively demonstrated. In addition, we continue to be influenced by deeply entrenched ethical frameworks that favor purity over mixed forms. Even where *margins* and *marginality* have been the metaphors of choice, the dream of a "wild zone" or separate voice—and the idea that (white) patriarchy denied both—have acted as shaping principles. But more recent American feminist criticism tells a different story of women's writing. This story accepts the reality of limits and advances the idea of working between dominant and marginal systems through simultaneous acts of accommodation and critique. To organize this story, I have chosen the metaphor of negotiation. To my mind, no other word so fully explains the dialogics and dissonances of feminist criticism and American women's fiction.

The appearance of negotiation as a term in recent criticism suggests as much. In reviewing these deployments of negotiation, my purpose is not to erase the significant differences between practitioners. As we will see, each critical writer's staging of the term is occasioned by her particular context. I selected certain critics because of the degree of self-consciousness that accompanies their use of negotiation and because they sustain the term in their own riffling over the politics of feminist reading. Clearly, I have not sought to be exhaustive. Several of the critical texts that I examine appeared between 1989 and 1993 (Meese, Miller, Spivak, Flieger, and Snitow), suggesting the emergence of a third stage of feminist criticism. These practitioners draw from the larger body of feminist theory. Indeed, their writing can be viewed as exemplary of two notable shifts in feminist discourse beginning in the 1980s. On the one hand, Elizabeth Meese and Nancy K. Miller are influenced by deconstructive techniques that explore the "gap" or the "between" in order to interrogate reigning binaries. Gayatri Spivak's work is also influenced by deconstruction but emerges as well from the race, class, gender thinking of recent years, beginning with a recognition of recalcitrant differences among women. Jerry Aline Flieger and Ann Snitow canvas both of these shifts and demonstrate a wish to get past the political impasse of strict identity politics.

In *(Ex)tensions: Re-figuring Feminist Criticism* (1990), Elizabeth Meese hopes for a "theory and practice of nonhegemonic, negotiating feminism."[8] But what does she mean to imply by "negotiating" and/or what images and arrangements are implied by her usage? In a chapter on Adrienne Rich titled "Negotiating the Metalogic," Meese charts the poet's "kaleidoscopic positioning and repositioning as thinking, feeling, and writing subject." Among these positionings and repositionings, "Rich negotiates the tension between the exclusion of the masculine" and "the more pragmatic need for . . . negotiated coexistence" between male and female. Like Nancy K. Miller, who figures feminist difference as acquired through movement between central and marginal positions (quoted in my preface), Meese's usage conjures an individual shuttling between two points on a political continuum, one more conciliatory (or accommodating), one more radical (or separatist).[9] To be more precise, Meese represents Rich as always engaged in a series of overlapping negotiations, "negotiating" coexistence with men and maleness, for example, but also negotiating between that project and a more separatist feminist poetics.

Furthermore, Meese's usage recommends the modality of negotiation to describe feminist positioning and repositioning *within* feminism as well as *between* feminism and other criticisms, politics, and identities. Both Miller and Meese deploy negotiation evaluatively, suggesting the usefulness of this metaphor which legitimates the often polarized strategies of accommodation *and* resistance.

Elsewhere in *(Ex)tensions*, Meese goes further, suggesting that a negotiating feminist poetics will, among other things, make us cognizant of our own uses of others. She writes, "There can be no interplay (an unexplored potential of the 'double agent' or 'go-between' as shuttle) between feminist literary criticism and [other criticisms] . . . if feminist criticism refuses to be as accommodating as it asks deconstruction to be or if feminist criticism installs itself in a position of denial, refusing to explore the repression it works in the interest of securing its difference."[10] Meese chooses decidedly dangerous imagery—since "go-between" and "shuttle" both risk a return to the female as sexual accomplice. But Meese's point is that feminism may already be an accomplice in *other* repressions. Picturing the feminist critic as go-between, Meese here confirms the imagery put in play by Miller. Negotiation is imagined as a feminist intellectual's movement between opposing or unequal positions, both of which she owes something to. More accurately, Meese pictures a community of writers ("feminist criticism"), and not just the individual critic, as gaining volume and substance through coalition and critique. Thus feminist writers do not visit the mainland (deconstruction, the academy, the canon) merely to resist and oppose. They visit to appropriate, to borrow, perhaps even to solicit comfort or acquire backing. Meese suggests that feminist negotiations with dominant politics and poetics are both chosen and imposed. Feminist critics cannot deny that they are shaped by the critical contexts and national histories that touch their work. But they can make some choices about the *use* they will make of those influences and of the spaces they allow.

Ann Snitow's use of negotiation in her 1990 essay, "A Gender Diary," produces an imaginary landscape much like Meese's and Miller's. It is worth quoting Snitow at length:

> Feminism is inevitably a mixed form, requiring in its very nature . . . inconsistencies. In what follows I try to show first, that a common divide keeps forming in both feminist thought and action between the need to build the identity "woman" and give it solid political meaning and the need to tear down the very category "woman" and dismantle its all-too-solid history. . . . Second, I argue that although a settled com-

> promise between these positions is currently impossible, and though a constant choosing of sides is tactically unavoidable, feminists—and indeed most women—live in a complex relationship to this central feminist divide. From moment to moment we perform subtle psychological and social negotiations about just how gendered we choose to be.[11]

More than Meese or Miller, Snitow envisions negotiation as an externalized or open discussion between feminists who have chosen "sides." Her usage presages the negotiations between characters that I analyze in the following chapters. At the same time, Snitow makes the same critical move that Meese and Miller enact, transferring the practice of external negotiations—where one might take a "stand," onto the self—who sides with more than one position. In observing that feminist workers negotiate gender on a day-to-day basis, Snitow uses negotiation to represent the internalization of an outer oscillation between various positions on the social map of gender (whatever that may be in any particular person's context). What I find most intriguing about Snitow's last sentence is the phrase "just how gendered we choose to be." The feminist trope of *choice* appears to dominate Snitow's sentence, but the limit that underlies this phrasing is the unavoidable situation of negotiating gender. No one can step off the gender map, as Snitow makes clear with the words "just *how* gendered we choose to be" (emphasis added).

As with Meese and Miller, then, Snitow's negotiation suggests a critical juxtapositioning of feminist goals and the daily realities of a historically oppressive gender system *in the thinking* of feminist practitioners. Rather than a frontal assault on gender, this description supposes working alongside or within some of the motifs of gender identification in order to create a space for influencing change. But this negotiation of one obstacle or area of conflict is bordered by another area of interest and contention. One does not merely negotiate gender, one negotiates gender *as a feminist*, the last phrase also indicating a space of debate and multiple sides. Along these lines, Snitow's observation structures "most women's" worlds in the way Sara Ruddick describes "maternal thinking," as inflected by multiple interests which are always themselves sites of flux and argument. Writing in the field of philosophy rather than literary criticism or feminist theory per se, Ruddick imagines mothers "negotiating with nature on behalf of love, harassed by daily demands, yet glimpsing larger questions."[12] What Ruddick's vignette adds to the negotiated landscapes imagined by Meese, Miller, and Snitow is a glimpse of the reasoning and ethics behind many women's and many feminists' negotiations: the acceptance of responsibility for another person, a community, and/or a view of oneself as never entirely separate and free. While this reality is not directly foregrounded in the passages excerpted from Meese, Miller, and Snitow, it is often articulated in their work. In Snitow, for example, the motivation for tracing feminist conflicts begins with a conversation with a friend, one who experienced consciousness-raising in ways exactly opposite from Snitow. Meese defines Rich's feminism in terms of her transgression of personal boundaries and her poetic experimentation on behalf of other women.

This reasoning in feminism—the always necessary but nonetheless complex link between the personal and the poetical, the personal and the political—clarifies these writers' deployment of negotiation as a term, as a metaphor. In a straightforward way, negotiation stands for external, actual world practices of contentious dialogue on the subjects of canon formation, theory and feminism, and the usefulness of deconstruction. On the other hand, negotiation stands for tactical *and* heartfelt oscillations "between reasons," for *thinking* through one's interests in multiple identities and relationships.

Negotiating practices in the external world become for feminist readers a form of logic, an exercise in ethical reasoning. Gayatri Spivak's very intentional use of negotiation in her essay "Feminism and Deconstruction, Again: Negotiating with Unacknowledged Masculinism" (1989) illustrates this practical/theoretical link. Her primary argument is for feminist uses of deconstruction "without giving [deconstruction] up."[13] She calls this proposal "a more charitable position on the usefulness of deconstruction for feminism than I have supported in the past. . . . a negotiation and an acknowledgement of complicity." Going on, she tells her reader that the essay "is a result of my recent teaching stint in India, which persuaded me that the indigenous elite must come to terms with its unacknowledged complicity with the culture of imperialism."[14] Like the critics and theorists reviewed earlier, Spivak employs negotiation as a necessary modality in feminism because feminism itself is contradictorily situated: of Indian origin, Spivak is a female member of the cultural elite, teaching sometimes in India and sometimes in the United States and writing about the "female subaltern." Her actual world travels elicit her negotiated thinking.

The most obvious feminist tactic evoked by Spivak's negotiations is externalized or public borrowings from other criticisms. But Spivak, like Meese, does not imagine a pure or unfettered feminist critic who occasionally makes a foray into the alien and corrupting territory of masculinist theory. Instead, Spivak recognizes her complicity with colonialist and masculinist arrangements before, during, and after any visitation with deconstruction. Thus Spivak's effort to theorize feminist negotiation with deconstruction is situated in personal and internal operations of accommodation and critique. As long as she is a member of the cultural elite, her work is "limited." But if she were not so limited, she could not write academic feminism.

If the broadest definition of negotiation is choosing and working within limits—creating from among imperfect scenes and tools—what Spivak shows us is that *a chosen and imposed* limit to her feminism is her location, at times, in places of cultural privilege. If we go back to my own beginnings—the feminist academic who lives somewhere between obscurity and a tenure track job—this limit is one that most of us aspire to. In this sense, feminist academics cannot escape their negotiations. This is what Spivak's essay confesses—but not in order to forget the workings of sexist discourse. Indeed she wants to "make clear how crucial it is not to ignore the powerful currents of European anti-humanist thought that influence us, yet not to excuse them of their masculinism while using them. This is what [Spivak is] calling 'negotiation.'"[15] Writing for a feminist audience, Spivak self-consciously formulates negotiation as a name for using prejudicial, even sexist material positively, without irony. She goes on to enact a negotiating reading by setting aside her earlier opposition to Jacques Derrida (his use of *woman* as a sign of indeterminacy) and using Derrida to define her own impure, but nonetheless antisexist, practice. Writing on Nietzsche, Derrida suggests that the reader should not excuse his texts for their use by the Nazis. Instead, Nietzsche's texts should be seen as available to that appropriation. This acknowledgment can then be followed by a reading from within the text, which, in Spivak's words, opens it up "towards an as yet unknown horizon so that it can be of use without excuse." "Let us," she says, "call this: negotiating with structures of violence. It is in that spirit of negotiation that I propose to give assent to Derrida's text about woman as a name for the non-truth of truth."[16]

Moving from Derrida's maneuver within Nietzsche to her own scene of writing, Spivak represents negotiation in the most dangerous way yet and places herself squarely in that praxis. Indeed, she supplies another example of negotiation within negotiation. On the one hand, her text negotiates Derrida and Nietzsche by "resting" the case against them and working nonironically "on their side," out of their texts. At the same time, she negotiates the limit of her own politics, theorizing the disenfranchised women of India (whom she names "gendered subalterns") *from her location* as an academic in elite Indian universities. Thus she recognizes that hers is also a text of violence; she allows Derrida his use of *woman* and in the same move names a woman who cannot speak in Spivak's place. But she does so in the hope that this situation of naming the disenfranchised woman will end. Spivak's acknowledgment of complicity *as she continues to write* demonstrates her belief that impure textual politics may yet influence change in the right direction. It begins to appear that negotiation, far from an enforced practice, is an achieved possibility in criticism and theory.

Here it is useful to return to Meese and her reading of Spivak. As Meese remarks, "Feminism's double bind is that it cannot speak 'for' other women, nor can it speak 'without' or 'apart from' other women."[17] She argues that feminism must create spaces for women who are not white and middle class, Anglo or European, to speak and write. My chapters on Zora Neale Hurston and Marge Piercy demonstrate how American women's fiction anticipates this need. Meese goes on, quoting Spivak: "'However unfeasible and inefficient it may sound, I see no way to avoid insisting that there has to be a simultaneous other focus: not merely who am I? but who is the other woman? How am I naming her? How does she name me?'" In her own words, Meese concludes that in this double step—"who am I? who is she?—Spivak's questions point us in the direction of negotiating mutual respect across boundaries."[18] In this discussion, Meese reverses her exterior/interior imaging of negotiation. Earlier, I showed that Meese and others represent the internal nature of feminist negotiation—our difference within. But Meese and Spivak also argue for new, external displays of feminist/women negotiation. Both critics are keenly aware of the power imbalance that exists between academic feminists and many of the women feminism theorizes. And yet—"however unfeasible and inefficient it may sound," they argue in favor of this "double step": looking at the self/looking at the other; speaking from one's position/inviting speech from other positions. This double step is not imagined as leading ultimately to synthesis but to more respect, to more accurate knowledge, about ourselves and about others.

Jerry Aline Flieger describes poststructuralist interpretation as I would define the critical mode of negotiation. Like "all good theory," she says, it "crosses the bar . . . between two apparently unlike terms, making a connection that manages to include them both, even while gaining in force from a maintained tension between the terms."[19] And yet, what all of these critics simultaneously provide and miss in their own writing is the metaphorical device of negotiation. Although Meese, Snitow, and Spivak appear to be self-conscious in their use of the term, none of these critics spells out a negotiating criticism. What they do provide—taken together—is material for a working map, for plotting negotiation as a concept and modality in criticism. My hope in the following chapters is to demonstrate a

The States of Feminist Reading

number of ways that negotiation can be read in American women's fiction as well as a number of ways that these fictions reread the negotiations in feminist criticism.

Let me elaborate on the various images and motifs that have circulated in these critical examples thus far. First of all, it is clear that these writers use negotiation to name a strenuous form of feminist work. What negotiation *is not* for Meese, Snitow, and Spivak is mere capitulation to the center, mere accommodation and concession. The imagined scenes of negotiation differ, but all three imply a view of negotiation as both an external, political practice, within feminism and between feminism and other schools, and as an internal, moral practice, a movement and conversation *within the practitioner* who desires a better world for women while recognizing the limits of her politics and the imperfect choices before her. Thus the situation of negotiating grounds one epistemologically—one is always related to other subjects and not just in the interest of self-enhancing exchange, a scenario that always reduces other subjects to objects. Instead, negotiating as a state of being and knowing leads to a recognition of otherness within and of selfhood in others. Whether external or internal, negotiation as a thinking process is accomplished through analytical sifting and juxtapositioning. Even when negotiations are imagined as external and participants are thought to choose sides, these critics argue for the simultaneous work of identifying some common situations, tasks, and modes of thinking that connect feminist and feminist, feminist and other workers. Where negotiation is plotted on an internal landscape, the poet-critic is herself the scene of these juxtapositions or "sidings." Her own life is both subject and object of feminist negotiations. What qualifies these negotiations as feminist is not the worker's uncompromising commitment to one utopian program or goal but her commitment to improving women's lives by tangling with all sorts of corrupt and imperfect systems in light of a utopian ideal.

The one tactic these critics avoid is systematic denial of *any* value or good in other positions. That violence can only lead to forgetfulness: of one's own limits and complicities. If feminist negotiation is a more moderate, more patient program than cultural subversion or separatism, these critics suggest that it may also provide a closer analogy for most women's lives, reconnecting analysis with actuality.

To further describe what negotiation denotes for these critics, we might turn to their tone. Though each argument originates on women's sides, these writers do not imagine a pure position. Instead, they demonstrate Donna Haraway's claim that "the standpoints of the subjugated are not 'innocent.'"[20] If we were to say that all positions originate in negotiation, we would mean by that—drawing from these writers—that all positions are already touched by the instruments of power. This recognition, however, is coupled with a view of the self as capable of shifting power relations somewhat. Thus a self-reflexive faith marks these critics' voices. What makes their uses of negotiation more than another name for savvy appropriations—the subordinate's ability to use the master's tools to dismantle the master's house—is that they argue against the vertical plot of dismantling (where things high are brought low), or even of deconstruction and reconstruction. Instead, they sound a narrative of horizontal relays between positions in order to enlarge some in-between areas on the social maps of gender, class, race, and sexuality. Thus, they risk scenes in which the feminist worker or mother or woman sometimes stands on the opposition's side and not just in a posture of irony.[21] Meese's use of the phrase "negotiated coexistence" suggests the possibility of a working relation that is more than a mere marking of time until the opposition crumbles. Because the selves of these critical texts recognize their own otherness, they rethink the possibility of victory over the opponent, even the possibility of bargaining at the other's expense.

Indeed, negotiation in all of these cases assumes a subject or subjects who belong on more than one side. One's interest is not located in one but in many, often antagonistically arranged, places. Insofar as these critics do choose a side, then, it is with other feminist women whose contradictory commitments make it impossible to abandon the (master's) house, sometimes literally (the slave narrative of Harriet Jacobs comes to mind). The logic of this subject's negotiations is neither winning (more) or saving (what little one has). Instead, this subject's logic is directed by the need to enlarge the space or territory habitable by women. This does not necessarily mean taking space *from* but opening space *to*.

Beginning with Miller, all of these critics remark on feminist negotiation as movement. Unified placement—even on the margin—is rejected in favor of multiple locations and dislocations. But it is the movement itself, the crossing back and forth, that allows the practitioner a different view. On the one hand, these deployments represent the feminist poet-critic as a player who moves from location to location. On the other hand, she (or sometimes he) is the place through which ideas, politics, and identities move and find expression. In other words, because feminist critical negotiations are internal, even the places feminist subjects oppose move within them. The figures of shuttle and go-between, are not, then, provisions for a balancing act. Instead, they suggest tangling, argument, dancelike improvisations.

The States of Feminist Reading

Yet another structuring element in these negotiations is self-conscious *setting aside*, an operation that results in certain generosities. The generosity Spivak extends to Derrida, for example, circles back to her own scene of writing, momentarily allowing her reprieve (from the immobility of constant apology) and providing her the space of composition. If negotiation is preferred by these writers to compromise or separatism, it may well be because negotiation allows the double opportunities of rest and movement, collaboration and critique. The decidedly dangerous *side* allowed by this modality is the other's need for accommodation. Thus a risky generosity accompanies negotiating operations both within feminism and between feminism and other criticisms.

Negotiation as a term emerges from these scenes of writing as a personal and political mode of attending to numerous, contentious interests and concerns. Whichever comes first, the personal or the political, negotiation names a form of thinking, a philosophy. Its methodology is one of recycling rather than overturning—Meese and Flieger, for example, risk the use of shuttle and go-between—while its tools are double voice, setting aside, appropriation, accommodation, juxtaposition, and annexation.

Finally, all of these negotiations assume a utopian horizon. Spivak, for example, closes her essay thus: "Today, here, what I call the 'gendered subaltern,' especially in decolonized space, has become the name 'woman' for me. In search of irreducibles, after the chastening experience of coming close to the person who provides that imagined name, I want to be able not to lament when the material possibility for the name disappears."[22] Anticipating a time when "the material possibility" of naming the subaltern disappears, Spivak seems to point to a radically altered future, in which Third World laborers are not in thrall to First World markets and (as a consequence) not only world economies but academic institutions are radically reorganized. Thus negotiation is always motivated by the hope of a nonsexist, nonracist, nonimperialist world.

Having worked through these recent deployments of negotiation in feminist writing, I propose that we call *negotiating* the process of working between authorities, histories, and disciplines, where sides are not equal but neither are they simply opposed. Instead, a subject makes use of conflicting and imperfect cultural fields through simultaneous acts of discrimination and new conjunction. Without giving up her multiple affiliations, this worker assembles a space for influencing the course of change. In this mode of production, writers (one kind of feminist worker) do not trade *this* for *that*—feminist for womanist (Alice Walker's term for black feminist), heterosexual for lesbian, even masculinist for feminist—but instead allow their voices to be the space of argument and coalition in the interest of less oppressive, more female-loving systems. Exemplifying this worker, bell hooks maintains connection with her black southern experience while searching for new questions and connections offered by the decentered subject of postmodern feminism.

With this framework, we can turn to feminist-writers-workers who do not use the metaphor of negotiation but whose texts, nonetheless, contribute to a negotiating feminist criticism. In "La conciencia de la mestiza: Towards a New Consciousness," Gloria Anzaldúa quite forwardly "choose[s] to use some of [her] energy to serve as mediator."[23] To activate a mediating sensibility in her reader, she writes in Spanish and English, a strategy that dramatizes Anzaldúa's own oscillations between histories and identities. This language choice literally sets English-only readers in motion as they go in search of a Spanish-English dictionary or seek out a colleague in the Foreign Language Department of their college or university. Throughout her essay, Anzaldúa demonstrates how far feminist negotiations are from settlement or even trade. Instead, she works between and across the Mexican and U.S. border to fabricate the coalitions and dialogues that are necessary for her life. Rather than a rarified "third" tongue or sure position, this other option clearly demonstrates the imbrication of the other with the self, of the opposition with the position. Without giving up on deconstruction, place, *or* identity, Anzaldúa draws on past histories and geographies to invent a negotiated homeland:

> As a *mestiza* I have no country, my homeland cast me out; yet all countries are mine because I am every woman's sister or potential lover. (As a lesbian I have no race, my own people disclaim me; but I am all races because there is the queer of me in all races.) I am cultureless because, as a feminist, I challenge the collective cultural/religious male-derived beliefs of Indo-Hispanics and Anglos; yet I am cultured because I am participating in the creation of yet another culture, a new story to explain the world and our participation in it, a new value system with images and symbols that connect us to each other and to the planet. *Soy un amasamiento*, I am an act of kneading, of uniting and joining that not only has produced both a creature of darkness and a creature of light, but also a creature that questions the definitions of light and dark and gives them new meanings.[24]

Anzaldúa's prose demonstrates negotiation by refusing whole systems of oppressive thought (Western religious ideologies) and yet sifting through them for redeemable characters, symbols, images. This practice demonstrates an important angle in feminist negotiations. They are both selective or partial and at the same time capable of larger unitings and joinings. Like bell hooks, who draws from "a working-class Southern black folk experience while incorporating meaningful knowledge gained in other locations, even in those hierarchical spaces of privilege,"[25] Anzaldúa provides more feminists, more women, with more tools and more space.

Anzaldúa frankly states her disenchantment with the "counter-stance" because it is not a livable posture and because it does not work. In her negotiated homeland, "it is not enough to stand on the opposite riverbank, shouting questions, challenging patriarchal, white conventions. A counter-stance locks one into a duel of oppressor and oppressed," reducing parties "to a common denominator of violence" alone: "it is not a way of life."[26]

In an actual staging of diplomacy, Anzaldúa addresses white readers: "Admit that Mexico is your double, that she exists in the shadow of this country, that we are irrevocably tied to her. Gringo, accept the doppelganger in your psyche.... tell us what you need from us."[27]

Again we see the active, riffling nature of feminist negotiation, what Anzaldúa identifies as *mestiza* thinking. First Anzaldúa connects herself with Mexico, urging whites to admit "*your* double" (emphasis added). But she also includes herself in the "we" who are being called on (by her rhetorical voice) to confession ("*we* are irrevocably tied to *her*" [emphasis added]). In the next two sentences, she moves back to Mexico and speaks to "Gringo": "tell us what you need from us." This oscillation can hardly be mistaken for feminine indecision or the subordinate's fear of reprisal. Instead, Anzaldúa's project once again makes clear the potent work of juxtaposing, sifting, and double alliances that feminist workers practice. In my reading, Anzaldúa's *borderland* acts as a utopian edge for her thinking rather than as a point of pure origins. Like the other writers discussed earlier, this *mestiza* feminism is characterized by a tactical assemblage of unequals to advance present political systems in the direction of greater understanding as well as to achieve more space for feminist workers. In a generous gesture that is not at all ironic, Anzaldúa assumes the other's legitimate requirements: "tell us what you need from us." Anzaldúa's sentences suggest the peculiar or "queer" challenge of current feminism—how to progress without a clear identity or a common politics. At the same time, her negotiating mode of operation suggests some common lines of thinking among feminist workers. Her use of two languages in particular illustrates how a negotiating subject provides her own coalitions and seeks to extend them into the realm of public academic discourse. As with the literary critics examined so far, then, Anzaldúa demonstrates the inside-out nature of negotiation, the way in which engaging in negotiations—where one takes more than one side—becomes a way of thinking, a production of the self.

Another writer who negotiates critically but without using the word is Elisabeth Däumer. In "Queer Ethics; or, the Challenge of Bisexuality to Lesbian Ethics," she imagines instances of theoretical negotiation where lesbian critics tangle with the subject of bisexuality. "Our ability to respond to diversity *within* lesbian community," she writes, "is linked to our capacity to articulate and reimagine the complex relations and interactions, as well as the shifting boundaries and allegiances, *between* communities."[28] In the go-between or mediating position, bisexuals are "always both inside and outside a diversity of conflicting communities," providing a perspective for revisioning not only both sides but for revising the uses we can make of go-between personas. Däumer would, I think, recommend negotiation as a critical fiction because it allows an interpolation of the everyday self within the feminist thinker. It validates feminist work that is both utopian and this-world directed. As I have already indicated, I advocate negotiation as a metaphor because it provides some methodological common grounds while it proliferates feminist voices and identities.[29]

Certainly it matters who is negotiating with whom and where. Thus we can never settle the contours of a feminist negotiating criticism, and such a criticism certainly cannot be used prescriptively. At the same time, as we have already seen, negotiations are shaping our work in some common ways: common in the sense that these are everyday dilemmas that we grapple with and common in the sense that all of these writers create imaginary landscapes that construct negotiation as a moral and epistemological practice, a progressive movement constituted through visitations across scenes of power. Even if we discover (why should we be surprised?) that it is privileged feminists and women who have the most room to negotiate, such a realization should not deter us. Instead, feminist critics should commit ourselves to creating more spaces for more feminist workers to bring their negotiating knowledge into the marketplace of ideas.

Travels between Cultural Realms

I have been thinking about my own geographies in conjunction with this project. I was born in Ogbomosho, Nigeria; my parents were Southern Baptist missionaries, an identification I have learned to silence. When I was born, I was bequeathed two sets of names, one by my parents (necessarily followed by my father's family name) and one by Yoruba well-wishers

The States of Feminist Reading

(who had prayed for a son for Mr. Neil, my father). My first family-given name is a name I will not call myself. No one else, including my mother, has ever called me "Miriam," though I have to use it on legal documents and insurance claim forms. It was my aunt's name (my mother's sister's), and Moses' sister's name, of course. But my second name, "Elaine," was always mine because my mother "just liked it." Due to her admission, I have always considered my mother to be my namer. As an adolescent, I thought Elaine homely—because I thought of myself that way—but as I matured I began to like it. Indeed, the name began to seem elegant to me even before I learned its Greek origins and its associations with Helen. My last name alone aligned me with my father (Neil). But it was a close alliance, partly because my body resembled his: growing up I was tall, lean, and flat chested; our legs and arms, I thought, were long and graceful; we were both athletic, swimmers and runners.

My Yoruba names, unlike my European and biblical ones, told stories I found interesting from the start, largely because of their sound. Whereas my parents' names or naming led to the development of a story through our living together, these names assumed a past and a future in the moment of their giving. Once I was old enough to think about it, I considered my second Nigerian name, Funmilayo, to be confessionally given. "She brings joy to the house" seemed a revision of the prayer for a son and thus harks back to a relation—and a struggle—that began before my birth. Or perhaps the Yorubas in attendance witnessed my parents' pleasure (and relief; I was a month overdue), and the name described a process that culminated in my birth (whereas I, of course, think of my life as beginning at that moment).

The first name, Bamadele, like my second European name, Elaine, is the one I have taken to heart. Meaning "come home with me" and spoken kinetically—with arms outstretched, beckoning—Bamadele is an invitation by the Yoruba speaker to one who is born away from home. I took the naming seriously by adapting to my Nigerian birthland: I took to Nigerian rivers, paths, trees, smells, sounds, flora, and fauna like a natural. Yet, an unnatural buffer—my white American appearance and the fact of my U.S. citizenship—shielded me from hunger and homelessness, the idiosyncrasies of the Nigerian marketplace, and finally the Biafran War. And yet the shield was not so total or complete that it kept out all dangers or sideways glances. When I was five, I suffered an acute bout of filaria (filaria, like malaria, is carried by mosquitos; larvae hatch in one's bloodstream, causing engorged limbs). Very likely, this childhood disease contributed to the later onset of juvenile diabetes. When I was eight and playing in my sandbox on the missionary compound in the village of Eku, I regularly viewed unclaimed bodies being carried to an unmarked grave among the rubber trees that edged our deep front yard, a viewing that was not mediated by church services or anyone's comforting words. I cannot say how, exactly, I am marked by the drumming that lulled me to sleep in Ogbomosho, or by my participation in Uhrobo Baptist church services in Eku, where English was the translated language. Though I know that these events—and the negotiations of language and context that they occasioned—even now shape and lace my dreams. As I write this, I remember that last night I dreamed of Nigeria. I was walking in the predawn light, lost, searching for something, for a child, I think, though often, in recurring dreams, I *am* the child, searching for something I have buried and which I believe I can still find if I look in the right location. I have come to think of this dream as a search for a second self, a second voice, a doppelganger who is both me and not me, like me and not like me.

Taking "Bamadẹle" to heart means, I think, that a part of my center, my self, is Yoruba-given. This does not make me American-African or gloss the colonialist impulses that are also at my center, but it does imply a nonironic relation to other people of African origin. One way to speak about this is to remark on my foreignness in the United States. I remember vividly the first time I saw myself as other, as one who had become *too* at home in Nigeria. I was nine years old, and my family was preparing to return to the United States for a year's furlough. I had not been to the States for three years. Prepubescent and distant from the commercializing images of the United States, I had not yet learned to see myself as a female object on view. On the evening in question, I was sitting cross-legged in our living room in our ranch-style house in Eku. The sisal rug rubbed uncomfortably against my exposed legs while I studied a Sears Roebuck catalog. I turned to the girls' clothing section and my eyes came to rest on the-girl-I-should-be but was not. Blond and light skinned, she was my age and she looked into the camera boldly. My wispy hair was cut just below my ears in a pixie; her hair was longer and flipped up slightly at the ends. She wore a perfect white short-sleeved shirt tucked just so into a pleated, navy blue skirt. Most important, her face displayed perfect symmetry, in contrast to my round cheeks, high forehead, and odd assortment of freckles. That was 1965, and the furlough year was a failure for me. I could not make myself middle class and white enough in the grade school where I was enrolled in Easley, South Carolina. Four years later in 1969, no one mistook me for a member of the local white middle-class elite when I enrolled at Decatur High School, Decatur, Georgia. Even when I learned to groom myself passably according to white middle-class U.S. feminine standards (no small feat), I could not erase my cultural queerness. I did not know the language of popular culture so I was silent when I should have been talkative. I remember being taught by a patient acquaintance what "groovy" meant. But I could never get a handle on actually using the term. My comfortable silence in Nigeria—where I listened to the Yoruba and Uhrobo languages as music—was replaced in Georgia with the uncomfortable silence of an unnamable outsidership. I was white; I should have known the language; I understood the words, but I could not urge myself to play the part. There was too much to leave behind: the untamed grounds of the missionary compound, where the grass grew high and guava trees yielded a fruit that still resists domestication (mangoes I can now buy in my local market); the lights and the smoke of the night market in Ogbomosho; the women who came to the Eku compound to collect palm nuts; Mrs. Adebimpe's brilliant Yoruba clothing, which far outstripped the Western smocks she sewed for me; the Western-style shop where one could buy kola nuts and fine English toffees.

Much later, I came to own my husband's family name when I married at age twenty-two. After entering into academic feminism in the early 1980s, I considered giving it up. But *my own* last name was also a man's name, and, thus, I found myself like many without an obvious or uncompromised option. Some women were choosing hyphenated names. But I did not, at the time, imagine Neil-Orr as less compromising than either name alone. Instead it seemed to up the ante of male genealogy. I imagined that something could be said by way of writing as a feminist who nonetheless adopted her husband's name. That contradiction seemed to hold the most confusion and thus the most potential. My name, Elaine Orr, tells only the European story, but the European contradictions are crossed with the Nigerian affiliations that name the spiritual and psychological negotiations that I exercise every day. My whiteness is neither pure nor simple.

As my names suggest (in a kind of outline fashion), my identity, knowledge, and experience do not break down along binary divides. I have always experienced strong affiliations (positive and negative) with both parents. Indeed, their characters do not match feminine and masculine constructions. For example, it was due to my mother's childhood aspirations, not my father's, that any of us showed up in West Africa.

Furthermore, I have experienced the othering that postcolonialists associate with the "native" position.[30] Visiting the United States when I was a child, my family and I were the subjects of fascination and revulsion. I was often called out and looked at but then not invited to the intimate party. The most potent naming I received in the ninth grade (the year in Georgia) was "queer."

I know in my adulthood that the self-forgetfulness of my first ten years was provided, in part, by the machinery of colonization. And yet that realization does not cancel my cross-cultural upbringing. Nor does it erase all possibility of generous intentionality on the part of Nigerian neighbors and hosts. In the ritual of naming, for example, the men and women who chose Bamedẹle (inviting the invader; it was 1954 and Nigeria was still a British colony) might have been mimicking our colonial relation.[31] But how can I assume their absolute or totalizing cynicism? And after all, the question is not only "Who are they?" The question is also "Who am I?" and "Who am I as a consequence of that interaction?" Finally, the question is "Who will I help—in these chosen and imposed relations, in these contradictory and yet somehow useful connections, in these buffered, impure, and sometimes common spaces?"

There is more, to be sure: my high school years in Arkansas, a place of so much foreignness that I can hardly remember speaking for two years. A son—born prematurely—who remained nameless for four days because I had been too preoccupied with surviving graduate seminars to solve the riddle of *his* naming. The nearly two decades of work for academic title and placement, with years of translating what I knew into a suitable critical tongue. I am translating even now as I revise this chapter yet again for publication. The negotiations multiply: between my son and my dissertation; between feminist and familial claims; between models of collaboration and the requirements of competition; between daily insulin injections and the presentation of a professorial self. Some readers have urged dropping this section. But I hazard this autobiographical information because it may provide some negotiated grounds which other sections of this chapter do not.

Feminist Reading as Negotiation: Toward a Topology

Third stage feministics—after the search for equality and the articulation of difference—requires an interpretive model that acknowledges common ground and real disagreement. Go-between maneuvers like those described by hooks, Däumer, and Anzaldúa conceptualize female agency in the complex and local operations of displacement and placement, deconstruction and synthesis, appropriation and critique. This view of female and feminist self-making provides a common model for feminist critics at the same time that its local enunciations provide a means for recognizing differences

The States of Feminist Reading

among feminist readers and female protagonists. Produced through readings of female negotiators and go-between operations, a negotiating feminist criticism invites articulations of "crossed" loyalties that nonetheless bring us closer to a nonsexist, nonhomophobic world. Readings that are merely oppositional (whether the opposition is *inside* or *outside* of feminism) only exacerbate the splits rather than putting them to use. Such readings call *feminist* only those practitioners who can afford a politics of subversion. The woman with the forked tongue, the bisexual, the dually aligned accomplice remains a suspicious character. She is not committed enough, not feminist or lesbian or postcolonial enough.

But a view of feminist criticism in the go-between or negotiating position leads to the interesting discovery that subversive and separatist strategies have serendipitously expanded feminism's negotiated homelands. Approaching feminist reading from this perspective, it seems necessary to ask how a negotiating criticism is to be self-consciously crafted and practiced. How can differences that we find valuable be both preserved and negotiated?

If a deconstructive feminist criticism enjoys a wry celebration in the gap, in (the) difference (between power and powerlessness, masculine and feminine, white and black, colonist and subaltern), a negotiating feminist criticism looks for go-between antecedents, for figures that demonstrate not only the difference within but the overlap inside and outside. This point of view informs my method of rereading female-authored fiction for instances of negotiating plays: grafting, welding, annexing, bridging, sifting. Like the figure of border crossing(s) but even more vividly, such negotiating images demonstrate the presence of overlap and the inevitability of consort.

In my critical story, the twin actions of resistance and construction (or resistance and accommodation) characterize feminist writers' and female characters' negotiating practices. As Elizabeth Meese writes, quoting Adrienne Rich, "The function of the poet, the woman, the feminist fuse in the imaginative and pragmatic quest to determine 'how we can use what we have / to invent what we need.'"[32]

Moving toward a feminist topology of narrative negotiation, let me remark on some common features of the novels I read. Wharton, Hurston, Welty, Morrison, and Piercy advertise their own negotiating sensibilities by creating female "leads" who make inventive use of their relations to both a dominant and a subordinate identity and place. These leads may not be the novel's protagonist; in Wharton's case it is the protagonist Lily Bart but in Morrison's novel this part is played by the protagonist's ancestor Pilate Dead. In every case, the novels I read resist the plots of climactic upheaval or peaceful resolution. Instead they are instances of what Ursula Le Guin describes in "The Carrier Bag Theory of Fiction": "Conflict, competition, stress, struggle, etc., within the narrative conceived as carrier bag/belly/box/house/medicine bundle, may be seen as necessary elements of a whole which . . . cannot be characterized either as conflict or as harmony."[33] Le Guin's description of plot as process which includes elements of stress and competition can be likened to my fiction of feminist criticism as a negotiating reading practice that includes elements of subversion and separatism.

Le Guin's imaging of narrative through the metaphor of "carrier bag" serendipitously evokes the mysterious bag of bones and rocks that comes to identify Pilate Dead in Toni Morrison's *Song of Solomon*. Without trying to hold everything (that is Macon Dead's approach), Pilate proposes picking up odd mementos along the way as a reminder of where one has been, the debts one owes, and the life one hopes to invent. A view of feminist criticism and feminist narrative as negotiation leads to a focus on everyday inventions rather than grand resolutions. Such a preference may lead one to emphasize the frame narrative in Hurston's *Their Eyes Were Watching God*—where we witness two women engaged in feeding, washing feet, and telling stories—rather than to read the inset narrative of Janie's triumph alone. Shuttling back and forth between these textual locations, I hope to discover how Hurston herself negotiates the frameworks of race and gender in telling her tale. The novel, which appears to close with Janie's achievement of individual voice, actually depends on the device and reality of an accomplice who is neither free nor beautiful, neither wealthy nor vocal. Her presence ripples the waters of Janie's placid demeanor, creating a remembrance of the places Janie has been, the debts she owes, and the "interests" she still exercises in more than one economy. Not insignificantly, Hurston's heroine has money in the bank. Indeed, the frame—where Janie accepts Phoeby's gift of rice and audience—results in a narrative grafting of a utopian figure with the textually and historically "bound" go-between who points back to the heroine's achieved "limits." This unequal relationship can never be rejected by the novel's telos since it is the device for Janie's enunciation. Thus Hurston's novel on a whole narrates the ongoing process of negotiating between actual world realities and utopian hopes, between day-to-day relationships and individual dreams.

My brief discussion of Janie and Phoeby brings me to another narrative feature shared by the novels under consideration. Fictions that invite a feminist negotiating criticism operate through simultaneous appeals to ac-

The States of Feminist Reading

tual and utopian worlds and points of reference. They are generically and politically impure, asking the reader to sympathize with characters' conventional as well as progressive longings. Connie Ramos from Piercy's *Woman on the Edge of Time* provides an excellent example. The novel itself grafts utopian and realist writing to represent Connie's heartfelt oscillation between the desires of biological mothering and the progressive programs of a future state. In Connie's actual world, her (bad) mothering is the reason for her brutal incarceration. But she and the narrator insist on the value of her dream to be biological *and* social mother.

I read these novels as Nancy K. Miller reads women's writing "for the places . . . where the female (I really mean to say feminist) . . . constructs herself in language—precisely at the intersection of cultural codes about women."[34] I approach female-authored American fictions and feminisms as they challenge the imperative of the counterstance, convening instead subjectivities that operate between the poles of oppressor and oppressed, light and dark, colonizer and colonized. Imagining these texts as "subject to negotiation," I choose the option of elaborating on their success, even where it is limited, as in the case of Lily Bart. I do not read these novels to establish a scale of more and less successful plottings of negotiation, even though, perhaps not surprisingly, we find more success the further we move through the twentieth century.

I hope to demonstrate these authors' preference for go-between subjects and negotiating options. The writers, characters, and readers who are brought together in these pages may negotiate as agents of resistance, but they may also negotiate as agents of coalition and novel connection. To theorize negotiation *only* as resistance is to return to the "purer" rhetoric of subversion where the only female-authored practices that can aspire to feminism are necessarily deconstructive or utopian.

My approach to the novels is to read them as dramatizing a negotiating authorial subjectivity. This angle in reading is developed from my second and third critical fictions: the authors I study are positioned between competing and unequal "worlds," both or all of which contribute to their vision; and the writers' negotiations of authority and history are published through their characters' thinking across contested lines. The descriptive categories I propose for viewing narrative negotiation sketch a heuristic. I do not presume that my theorizing masters the multiple ways in which negotiation can be read. Neither do I intend for my readings to deny the insights of other approaches. My critical direction, however, makes palpable a fictive design that elucidates otherwise troubling features of each text. For example, Lily Bart has generally been read as a necessary sacrifice in Wharton's uncompromising critique of New York manners. But a negotiating criticism brings to light Lily Bart's need for "accommodations" between exclusive social systems. This narrative argument alters our angle of vision. Rather than reading Lily as a sacrifice, we can read her as a precursor in the feminist argument for positive productions between scenes of power.

Needless to say, significant overlaps occur in the following five narrative categories. Nonetheless, this topology helps us focus on the particular aspects of negotiation that will structure my reading and the rest of this book.

First, negotiating feminist fictions (including our critical ones) feature significant go-between characters who choose to remain connected to both dominant and subordinate worlds, knowing that these designations are themselves slippery and changing. What dominates in one location, may not in another. Without guarantee of success, this double connection is chosen in the interest of shifting power relations somewhat and with the understanding that one must have some grounds even as one acknowledges their impurity. It also suggests a characterological faith in small changes. Operating between scenes of power, such characters create a play between difference and similarity—not to homogenize identities but to foster opportunities for coalition and to create habitable spaces for women.

Second, negotiating feminist fictions are organized through characters' back and forth rather than linear progressions. This improvisational movement suggests neither ideological resolution nor political stasis but a poetics that does not give up on its "crossed" resources: for example, black performance and white sponsorship, lesbian theory and "motherist" politics.

Third, negotiating feminist fictions feature dramatizations of generosity—or setting aside—initiated by a "subordinate" character. These moments are not merely bluffs or tricks; rather they express a subject's awareness of her own need to draw from both sides in power relations. At the same time, they operate to give the subject a tool with which she can make narrative and critical progress. This characterization of subordinate players anticipates Spivak's and Meese's arguments that feminism should make a place for "other" women to speak.

Fourth, negotiating feminist fictions produce a negotiating reason, a logic that harbors contradictions and operates through generic recyclings. This logic does not begin by refuting the opposition and is not motivated by the desire to overturn literary power relations. Instead, it begins by taking inventory of all that is good and useful in whatever locations one has

The States of Feminist Reading

access to and is motivated by a desire to bring more women into contact with the literary goods they need. In terms of narrative, negotiating reason produces intratextual revisions of key tropes and dramatic scenes. This staging of revision demonstrates the writer's own poetical and political oscillation, her own reluctance to give up identities and voices that may yet be useful.

Finally, negotiating feminist fictions enact a kind of shuttle diplomacy, carrying the reader back and forth across competing fields in feminist and other debates. This narrative structure does not yield to resolution though it may offer moments of achievement, as, for example, in Janie's voice. However, the plot always moves "forward" through narrative alliances with opposing truths or perspectives. We might say that negotiating feminist fictions always carry their dead (as Pilate does). They do not give up on the possibility of remaking history, even the history of white men.

I employ the foregoing topology throughout the book, although each chapter draws from some of these features more than others. Thus I read *The House of Mirth* in terms of Lily's go-between character, her actual, everyday movements across social fields, and the production within of a negotiating sensibility. In looking at *Their Eyes Were Watching God*, I focus on Phoeby as textual go-between and on the movement of the story across audiences and their interests. With Wharton and Hurston, I emphasize the accommodations in feminist reception. I read *The Optimist's Daughter* and *Song of Solomon* in terms of a "generous reason." In Welty's novel, this reason must be read from the inside out, from Laurel Hand's thinking toward the horizon of feminist reception. In Morrison's novel, this reason can be read from the outside in, from Pilate Dead's intercessional practice to the knowledge she embodies, her "bag." Finally, I focus my reading of *Woman on the Edge of Time* on the novel's shuttle structure, its plotting of character through the device of time travel.

Each chapter is staged in terms of chosen narrative elements and analogies. I read *The House of Mirth* in terms of setting and draw an analogy with authorship. *Their Eyes Were Watching God* I approach in terms of audiences within the novel and draw an analogy with audiences outside the novel. Welty's *The Optimist's Daughter* I consider in terms of character and draw analogies both with Welty's authorship and with the history of feminist reading. Likewise, I read *Song of Solomon* in terms of character but draw analogies from the civil rights movement. Finally, I study *Woman on the Edge of Time* in terms of plot and locate my discussion in feminist debates on the subject of mothering. Methodologically, my analysis moves between thematic, discursive, and historical readings.

Negotiated Homelands

For the most part (that is, with the exception of Welty), I have chosen novels that are central among feminist readers, in large part to show what new productions are possible with a negotiating criticism and to demonstrate how epistemological and philosophical negotiation is the context for subversive reading and writing strategies, not the other way around. I realize that I risk further ensconcing of *major* women writers. But, in fact, my reading method in many ways demythologizes these writers, demonstrating their historical contingency and their reliance on cultural and textual models at hand. The choice of Welty, who is less acclaimed among feminist readers, works a bit differently. By reading her as feminist, I broaden the purview of feminist fiction writers and demonstrate how feminist readers may have limited their authors by applying too narrow a definition of feminist.

Readers who approach this book for a chapter on a particular author should be able to read selected chapters without too much delving into chapter 1. Readers from neighboring critical schools may need to acquaint themselves with the novels, if they have not read them, in order to follow my arguments regarding individual texts.

My deepest hope is that I will hear back from some readers, that in striking sometimes a nerve, sometimes a chord, I will elicit your consideration. There, I have crossed that bar. I have told you what I need, what I yearn for.

2

Negotiation Our Text
The Search for Accommodations in Edith Wharton's *The House of Mirth*

But you belittle me, *don't you, . . . in being so sure.*
—Lily Bart

MY AIM IN this chapter is to demonstrate how negotiation makes palpable the political and aesthetic adjudications represented in Edith Wharton's *The House of Mirth* (1905), thus "negotiation our text."[1] Responding to previous feminist readings of the novel, I argue for a shift in our view of Lily Bart. Rather than insist on the inevitability of her death and of Wharton's sacrifice of her heroine, I emphasize Wharton's argument, through Lily, for "accommodations." In my view, *The House of Mirth* thematically represents both the hazard and the potential for women in negotiating social "scenes of power." In terms of its writing, Wharton's narrative style indicates her own productive uses of lady authorship and modernist prose while Lily Bart's musings throughout the novel suggest a grafting of male and female occupations and identities. Viewed in this light, the novel operates as a solicitation *for* "negotiating feminisms" and not solely as a criticism of power relations. Lily's death may be read not as Wharton's stoical acknowledgment of immutable hegemonies or as her resignation from ladylike ambition, but as a signal of her belief that women must achieve multiple attachments in order to proceed in the world.

Locating my argument in relation to other feminist readings, I stage the kind of interfeminist argumentation and debate that chapter 1 discusses. This strategy of reviewing other readings to create a space for one's difference is an operation feminist readers negotiate even as we seek to work more collaboratively. I undertake this review to demonstrate how the containment/subversion binary has overdetermined feminist interpre tation and to argue that a negotiating line of thought opens the novel to a new horizon of possibility.

In my reading, *The House of Mirth* dramatizes a series of overlapping gender and class negotiations which Wharton represents as necessary for her heroine's survival: negotiations between male and female occupations, domestic and public space, and the rhetorical modalities of sympathy and critical judgment.[2] Interpreted in these conjunctions, Lily becomes an agent of Wharton's own search for some *middle* way between the feminine voice of the domestic novelist and the feminist voice of the public suffragette. Like Elaine Showalter, I read the novel in relation to Wharton's life and the transitional moment of turn-of-the-century politics. But I view Lily as affiliated with Wharton in the operation of negotiation: taking sides with culturally opposed options, for example, female friendship and heterosexual romance. Rather than reading Lily as "stranded," I remark upon her peripatetic linking of agonistic spheres.[3] This *movement* suggests Wharton's sometimes cautious politics, her need for approximate spheres of self-design, and her tendency to fashion narratives that operate through horizontal linking of social scenes rather than vertically through the acceleration of action. I take very seriously her own personal maneuver of writing in the morning and receiving guests in the afternoon.

But as I have indicated, prior feminist readings of *The House of Mirth* have been devoted to establishing Wharton's non-negotiating poetics, her narrative representation of unyielding social structures. Indeed, most feminist readings comment on Wharton's production of "totalizing systems," thus interpreting the writer's sensibility in terms of philosophical absolutes. Wai-Chee Dimock, for example, has argued that the novel is fueled "by an almost exclusively critical energy directed at the marketplace Wharton disdains." In Dimock's view, *The House of Mirth* reflects Wharton's political "bleakness of vision" in regard to "a totalizing system" from which there is no escape."[4] Indeed, "the power of the marketplace resides, . . . in its ability to reproduce itself, in its ability to assimilate everything else into its domain. As a controlling logic, a mode of human conduct and human association, the marketplace is everywhere and nowhere, ubiquitous and invisible. Under its shadow even the most private affairs take on the essence of business transactions, *for the realm of human relations is fully contained within an all-encompassing business ethic.*"[5] Assuming a constant and nonproductive tension between a number of oppositions—capitalism/personal relations; business/love; male contamination/feminine purity—Dimock argues the full absorption of one by the other.

Other feminist readings of the novel similarly suggest such totalities.

Nancy Topping Bazin, for example, argues that "as in all money-centered, non-androgynous societies, every choice offered Lily requires that she compromise her dignity and self-respect." Roslyn Dixon writes that "Lily's choices are reduced to absolutes: she can survive by compromising the ideal, or she can honor the ideal by sacrificing herself." Along similar lines, Robin Beaty suggests that Wharton "could not bear to see [Lily] compromise by choosing only one of the prizes to which she aspired." Finally, Elizabeth Ammons claims that in the end, "Lily has been forced . . . to give up all ambition for independence; the social system has triumphed."[6] But does Wharton's masterpiece silence Lily's utterance that "[m]oney stands for all kinds of things" or her personal knowledge that "the door [out] . . . stood always open?"[7] I will show that it does not. Instead, and in sympathy with a character who is neither obsequious nor subversive, Edith Wharton challenges feminist criticism to read *negotiation our text*.

Some critics have theorized Wharton, if not Lily Bart, as actualizing her authorship through canny appropriations of rival domains. Susan Goodman argues that Wharton learned to balance the traits of femininity and cleverness "in a society that tended to see them as mutually exclusive."[8] And Amy Kaplan demonstrates how Wharton's self-presentation was accomplished through a series of negotiations with apparently exclusive models: family history and emerging capitalism; domesticity and publicity; leisure and production; lady and writer.[9] Yet Kaplan's reading of Lily confirms earlier analyses that find in the textual woman only the inverse of the writer's success. Indeed, Kaplan reads Lily's failure as a price Wharton must pay for narrative realism: "Wharton saves Lily from Rosedale's plot [blackmailing Bertha] by extracting her from the circuit of exchange; yet outside that circuit [Lily] can have no self. . . . In burning [Selden's] letters [Wharton] replaces them with Lily, who ends her life."[10] This interpretation abandons the negotiating logic of Wharton's authorship, where antithetical landscapes are grafted as a space of self-presentation, and embraces once again a logic of pure oppositions, one that requires that something be given up in order for something to be gained: in this case, Lily's life for Wharton's authorial integrity.

My reading of Lily begins with the question of how our criticism repeats rather than alters the terms of Lily's *actual* world; how our readings undervalue her *possible* world logic of influencing recalcitrant systems through social negotiations.[11]

We first see Lily as Selden does, between trains and with time to spare. The question she raises for herself—and by implication for him—is "what's to be done in the interval?" Thus the novel begins by inviting the reader to a threshold position and sets the stage for Wharton's interest in *accommodations*. In my reading, Lily's thinking leads to a possible world geography in which coalition would provide some footing but without requiring her to buy in altogether.

Unfolding the novel's numerous threshold scenes, I argue that *The House of Mirth* communicates, however indirectly, Wharton's negotiation of enclosed spaces and divergent priorities. Indeed, *The House of Mirth* signifies an authorial argument *for* accommodation, for some generosity between oppositions and for some landings on which one may stand as one seeks to expand the social field for women. Although this reading might seem to ignore Wharton's ironic title, it brings to the fore Lily Bart's imagination as well as Wharton's methods of narration. Following their line of thought, my reading practice here establishes my terms for the rest of the book. While the secondary characters argue for exclusive spaces and commitments, Lily as inside/outside subject argues for hybrid commitments and produces a logic that accommodates *faults*. In the interest of this representation, Wharton draws rhetorically from the fictive storehouses of both sororal relations and heterosexual romance.

Readers are no doubt familiar with Lily's situation: at the ominous age of twenty-nine, she continues to refuse any one of the marriage arrangements available to her even though her options are diminishing. Without real financial backing, she depends on the goodwill of fickle and demanding *friends* to see her through to a suitable marriage. Among these wealthy sponsors, Judy and Gus Trenor figure the distinctly gendered fields of social life and business. Just beyond the wealthy circle is Selden Lawrence, the most fickle and most desirable of Lily's possible suitors; but he is too poor—whether in imagination or money is up to the reader to decide. Then there is Gerty Farish—Selden's cousin and a social worker—who appears to love and despise her beautiful friend. One of the wealthiest of Lily's callers is Simon Rosedale, a rising Jew whom Lily alternately abhors and pities, perhaps because his ambition, like hers, shows. Beyond these three, most of Lily's acquaintances are players in the field of upper-crust New York, the really rich who plan extravagant parties, play cards late into the evening, and cover their affairs by merely ignoring them. Lily does, however, establish some significant contacts among the working-class women of New York, not only Gerty, but also Nettie Struther, a "girl" she meets from the millinery factory. The entire novel is plotted through Lily's walking or driving from place to place, a narrative movement that parallels her attempts to create workable but not fully containing coalitions among the positions her acquaintances occupy.

Wharton's *The House of Mirth*

What Lily longs for—even if she is not always conscious of her self-disclosures—is a negotiation of female friendship and male sponsorship. Thus Wharton stages the social question: what lies between resignation to marriage—full complicity with male systems—and escape from heterosexual designs—uncompromising critique of the sexual economy? At the level of writing, the question translates: what lies between the domestic plot of feminine sacrifice and the new plots of female resistance? As I will show, the novel exaggerates the scenes of marriage and sorority to illustrate their indifference *as opposites* and then to use them as sites of authorial and character negotiation.

Between Sorority and Marriage

We might consider Wharton's relation to architectural design as an entry into her novel. Houses functioned as Wharton's touchstones both literally and figuratively. When one visitor to The Mount, for example, commented on the perfect accommodations in her room, Wharton replied, "Oh, I am rather a housekeeperish person."[12] At the same time, as Amy Kaplan argues, Wharton's first book, *The Decoration of Houses*, "served as a metaphor for [her] developing views of professional authorship."[13] In her metaphor of "interior architecture," Kaplan suggests, Wharton "appropriat[ed] a traditional male discourse of architecture to transform a traditional female discourse of interior space. 'Interior architecture' turns domestic space inside out, to project a borderline area at the intersection of the private home and the streets of the public marketplace."[14] Kaplan's description *re-views* Wharton's authorship from the position of threshold or conjunctive spaces. At the same time, it indicates how Wharton's negotiation of identities and spaces is more than passive imbibing of difference or stoical balancing of imposed systems.

In *The House of Mirth*, Wharton allows Lily to appropriate sororal discourse in her enunciation of male/female friendship. Thus sorority is turned inside out, creating an overlap with heterosexual engagement. In a parallel move, Wharton inflects sisterly and maternal embrace with elements of heterosexual erotics, taking to heart the possibility of a nonsexist heterosexuality. Thus Wharton's rhetorical negotiations shadow her heroine's interpersonal ones.

But before turning discourses inside out, Wharton must establish them in their recognized forms. She depends on Lily's closest associates—Selden, Gerty, and Judy—to represent the lexicons of patriarchal marriage, on the one hand, and sororal affiliation on the other. As the novel begins, for example, Selden projects the objectifying terms of marriage. Alluding to the heroine's planned visit to Bellomont, he remarks, "Ah, well, there must be plenty of capital on the lookout for such an investment" (18). Drawing on the metaphor of vision ("on the lookout") and laying out the terms of marriage ("capital" and "investment"), Wharton succinctly inscribes the contractual erasure of woman in late-nineteenth-century gender arrangements. In the logic of capital looking for an investment, Lily cannot be seen except as the value she represents. Although there are no actual men in Selden's sentence, "capital" and "investment" cohere to his side, leaving no feminine position in the arrangement. Like his voice, Selden's vision trades in women and pretends no part in the arrangement. Not only is Lily commodified in his view, but so are all the "ugly people" who "produce her." Left out of his calculations is his own enforcement of this law. But Wharton reveals his "luxurious pleasure in [Lily's] nearness: in the modelling of her little ear, the crisp upward wave of her hair—was it ever so slightly brightened by art?" (6). Assuming that all of Lily's motions are directed toward successful marriage, Selden, like most of Lily's friends, thinks and speaks in ways that solidify this design. To his mind, Lily's "discretions . . . as much as her imprudences . . . [are] part of the same carefully-elaborated plan" (6). But even in this thought, Selden's logic admits an alternative, for he supposes Lily's agency in this design, a possibility effectively erased in the equation capital = investments. In an odd way, then, Selden becomes a figure for feminist criticism's reception of Lily: its simultaneous description of the heroine's containment *and* her failure to act.

Interpreting Lily's oscillations as calculation toward *immobility*—marriage—Selden represents the pure logic of separate and immutable categories. One is either free or bound, participant or exile. An apparently passive witness to marriage—he is too poor and too free to consider such a contract—Selden's words in fact insist on its reduplication. The novel clearly critiques his *neutrality*, showing his *objective* witness to be nothing other than a denial of Lily's more negotiated reasoning. Given this difference—between Lily and Selden—it is interesting that feminist critics also view Lily as tragically situated between exclusive commitments. This approach fails to follow Lily's train of thought, a colonizing gesture toward Lily that inflates male power—men are the culprits *and* they remain in power—and a new subordination of Lily—she is only the inverse of what feminist readers hope to be. She is buried by men in her *actual* world and by feminism in the *possible* world of female authorship.

Lily's voice in these early scenes expresses her desire for an acceptable negotiation of her contradictions. "Taking the risk" of having tea in Selden's apartment, she makes plain her situation even as she appears to thwart her own purposes: "I am horribly poor," she cautions, "and very expensive" (14). Though Selden thinks otherwise, in no case are Lily's choices mere calculation. She is, for example, looking for respite from boredom, heat, and loneliness, not only for a husband. And she tells Selden her problems with a fair amount of candor. Furthermore, in her intercourse with him, she frees him from any fixed place in a male continuum: "I don't think you dislike me—and you can't possibly think I want to marry you" (11). Finally, she self-consciously introduces the category of friendship as a negotiated alternative to sexual and monetary arrangements. Resisting Selden's flattery, she makes clear her meaning: "Don't you see, . . . that there are men enough to say pleasant things to me, and that what I want is a friend who won't be afraid to say disagreeable ones when I need them?" (12).

Shifting her terms from "men" to "friend"—there are "men enough" —Lily's words paint a possible world where she and Selden might romance one another as *sisters*, both comforting and challenging one another, not solely one or the other: "there are men enough to say pleasant things to me." This implied sorority differs from the female-female friendship described by Carroll Smith-Rosenberg in her study of nineteenth-century women since it encourages critique and not only sympathy.[15] But it is equally distinguishable from a model of marriage that depends for its logic on the opposition of women and men. Thus Wharton draws from the traditions of female friendship and heterosexual romance to envision a scene of male/female friendship. "I shouldn't have to pretend with you or be on my guard," Lily remarks, followed by her most direct address to Selden and the reader: "You don't know how much I need such a friend" (13).

A brief study of Lily's sororal contacts further demonstrates Wharton's choice to negotiate gendered discourses and spaces. Like Selden's marriage proposals, Lily's female friends require strenuous commitment to singular goals and are unaccommodating of Lily's contradictions. Gerty Farish provides one model of sisterhood. The unambiguous figure of the New Woman, Gerty suggests an uncompromising feminism dedicated to the strict party line of egalitarianism. As a participant in the female support networks that were springing up at the turn of the century, she can also be read as an equivalent for the separatism of second stage feminist criticism. New Woman or Old, she cannot, it seems, choose love and work, leisure and professionalism, certainly not children and political commitment.

Wharton provides another (and older) depiction of sororal intercourse when Lily joins Judy Trenor in the domestic world of letter writing, a representation that suggests nineteenth-century women's domestic fiction.

A form of feminine language that reinforces distinct gendered spheres, the writing of notes is as unappealing to Lily as is marriage with the wealthy Percy Gryce or a flat like Gerty's. None of these *choices* contradicts the established order. Indeed, as other critics have argued and as Wharton makes clear, Judy works for other women's marriages. Her writing, then, functions as a double rebinding of woman—both economically and linguistically—rather than as the bridging of oppositions for the purpose of evoking more liberal friendships and life plans.

Chapter 4 begins with the note Judy writes to Lily, requesting her help: "Dearest Lily," it runs, "if it is not too much of a bore to be down by ten, will you come to my sitting-room to help me with some tiresome things?" (61). According to our narrator, Lily "[knows] too well the nature of the tiresome things in question . . . notes and dinner-cards to write, lost addresses to hunt up, and other social drudgery" (61–62). Whereas Wharton managed to negotiate lady/writer by composing in the morning and giving her afternoons to social engagements, Lily's actual world does not allow such an accommodation. Lily must help Judy because in doing so she repays her for the kindness of keeping her on, of replenishing her wardrobe and arranging her opportunities with men: "it was one of the taxes she had to pay for [her] prolonged hospitality" (41). Our visual introduction to Judy concludes with the remark that "it was difficult to define her beyond saying that she seemed to exist only as a hostess" (63). Referring to the "chaos of letters, bills and other domestic documents" on her writing table as "such lots of horrors," Judy Trenor portrays the author's distaste for domestic and sororal ties that deny any opportunity for "crossing" to another discursive and social location.

Indeed, as domestic writer (writing notes and invitations), Judy adapts her actions and desires to a single line of vision—hostessing. The literal tax that this exacts from Lily—in the forms of note writing and card playing—signifies a taxation of character. Thus female-female alliance, along these lines, is as stultifying as the marriage contract and assumes the same linear exchange: *this for that*. The apparent opposite of Selden, Judy Trenor actually offers Lily the same deal, reestablishing gender divisions and hoping for Lily's containment in the private sphere. Her retort to her friend when Lily fails at her chance with Gryce makes clear Judy's thinking within exchange contracts: "I'm sure everybody played fair! . . . Even Bertha kept her hands off—I will say that—till Lawrence came down and you dragged him away from her. After that she had a right to retaliate" (119). Assuming fair play, rights, and essential roles, Judy warns Lily that she'll "never do anything if [she's] not serious!" (120). This division of work and play, of seriousness and frivolity thwarts Lily's more negotiating logic. Beyond what she says, Lily's skirting of female plots—like her skirting of male ones—portends an alternate or possible world in which she might participate on both sides of the equation, taking to heart the roles of hostess and intellectual, lover and critic.

"The horror" on Judy's desk—suggesting the indiscriminate submerging of female energy beneath sisterly expectation—is matched by Gerty's *tastes*. Recalling the meager accommodations of Selden's cousin's apartment, Lily confesses to him that Gerty's "cook does the washing and the food tastes of soap" (10). The reduction of tastes to "soap"—a clear domestic marker—indicates how little the New Woman differs from the Old. A member of the new class of professional women, a woman committed to Working Girls' Clubs, Gerty's understanding of female responsibility is no more flexible than Judy's. Both women direct Lily's desire toward contained locations rather than providing bridges for her movement between occupations.

In Lily and Selden's discussion of success, Lily herself registers the indifference of masculine and feminine roles, of sorority and marriage, enunciating, by contrast, her desire for the progressive option of friendships. She ends her definition of success interrogatively—"Success? . . . Why, to get as much as one can out of life, I suppose. It's a relative quality, after all. Isn't that your idea of it?" But Selden proceeds declaratively: "My idea of success, . . . is personal freedom" (108). To his definition—which requires escape from one place to another, or giving up of one significance for another—Lily replies: "Ah, you are as bad as the other sectarians." She exclaims, "Why do you call your republic a republic? It is a close corporation, and you create arbitrary objections in order to keep people out" (113). Lily's question points out the insufficiency of all self-fashionings that are simply "for" or "against." In a voice that is better described as coalitional, Lily goes on, "Don't you think, . . . that the people who find fault with society are too apt to regard it as an end and not a means, . . . Isn't it fairer to look at [it] as [an] opportunit[y?]" (111). In this return, Lily's voice opens the window to a possible world of conflict and dialogue while Selden's continues to obey the actual world of gender and class distinctions. Lily needs the pieces of a mixed solution: some freedom, some dependence; some criticism, some sympathy.[16] Selden recommends renunciation of material goods for a life of intellectual freedom, but Lily understands this as the same predetermined contract that all of her associates offer: her resignation, his freedom.

Lily Bart's dilemma is fashioned in the imperative to negotiate professional and personal relations, making her a compelling figure for contemporary feminism. Without mother or father or fixed income,[17] she dreams—if haltingly—of a possible world in which she could critique the coarser aspects of the marketplace but without giving it up altogether. Selden's "freedom *from*" (108, emphasis added) will not do because it too is developed through an exclusionary logic, leaving Lily no ground to work from, no space for the more elastic practice of negotiating multiple territories. *Friendship* is her objective correlative for gender arrangements in which one would be allowed to retain some ties to the status quo while experimenting with new femininities, new masculinities. Even as Lily becomes aware of the artificiality of marriage arrangements, she needs to retain a feminine space and voice in order to annex other spaces and voices. Unlike the mythical Lilith, she cannot simply step out of the dominant field. As friends, Lily and Selden would not be free of *normal heterosexuality* but neither would they be closed off from the territory of intellectual critique or the space of sisterly caretaking.

Wharton broadens and deepens her text's negotiating thematics in Lily's pondering of her social world in the image of a "great gilt cage." Although this passage appears to confirm a "totalizing system," in fact Wharton's narration further demonstrates Lily's awareness of the porousness of social and economic systems. Within the gender system of upper-class New York, Lily must create herself as a woman-to-be-married and then as a married woman. The logic of this construction is linear and uncompromising. In her early meeting with Selden, Lily complains about the constraints: "Ah, there's the difference—a girl must [marry], a man may if he chooses" (17). Between "must" and "may," Wharton indicates the closed nature of this exchange for women. Indeed, in the text's actual world, a woman must hope for closure in her dealings with men.

But Lily's later musings about the cage revise the closure of this exchange, indicating again Lily's bid for friendship and border crossing. The full passage merits our attention:

> Miss Bart was a keen reader of her own heart, and she saw that her sudden preoccupation with Selden was due to the fact that his presence shed a new light on her surroundings.... [H]e had preserved a certain social detachment, a happy air of viewing the show objectively, of having points of contact outside the great gilt cage in which they were all huddled for the mob to gape at. How alluring the world outside the cage appeared to Lily, as she heard its door clang on her! In reality, she knew, the door never clanged: it stood always open; but most of the

captives were like flies in a bottle, and having once flown in, could
never regain their freedom. It was Selden's distinction that he had never
forgotten the way out. (86–87)

In a significant authorial change of mind, Wharton first closes the door
and then reopens it, apparently dramatizing Lily's desire for escape. But
a textual ambivalence denies this conclusion. The images of "clanging"
and "flies in a bottle" hinge on the resounding "never": "never clanged,"
"never regained." The negative overrides the apparent difference between
staying and escaping, establishing as subtext or alternate myth the freedom
to negotiate oppositions, to come and go, to cross over and return. To get
"out" of the cage on Selden's terms is impossible, as Lily makes clear. She
has no means of supporting herself alone on the fringes of society. And yet,
it is because Lily sees Selden as "out" that she is led to imagine some mode
of intercourse that is not contained by the cage. In this way, Lily negotiates
Selden's logic just as Wharton negotiates the public sphere of authorship.
She recognizes a good on his *side* but without buying in altogether. Indeed,
she takes to heart the idea of gaining independence but she does not separate freedom from the material conditions of her life. What Lily wants is a
relation with Selden in the threshold, a space of contact which will not
require her to *trade off*. This, of course, is exactly what feminist criticism
wants: a working relation to the institution that still allows coalition and
critique. Few feminist critics, in other words, desire absolute freedom or
silent partnership.

Wharton's critique of marriage and sorority solicits a negotiating feminist critical paradigm. Rather than insisting on the essential corruption of
either institution, Wharton's text negotiates the stubborn but nonetheless
pliable social structures that her characters encounter. Lily's voice may not
be strong enough to subvert the status quo, but her multiple contacts and
pedestrian habits recommend the liberating option of critique and accommodation or, more precisely, of adequate accommodations from which
one can exercise thoughtful critique and generous reasoning.

Friendship

The image of the slightly open cage is the most dramatic of Wharton's
threshold scenes. But again and again, the narrative returns Lily to points
of intersection, developing Wharton's rhetorical inscription of gender and
class negotiations. The author's recounting of her own longtime friendship
with the advocate Walter Berry suggests a bridging of sympathy and criti-

cism: "No critic was ever severer, but none had more respect for the artist's liberty. He taught me never to be satisfied with my own work, but never to let my inward convictions as to the rightness of anything I had done be affected by outside opinion."[18] The argument against "outside opinion" locates Wharton and Berry in domestic interiors whereas the argument against "satisfaction" suggests the requirement to broaden one's field. A comparison with Wharton's writing of the great gilt cage illustrates my claim that Wharton sought a third or middle option. The description of her friendship with Berry is accumulative rather than depleting. Though the poetic cadence of the phrases turns on the conjunction "but," the effect of the juxtaposition is additive. The uniting and joining of opposites—which remain oppositions but now annexed in the figure of *friend*—point to an evolution of thinking. Berry provided judgment and freedom, resistance and affirmation. The rhetorical negotiation patterned in Berry's friendship is not based on trade—*this for that*, but on enfolding and oscillation—*this* and then *that*. If we return to *The House of Mirth* with this discursive pattern in mind, we find that Wharton speaks it often.

Selden and Lily's walk along the wooded path above Bellomont, for example, might be interpreted as resistance to the marriage plot. But it also operates as a textual expansion of Lily's character by building the discourse of a nondepleting interchange. Lily needs male sponsorship; that is why she stays *in* the game. Yet she does not want the traditional marriage of separate spheres and antagonistic bargaining, and that is why she always defers. Though Selden's voice reinstates the same terms, the narrator insists on Lily's desire: "[Selden] himself did not know why he had led their talk along such lines; it was the last use he would have imagined himself making of an afternoon's solitude with Miss Bart. But it was one of those moments when neither seemed to speak deliberately, when an indwelling voice in each called to the other across unsounded depths of feeling" (114). Wharton's appeal to an "indwelling voice" suggests the sympathetic tone of domestic fiction, but the writer employs it here to institute a new mode of male/female friendship. This "calling" depicts the laws of gender and sexual division as transgressable, and not just in irony or jest.

This possibility or dream is expanded in other meetings between Lily and Selden. For example, the two escape to the garden after the tableaux vivants, a space between the world of business and the world of domestic interiors. The tone of Wharton's narration is decidedly romantic in a novel that generally prefers a realistic tone: "Hanging lights made emerald caverns in the depths of foliage, and whitened the spray of a fountain falling among lilies. The magic place was deserted: there was no sound but the plash of the water on the lily-pads, and a distant drift of music" (221). Again the narrator turns to silence for what is hardly writable in this scene, the only sound being "the plash of the water on the lily-pads." The Lily of the tableaux vivants—woman as consumable object, woman as man's opposite—is displaced onto nature as if to insist on the greater naturalism of transitional space and friendship. Between the Welly Brys interior and the public space of business, the garden again opens the question of Selden's and Lily's "identities in dialogue."[19] When she turns to remind Selden of her dream—"Why can't we be friends?"—Lily "raise[s] her eyes with the beseeching earnestness of a child" (222). Though Selden can only answer with "love," Lily's question recurs to her earlier desire for critical coalition and more fully discloses the possible world she is trying, paradoxically, to invent and inhabit.

In Lily's childlike look, Wharton implies the less determined sexuality of girlhood as well as Lily's desire for friendship. This idea is played out in the turn of Lily's face to Selden's before they kiss, an action likened to "the soft motion of a flower." This naturalization of Lily's name expands the sexual ambiguity of the scene since lily or lotus may refer both to genital magic and to virginity as well as to the self-fertilizing power of the vulva.[20] In all cases, Lily's representation in this transitional moment wavers between fixed points in the sexual field. This instability is not taken seriously by the realism of the text (this scene is described as "unreality") or by its chronological plot (Lily will soon be restored to the Welly Brys interior). Instead the indeterminate sexuality of the scene implies the text's alternate world of collaboration and accretion, what Lily calls "friendship." If Wharton is making a gesture toward the feminism of her age, she seems to be rejecting both the *choices* of the past and the *choice* of the future. In the perplexing "unreality" of this passage—before Lily is returned to the text's actual world and her *sex*—Wharton implies that the way out of the great gilt cage is to linger in the doorway or corridor, between the options of separation and subversion. Unlike anthropological descriptions of liminality, however, this discursive hovering of personas in transition is not accompanied by paring down but by piling up.[21]

The description of this space is excessive: "hanging lights," "emerald caverns," "depths of foliage," "a fountain falling among lilies." Wharton seems to insist that a middle voice is not a compromise and that accommodation of difference does not represent poverty of imagination or inheritance. By negotiating marriage and sorority—two similar models that cannot be exchanged because they are already the same—Wharton argues for a use of each, or some aspects of each, in the project of inventing more flexible, more supportive male/female relations. Thus, *negotiating identities* leads to more not less: more connections, more space, more presentations of the self.

In the first chapter of the novel's book 2, Selden again comes upon Lily at the train station, again in transition. But according to his view, "a subtle change had passed over the quality of her beauty" (307). He remembers their last parting "on the threshold of the Brys' conservatory; . . . [t]hen [her beauty] had a transparency through which the fluctuations of the spirit were sometimes tragically visible; now its impenetrable surface suggested a process of crystallization" (307). Selden's observation is prejudicial and contradictory but still useful to my critical purposes. If Lily's beauty has distilled into a hard surface, the transparency through which the fluctuations of her spirit sometimes showed was not her tragedy. His analysis—"that she had at last arrived at an understanding with herself: had made a pact with her rebellious impulses, and achieved a uniform system of self-government, under which all vagrant tendencies were either held captive or forced into the service of the state" (308)—is once again insightful but erroneously concluded. Having seen Lily through the scenes with Trenor and Mrs. Penniston (both of which register Lily's failure at uniformity and advertise her vagrancy), readers are aware that Lily's Mediterranean tour with the Dorsets simulates her earlier attempts to remain attached without being bought, to negotiate the marriage market and female friendships without surrendering entirely to the terms of either.

Lily's night with Gerty in the novel's pivotal chapter 14, like Lily's numerous encounters with Selden, illustrates again Wharton's rhetorical negotiations: of sorority and heterosexuality, private and public space, critical and sympathetic modes of discourse. It is prefaced by the women's meeting in transition in chapter 10. Lily has run into Gerty "just [as she has] left the committee-meeting of a struggling charity in which she [is] interested" (179). Lily herself is just leaving the shop that Gerty is entering. In a moment of "rare deviation" (438), Lily has just deferred purchasing a coveted dressing case until she pays off some debts. But a sudden "vision" of herself leading the life of Gerty's "cases" leads Lily to "slip . . . a liberal fraction of [her dress money] into Miss Farish's hand" (179–80). Like Lily's meeting with Selden in the garden, this passage is clearly unrealistic and has been quickly discredited in past readings. And yet it originates in Lily's vision, which is itself born of her propensity to join material from one territory with information from another. Her gesture at charity may be clumsy, but it is nonetheless noble and certainly *real* because it is exactly the sort of gesture that is so difficult to make in a decidedly territorial world.

Wharton's *The House of Mirth*

When Lily escapes to Gerty's after Trenor's attempt to collect on his "loans," the narrative negotiation of sorority is expanded. Gerty's apartment serves as an interval space since Lily will leave it to return to Mrs. Penniston's, and the scene begins with Lily at Gerty's door. Before Lily's entry, Gerty had thought of her friend as wanting only "the taste of new experiments," but with Lily before her, Gerty's "compassionate instincts" sweep "aside all her reluctances" (263). While the textual realism—or Lily's actual world—continues to offer a *stable* Gerty, the passage plays upon the possibility of connecting these very dissimilar women. Indeed Wharton appears to overwrite the women's difference in order to establish their need for negotiated relations in this moment.[22]

In their spoken interaction, Lily beseeches Gerty: "if I went to [Selden], if I told him everything ... would he loathe me? Or would he pity me, and understand me?" (268–69). Gerty, who loves Selden herself but knows her homeliness is no match for Lily's beauty, chooses to present Selden in the best light—for his sake as well as Lily's. "He will help you," she declares (269). The sorority figured here is less exclusive than the sisterhood that Gerty's figure usually demonstrates. Her heart leans toward her own abandonment, Lily's anguish, and Selden's infatuation.

As in the spatial intervals dramatized with Lily and Selden's meetings, this scene depends less on the women's speech than on their silence. We have already been told that "what Lily craved was the darkness made by enfolding arms, the silence which is not solitude, but compassion holding its breath" (240). Lily briefly provides the voice that draws the curtain on their actual world, appealing to Gerty to hold her: "All I want," she says, "is to feel that you are near me" (266–67). The embrace between Gerty and Lily offers a potential analogy for the complexity and often factiousness in contemporary feminist criticism. The two women's differences strain easy categorization just as lesbian and heterosexual, black and white, working and middle-class differences threaten the terms *female, woman, feminist.* Yet in their mutual struggle for attachment and freedom, these two rivals "become the means for each other's moral growth."[23]

Together in Gerty's bed, the two "girls" are distinguished from one another by Lily's decided femininity. Her hair and fragrance stand in sharp relief against Gerty's rigid body. But this predictable and stable defining of woman in both of her "other" aspects (as sex and as domestication) is adumbrated by the sensual and maternal imagery of the passage: "compassion holding its breath." In the first of several scenes showing this posture, the chapter ends with an uncanny assemblage of the two women: "[Lily] moaned; and Gerty silently slipped an arm under her, pillowing her head in its hollow as a mother makes a nest for a tossing child. In the

41

warm hollow Lily lay still and her breathing grew low and regular. . . . her head sank deeper into its shelter, and Gerty felt that she slept" (270). Like the garden corridor shared by Selden and Lily, this bedroom scene links friendship with indeterminate sexual iconographies—"warm hollow," "deeper . . . shelter." But the most significant revision comes in Wharton's grafting of female friendship with maternal symbolism; the women's embrace is a nesting, Lily's "low and regular" breathing a reinstatement of necessary emotional securities.

In book 2, chapter 8, Gerty remembers this scene, a discursive recursion on Wharton's part that suggests the significance she attaches to it. The internalized scene begins with Gerty's sense that Lily should "detach . . . [herself] from [her] old associations"; to the New Woman, Lily's "hold[ing] fast" to those contacts can only deter her "progress" (432). Yet the vision that follows is not of Lily's holding on to old associations but of her being held by her friend; Gerty has "not forgotten the night of emotion when she and Lily had lain in each other's arms, and she had seemed to feel her very heart's blood passing into her friend" (433). The sentimental rhetoric of this description again demonstrates Wharton's penchant to deploy *lady authorship* when it suits her purposes. Though Gerty does not believe that Lily remembers (a conclusion the novel later questions), her memory returns readers to the sexual intimacy of the earlier scene: "heart's blood" can be read in terms of uterine transactions, suggesting again the maternal character of the friendship, while the image of "passing into her friend" operates as another reference to heterosexual intimacy. As much as these scenes refigure sorority—by making a place for the mother and by allaying women of different classes—they also refigure heterosexuality, with Gerty as a feminized Selden. This revision of masculinity, like Charlotte Brontë's taming of Rochester, puts Lily and Selden on equal footing. Thus Wharton's rhetorical negotiations shadow the characters' interpersonal negotiations, setting in motion a critical dialogue between heterosexuality and maternity, commercialism and altruistic love. Through this thematic-rhetorical mirroring, Wharton not only states her preference for less rigid social boundaries but demonstrates her political savvy about the need to recirculate and adjust power relations.

Building on the already "unreal" vision of Lily and Gerty's embrace, this passage provides powerful evidence of the friendships that Wharton's text solicits even as it critiques the market in women and the new sororities of her day. Friendship begins to expand as a true negotiation of gender, class, and sex differences where participants respond to one another with affection and critique. While sorority and marriage have stood for enforced domestication and the production of the same woman (as wife or hostess or professional), friendship stands for complex relations to the differences within each character (or reader). This figure tolerates ambiguity, recognizing that even the opposition is *different* and the *same* and may offer materials, ideas, personas for assembling a new reality.

Lily's action is based in this knowledge, although she often effaces it. For example, she begins to think she is "bad" because she has trusted Trenor, and she imagines her faults to be attributable to "some wicked pleasure-loving ancestress" (363).

Toward the end of the novel, however, she seems less sure of these ready conclusions. For example, when Selden comes to save her from Mrs. Hatch, she reminds him that "there is very little real difference in being inside *or* out" (453, emphasis added). While Lily's claim may not hold true for all of her acquaintances, it is true for her because she needs access to both sides of the divide if she is to survive. She needs to be able to accommodate some of the requirements of her wealthier friends while also drawing what sustenance she can from her less prestigious working friends. Separatist ideals—whether Selden's or the reader's—deny Lily the option of "affirmative deconstruction" (Spivak), of seeing the fault in a system and yet drawing from its stores to see what other patterns can be invented.[24] Lily's awareness of this option—and her insistence on other ways of thinking about reality—is her strongest appeal to feminism.

The most prolonged representation of Lily's possible world of coalition or friendship is provided in the novel's closing pages, in scenes that critics have long found problematic. These are those moments when Lily discovers "human fellowship," first when she holds Nettie's baby and later when she imagines the baby beside her (510 and 522). Most readers have found this ending weak, a "compromise" on Wharton's part in which Lily's complexities are simplified and the situation of the working class is unconvincingly represented as the only alternative to the glamorous world that Lily has lost.[25] This critical conclusion, however, fails to take seriously the possible world of Lily's dreams and overlooks the negotiation implied in Wharton's revisions of the scene. In fact, Wharton intratextually revises both the Lily-Gerty bed scene and the Lily-baby dream scenes. In the latter, she revises Lily's interactions with Nettie's baby, first depicting the experience as sexual invasion and then rethinking the scene through maternal imagery.

In the literal moment of holding the baby, "the burden in [Lily's] arms seemed as light as a pink cloud . . . but as she continued to hold it the weight increased, sinking deeper, and penetrating her with a strange sense of weakness, as though the child entered into her and became a part of herself" (510). Wharton's language here appears to dramatize Lily's sexual objectification: "burden," "sinking deeper," "penetrating." But the imagery of this passage is uncannily synthesized in Lily's sense that the baby has "become a part of herself." Showing a breakdown of boundary and the hazard to self, Wharton nevertheless indicates the necessity *for Lily* to maintain this negotiating posture. Rhetorically and narratively, the scene urges readers' reconsideration of the imperative to befriend Lily, that is, to recognize a likeness with her, our own propensity to negotiate several sides. Like Lily, feminist critics often seek some safety and some liberty, some convention and some radical readjustment. Like her, the critics discussed in chapter 1 recognize their uncanny placement between distinct and often opposing parties.

The image of mother and child is doubly represented when the human mother is compared to the bird whose "nest [is] built on the edge of a cliff" (517). This recurrence interrupts Lily's actual world insistence on immutable categories and constant loyalties. Here—in the daring overwriting of the beautiful Lily, aloof and exotic, with the heavy material child—Wharton risks *quality* for experimentation and ideology for coalition. As Susan Goodman writes, Wharton "graft[s] . . . the artistic with the utilitarian," creating a new definition of woman.[26] Our uneasiness with this final image has much to do with our own desire to avoid a compromise but does not necessarily reflect Wharton's narrative pattern.

In Lily's later dream of the infant, she imagines "Nettie Struther's child . . . lying on her arm: she felt the pressure of its little head against her shoulder. She did not know how it had come there, but she felt no great surprise at the fact, only a gentle penetrating thrill of warmth and pleasure. She . . . hollow[ed] her arm to pillow the round downy head" (522). This version of the first dream vision shifts in emphasis from sexual invasion to maternal intimacy demonstrating in an *un*compromising way Wharton's preference to negotiate generic, political, and personal oppositions. What is so distinctive about these closing scenes is exactly this: their capacity to elicit a serious consideration of two opposing worlds, to act, that is, as a middle, if not fully synthetic, voice. If the passage operates idealistically, allowing Lily the friendship she has asked for throughout the novel, it also gives body to Lily's desire to belong without giving up, to negotiate her place without trading all of her selves. At the level of writing, this passage provides an analogue for Wharton's rhetorical negotiations throughout the novel, her narrative movement between the oppositions of celibacy and marriage, sorority and heterosexuality. Though in terms of plot, the novel fails to provide a middle space for Lily's grafting of upper and lower classes, of masculine and feminine spheres, of beauty and utility, the sentimental disruption of the realistic text *is* an opportunity or opening for readers to negotiate literary standards and to write beyond the ending.

Thus, Wharton's "weak" conclusion reverberates with new possibilities since in the negotiation between heterosexual, sororal, and mothering metaphors, other narrative contacts resurface. For example, we begin to see a whole set of textual moments in which Wharton dramatizes intervals, thresholds, and negotiation: Lily's *chance* meeting on the stair with the charwoman in chapter 1, her several run-ins on the street with Rosedale, Carrie Fisher's renewal of friendship on Fifth Avenue, Miss Kilroy's kindness in the millinery establishment. While none of these moments in isolation has the strength to challenge the female plot (marriage or sorority), read collectively they recommend possible world coalitions through which marriage and sorority might be altered and expanded.

Between Edith Wharton and Lily Bart, between Lily Bart and the feminist reader, the interval spaces of *The House of Mirth* open rather than close the question of *friendship*, of critical accommodations in which we show our need to belong even as we work for change. This is Wharton's challenge, and it remains the most important political question in late twentieth-century feminisms. How will we know women except in trade? How will we speak except in promotion? Is there an interval between feminist unity and masculinist cooption, between black womanism and white feminism? The future still waits for an answer.

3

Our Confounded Identities
Negotiating Audience in Zora Neale Hurston's *Their Eyes Were Watching God*

It is a well-known fact that no matter where two sets of people come together, there are bound to be some in-betweens.
—Zora Neale Hurston

CENTRAL TO MY concept of a negotiating criticism is the notion that feminist perspectives are produced through the imbrication of oppositions.[1] What most distinguishes feminist criticism is not its establishment of a separate field or a unique methodology but its go-between movements among a variety of fields and methods in the interest of providing space and agency to women writers, characters, and readers. To my mind, Zora Neale Hurston's fictive and autobiographical texts are characterized by just this sort of discursive activity. In this chapter, I will explore Hurston's textualizing of a racially gendered, in-between identity, in other words, her production of a female self through maneuverings between and among black and white territories, languages, and symbol systems. I will look, in particular, at her rhetorical handling of white and black female audiences and argue that, in her view, negotiation is the situation as well as the substance of the tale.

In chapter 1, I illustrated how negotiation has come to be a structuring motif in feminist criticisms. One outcome of this present mode is an increased awareness of differences in audience. Indeed, accommodating a number of *other* listeners is a rhetorical situation that increasingly characterizes feminist critical work. Perhaps third stage feminist criticism can be defined by *anxiety of audience*.[2] Having recognized the liabilities of a false *we*, feminist critics write with heightened consciousness of multiple audiences within our field and of the imbalances that characterize our relations.

In other words, feminist critics have become more aware of encroachments upon and witness by different feminisms within feminist criticism. In locations not specifically feminist—American Studies, for example—new essays on whiteness dramatize the false assumptions of critical projects that pretend a nonracialized subjectivity.³ By and large, this heightened awareness has led to greater integrity—and more modesty—in our work. And yet this new consciousness also carries new liabilities. Differences and imbalances can become so emphasized that the possibility of coalition, if not commonality, is assumed outdated and naive. As Michael Awkward writes, "Boundary transgression . . . has come to require either extreme theoretical naivete or perhaps unprecedented scholarly daring."⁴

For me as a white critic to write on Zora Neale Hurston today, especially in a project designed to emphasize a sameness within black and white feminisms, is a riskier endeavor than it would have been in the 1980s. I must try to ask what risks a negotiating feminist criticism poses for black feminists. Does my favoring of multiple sides and in-between situations, for example, romanticize in theory what is extremely difficult in the actual lives of women of color, including black feminists? Even if I narrow my responsibility to textual intercourse and not the vast horizon of cultural politics, might my approach distort creative texts by African-American women by searching for an accommodating tone, a *middle voice*? As Sandra Harding cautions, "Isn't it the worst kind of agenda to force women back into their traditional role of collaborators, their conventional position as . . . helpmates?" Michele Wallace formulates the problem just as powerfully, describing "the precarious dialectic of a [black feminist] creative project that is forced to be 'other' to the creativity of white women and black men."⁵

With an eye toward these conundrums I reread Hurston's *Their Eyes Were Watching God* (1937) to ask how Hurston fictionalizes her own personal, professional, and discursive negotiations.⁶ Thus this chapter demonstrates the negotiations of reception and race in contemporary feminist criticism by looking for antecedent graftings of oppositional audiences in Hurston's storytelling techniques. I follow the lead of black feminist thinkers such as bell hooks who boldly appropriate and reshape white and male discourses by fitting them to the contours of her intellectual history: "From small town Southern black life, from folk traditions, and church experience to cities to the university, to neighborhoods that are not racially segregated, to places where I see for the first time independent cinema," hooks shows that she reads and writes "critical theory" by working between racialized memory and the critical discourses that dominate academic studies

(Derrida, Michel Foucault, Frederic Jameson, Edward Said). In her words, "As we educate one another to acquire critical consciousness, we have the chance to see how important airing diverse perspectives can be for any progressive political struggle . . . [S]olidarity grows stronger in the context of productive critical exchange and confrontation."[7]

The particular focus of this chapter is the frame narrative in *Their Eyes Were Watching God*, a space in which Hurston represents her own critical exchange and confrontation with oppositional audiences. Looking closely at Hurston's female poetics and politics, I suggest that she negotiates the power imbalances between white and black women by enlarging the small woman—Phoeby Watson—and diminishing the porch sitters—a *mixed* and more distant audience. This choreography of audience gives priority to black women as the first hearers and speakers of the tale but also problematizes blackness through Phoeby's mulatto figuring and *secondary* significance. The model of *hearing through* a black woman suggests renegotiations of white feminism through black feminist thought.

My method of reading here is similar to my approach in the Wharton chapter. I argue for the appropriateness of *negotiation* by looking at Hurston's self-representation in her autobiographical *Dust Tracks on a Road*. I supplement my critical discussion with the historical horizon of black American migration in the first quarter of the twentieth century.

Hurston helps us think through the problematics of black and white feminist audiences by reminding us of the inscrutable nature of texts. According to Françoise Lionnet, Hurston's vigorous overwriting and hyperbole "caution her . . . reader to defer judgment about the explicit referentiality of her text. . . . Hurston is fully aware of the gaps and discrepancies that can exist between intention and execution, reality and representation, reason and imagination, in short, between the words . . . and the tune, which is the source of unity for the singers on the porch."[8] Lionnet goes on to argue that Hurston's autobiography constitutes a hybridized text, one that maps the writer's negotiations with discourse communities rather than her chronological, factual history.

According to Lionnet, *Dust Tracks* is a text "that attempts to create its own genealogy by simultaneously appealing to and debunking the cultural traditions it helps to redefine." Likening it to a folktale, Lionnet remarks that its "content is not rigid and unchanging but varies according to the tale-telling situation. It is the contextual frame of reference, the situation of the telling, that determines how the tale is reinterpreted by each new teller."[9]

Lionnet's description of *Dust Tracks* corresponds with my definition of feminist critical negotiations. The book is patterned on the twin movements of rhetorical accommodation and resistance, not resistance or subversion alone.[10] What is particularly useful from Lionnet in a feminist rereading of *Their Eyes Were Watching God* is her reminder that Hurston shaped her materials in relation to the African-American folktale, a form that both thematizes character negotiations—the folk find a way to survive without open revolt or mass insurgence—and which operates, in its delivery, as a discursive oscillation, a textual movement between listener and teller.

In *Dust Tracks on a Road*, Hurston narrates her early life with attention to the *accidents* of gender, race, and class. Later, she consciously *suits* these givens to dress herself as Hurston the daughter, Hurston the student, Hurston the anthropologist: a field worker at once participant in and observer of her culture.[11] Making herself her father's daughter ("some children are just bound to take after their fathers in spite of women's prayers"),[12] Hurston claims John Hurston's meanderings as familial signature. She tells us that he "had learned to read and write somehow *between* cotton-choppings and cotton-pickings" (emphasis added), a phrasing that deftly symbolizes black negotiations with the master's language, beginning with Frederick Douglass's trading of bread for letters. In Hurston, that rhetorical-political negotiation is more complex because she already inherits a literary history in which African-American tellers and writers have suited the English language to African-American uses. Thus Hurston's *anxiety of audience* spans not simply black traditions and white language but black as well as white authorizations of African-American letters.

We learn that Hurston arrived in New York in 1925 by way of a traveling theatrical troupe, after schooling in Baltimore and intermittent enrollment at Howard University. She studied for two years with Franz Boas at Barnard before returning south. In Robert Hemenway's words, "The New Negro cast her lot with America"; she "thirsted after higher education and the security it implied."[13] At the same time, she did not simply cast her personal or racial history aside. As Hemenway puts it, Hurston was becoming a scientist at Barnard (the women's division of Columbia), but "she did not abdicate the crown of the artist . . . [instead] a kind of vocational schizophrenia began to complicate her life, calling for a compromise between her college career and her literary interests. Barnard came to represent scientific discipline and academic respectability; the life of the Harlem Renaissance artist came to symbolize imaginative freedom, social progress, and liberating iconoclasm. Holding both worlds together was her commitment to the folk experience and the artistic forms it generated."[14] "Holding both worlds together" required sponsorship and, potentially, other compromises; Hurston found a patron in the wealthy white New Yorker, Mrs. R. Osgood Mason.

In 1927, Hurston signed a contract with Mason, which allowed her a monthly stipend of $200, a moving picture camera, and a Ford automobile in exchange for her field work in the South. Under this agreement, Mrs. Mason would read and approve Hurston's research before it was published. In "Looking for Zora," Alice Walker takes issue with Hurston's gracious recording of her relations with Mrs. Mason: "It pained me to see Zora pretending to be naive and grateful about the old white 'Godmother' who helped finance her research," she writes.[15] Mary Helen Washington explains Hurston's posing as purely economic: "Beneath all the subterfuge and posturing in [Zora's] letters [to Mrs. Mason] is one cold, inescapable fact: Zora was hard-pressed for the money for her career. She needed to travel to the South to spend time with people who knew the folk stories and would tell them only to trusted friends."[16] Hemenway, however, offers a more complex view of Hurston's relation with Mason, explaining that while Hurston was clearly pursuing material support in her contract, Mason and Hurston also "discovered some superrational relationship."[17] Throughout their contact, he explains, Hurston "chafed under Mrs. Mason's restraints and schemed with [Langston] Hughes about ways to circumvent them; yet she still revered, even loved, her Godmother. The relations with Mrs. Mason were humanly inconsistent. As Hurston went farther away, the psychic bond deteriorated, and her Godmother became a meddling patron. When she was closer, the bond was an operative force in her life, and Godmother was a soul mate, a woman whom Hurston could address as her spiritual progenitor: 'Flowers to you—the true conceptual mother.'"[18]

When Hurston returned to Florida as an academic field worker, she found herself shuttling between oral and written languages, between the *low* culture of her subjects and the *high* culture of university education. She cunningly conveys this negotiation in reports *of herself*: as a sometimes receptor—"the way the story told itself to me," as a future translator—"My landlady explained to me what was meant," and as cultural go-between—"I had store-bought clothes, a lighter skin, and a shiny car."[19]

Among other critical movements, Hurston's return south structured the writer's renegotiation of gender positions. In her young life, Hurston's father held the position of storyteller, but in her field work, Hurston occupies—in turns—both of the critical positions on the porch. She is Phoeby, the listener, and Janie, the teller.

Hurston's challenge to African-American and feminist critics from Richard Wright to Alice Walker lies in her accommodations of audience as well as in her willingness to identify with more than one position. While Wright repudiated Hurston's novel for the way it played to whites, black and white feminist critics have responded by emphasizing Hurston's radical poetics, in particular her subversion of white, male values. Neither approach looks at what is truly radical in Hurston's frame narrative. Beyond the apparent referentiality of the text, Hurston's rhetorical negotiations in the frame both elect and complicate black female agency. Phoeby's identity, in particular, signifies upon the author's straddling of cultures and her investment in a biracial women's discourse. Hurston clues us to her authorial negotiations in the novel's frame where Phoeby and Janie talk. Through the understated Phoeby, Janie's "little [listening] woman," Hurston figures her own deft navigation between and among competing and antithetical audiences. Henry Louis Gates associates the "little man or woman" with the trickster and the crossroads.[20] He or she "turns" the meaning of the text, making insignificance into significance. I want to argue that Hurston's Phoeby—who has been long overlooked in feminist reception—indicates Hurston's deployment of in-between possibilities. Rather than a single intersection of identities, Phoeby's location marks an overlap created through successive tellings of the story and crossings between audiences. Through Phoeby's hearing, Hurston self-reflexively brokers the power relation between herself and a number of witnesses as well as her own differences within. She also maps the negotiations of her inset narrative: between black and white, female and male, active and passive, local and national, individual and collective.

At first glance, Phoeby seems to suggest that Hurston privileges black female witnesses, and she does to a degree. But in Phoeby's function as an in-between, even go-between persona, Hurston produces several overlapping audiences—Phoeby, the porch sitters, and, by implication, all of the story's future mediators. Thus the text advertises its "both/and" logic, its affiliating and confrontational relation to a number of American identities and ideas. In this way, Hurston insists on the insider/outsider plurality of her art.

We are clued to Phoeby's significance and hence the significance of the frame through her self-effacement, her smallness, and her mulatto appearance. A crossroads character, the mulatto figure recommends a hybrid, negotiating—never pure—subjectivity. In Phoeby, Hurston insinuates in particular the indeterminate and mixed character of her audiences and thus her negotiating art. In other words, Phoeby is not a name for a separate African-American female aesthetic or origins, but a name for the culturally mixed context into which African-American women's art is delivered—and waits for a response. Phoeby's and Janie's peripatetic habits make this clear. Even sitting on the porch, Phoeby and Janie are never closed off from the broader, more contentious world since readers *overhear* the story in the wider circle implied in the porch and realized in the writing and publishing. Indeed, it is that contentious overhearing world which occasions the text, as it was Hurston's negotiation of worlds which gave shape to her literary productions.

Making this point dramatically, Hurston links her heroine and her audience to a mulatto identity and the habit of migration.[21] Janie's migrations are writ large, of course, while Phoeby's are represented in miniature: she migrates from porch to porch, a practice that mirrors Hurston's maneuvers as field worker as well as the dynamic quality of the folktale.

First elaborating Phoeby's position and then reading Janie's tale, we achieve a new perspective on Hurston's negotiated politics and poetics.[22] As Lionnet observes, Hurston views the self as "fluid and changing,"[23] in other words, as analogous to oral language, which itself *changes* between mouths and ears. Speech, as well as identity, lives in intervals—held open by the listener or narratee—and all conversation advances as a kind of expansive swapping and shifting. This poetics requires much more from the listener than a passive response or casual celebration of commonality. Instead it requires personal and collective responsibility for new negotiations of the tale and its politics.

Phoeby's Hearing

Part of the task in a feminist negotiating poetics is to give positive valence to a migratory, impure consciousness intent on survival and expression. Lorraine O'Grady provides positive naming to a negotiating black subjectivity: "Black artists and theorists frequently refer to African-Americans as 'the first postmoderns.' They have in mind a now agreed understanding that our inheritance from the motherland of pragmatic, 'both:and' philosophic systems, combined with the historic discontinuities of our experience as black slaves in a white world, have caused us to construct subjectivities able to negotiate between 'centers' that, at the least, are double."[24]

Hurston's *Their Eyes Were Watching God*

Hurston negotiates a number of *centers* in the figure of Phoeby, a "bosom friend" who can be interpretively linked to a series of Hurston's associates: her godmother, Mrs. Mason; her companion, Fannie Hurst; her mentor, Alain Locke; her associate, Langston Hughes; her numerous informants and Eatonville compatriots. In the simple act of naming, Hurston negotiates myth and history. Choosing the alternate spelling for her *small woman* (Phoeby rather than Phoebe), she mixes a number of possible allusions—to the moon goddess (alternately Phoebe, Artemis); to Phoebus (Apollo); to the ancient Phoenicians, and to the phoenix. This name, then, is crossed by a number of cultural *centers* and organizes an author-audience corridor that doubles (triples, quadruples) as negotiations between black (woman) and white (woman), female and male, African and European cultures, Greek and African myth, active and passive resistance. Although African-American and feminist critics since W. E. B. Du Bois have theorized double-voiced discourse, Phoeby's name covers mixed *hearings*, her identity as listener suggesting a manifold and complex aurality. As a name for Hurston, Phoeby can be construed both in her actual porch migrations and in the textualities which such movement engenders.

For example, when Phoeby approaches her friend, Janie claims that she "don't mean to bother wid tellin' [the others] nothin."[25] But immediately, she insinuates her desire for Phoeby to relay her story: "You can tell 'em what Ah say if you wants to." Phoeby's reply returns the desire to Janie: "If you so desire Ah'll tell 'em what you tell me to tell 'em" (17). Throwing "desire" back and forth between them, Janie and Phoeby end up conceiving a story, which is, in part, about how texts are constructed by the listener. The only unambiguous result of this textual migration is that readers surely know that Phoeby will tell the story *she* hears. Janie's "opened up" house ("let[ting] dis breeze get a little catchin") barely veils Janie's hope that her words will take wing (19). This vignette distills the negotiated nature of Hurston's inset narrative and of the novel as a whole. The word that is heard can never be the same as the one that is spoken because it lives in its reception. The text is always realized through the negotiations of sender and receiver, even when they are antithetically conceived (as are Janie and the porch sitters whom Phoeby has left behind). What makes this information so crucial for feminist readers, of course, is the positioning of multiple female and some male participants: Hurston (the writer), Phoeby (the implied audience), Janie (the heroine), the other women and men anxious to overhear (audiences outside the text). The tale may be well heard or misheard, and it is likely to be *over*heard. Rather than safeguarding the story between like-minded women, then, Hurston seems to be assuming a more contentious reception among and between members of a heterogeneous audience.

From her position, Phoeby knows the longing "to be there and hear it *all*" (16), a longing strongly suggestive of white interest in *hearing* (as much as viewing) black performance and art during the Harlem Renaissance. In *Their Eyes Were Watching God* (a novel written at a geographical distance from Harlem), Hurston composes her eager white and black audiences as bosom female friends, negotiating the question of sincerity with the "good thoughts" that she implants between Janie and Phoeby.[26]

With Janie's arrival in the frame, readers move with Phoeby to Janie's back porch where our listening is implied as an overhearing of the women's intimate talk. From front porch to back porch—and by implication to numerous other porches—*Their Eyes Were Watching God* simultaneously portrays a black female subjectivity blossoming between Janie and Phoeby and insinuates a hybrid and complex audience, "sitters-and-talkers" (284), listening in on the story. This "both/and" convening is implied in Janie's contradictory directions to Phoeby, as we just saw. Janie may not talk to all of us, but Phoeby will. Thus Hurston does not insist on the purity or unalloyed character of Janie's and Phoeby's interaction, a tactic that might translate into the identity politics of separatism (in relation to both maleness and whiteness). Neither does she depend on a white, male *other* to define her characters over against, a choice that would bolster an aesthetics of subversion. Instead she demonstrates Phoeby's and Janie's difference by producing an aural torsion between black female identity and the performance of self in relation to multiple invited *others*.[27] As a self-reflexive trope for Hurston's hearing, then, Phoeby introduces the author's agency in rhetorical negotiations that begin at home, as they did between Hurston and her father, and fan out to white and black spaces of privilege and struggle, to Columbia and Harlem.

Bearing "mulatto rice" to Janie when she returns to town, Phoeby advertises her role as a negotiating figure. Indeed, the rice operates as a metaphor for the author's poetics of adjudication. Within the frame, it acts as an actual world catalyst of interchange: Phoeby's rice elicits Janie's story.[28] But the rice that appears to circulate merely between those two creates a wider corridor in our reading. For example, the implied hyphenation of text-food points indirectly to Hurston's actual world need for physical and spiritual sustenance and thus signifies upon the author's critical and cultural negotiations: her relations with black male artists, white patrons and teachers, as well as the folk of her origins and the texts of these various groups.

As listener or audience, Phoeby marks the transformation of Janie's story from interior and latent gnosis—an unknown tongue—to exterior and publicized knowledge—a migratory word. Elsewhere, Hurston claims that there is "no agony like bearing untold stories inside you,"[29] but she might as well have written *unheard* and *uneaten*. In connecting Phoeby's body and the aural—the novel refers to her "hungry listening" (23)—the writer emphasizes the *secondary* character's evocation of and communion in the journey and thus the in-between status of the text. Janie's words are set on a road with Phoeby, becoming part of her ambulatory body. Thus speaker and witness, male and female, black and white, cannot be strictly separated or antithetically conceived in relation to this text as a whole. Neither, of course, can these categories be ignored or homogenized. Instead, these sets of difference are shown to be dynamically conceived and altered through Phoeby's negotiation of centers. For example, Phoeby—who moves between the demands of her husband and the needs of her friend—alters the power relations between those two *others* in the time that she listens to the tale. Phoeby and Janie together encroach on male territory by taking the public space of the porch and suiting it to their needs, thus enabling their stories but without actually turning any man out of doors. Phoeby's mulatto rice suggests a distant relation with white audiences, but in the actual world of the frame, black audiences are expanded and complicated so that *whiteness* functions here as a backdrop to *blackness* and not the other way around.

"In the beginning of this was a woman," Hurston writes in chapter 1 in a sentence that conjures a number of referents. Janie is the woman coming down the road, but readers are watching with Phoeby, Janie's narratee, who is sitting with her friends on the front porch (9). She will be the beginning of Janie's story, prompting her with food and flattery. Reading from this standpoint, we are reminded that Hurston's listener-reader outside the story and the woman of the text's origins is also Mrs. Mason, Hurston's New York patron. If we read the woman at the beginning of *Their Eyes Were Watching God* not only as the storyteller but as the story's audience, we can reconsider Mrs. Mason's influence through Phoeby's fictive role. This move allows us to examine Hurston's imaginative use of her relation with her patron. Rather than sitting at Mrs. Mason's feet—or on her footstool, as Hemenway records it—Hurston now has Mrs. Mason sitting in as her narratee.[30] And Hurston will speak her story—in liaison with Janie—without Mrs. Mason's editorializing. Thus, Hurston transforms the lopsided politics between herself and Mrs. Mason by making Phoeby at once a reflection of herself (the migrating listener) and a reference to her patron (a woman wealthy enough to begin things). This move transforms the white sponsor into Zora's handmaid. Thus a less dismissive reading of Mason's place in Hurston's genealogy might read her through Hurston's frame narrative, as a background presence revised through Phoeby's character. In this view, Hurston's *accommodation* of whiteness reveals her imaginative maneuvers within the power structure, allowing us to see that a negotiating posture on the part of the subordinate player can redress power imbalances and not merely facilitate them. Because Phoeby and her rice point both ways—toward white and black, home and journey, local and national audiences—Hurston creates through her position the shuttle movement of negotiating plots. This discursive adjudication transfigures Mrs. Mason's overhearing through Phoeby, allowing Hurston simultaneously to make the black woman larger and the white woman smaller.

Returning to the novel's beginning, we find that the time of day is gestured in porch sitting and sundown. In this liminal time, sitters witness Janie as she enters their frame. But if they are kin to her, their speech is an act of "mass cruelty." Thus Hurston begins with the undecidable sign of *woman* and a complex community of *blacks*. The novel's first speaking—omnisciently narrated by yet another originating woman, Hurston as implied author—comes from the space of the porch and is evoked by envy and desire: "What dat ole forty year ole 'oman doin' wid her hair swingin' down her back lak some young gal?—Where she left dat young lad of a boy she went off here wid? . . . why she don't stay in her class?" (10).

The last of the questions points to the real problem: Janie's not staying in place, a problem emblematized in her "swingin' down" hair. This *feature* points to Hurston's artistic migrations in New York, where she moved defiantly between black and white sponsors and resisted putting her folk art into the service of Negro politics *or* white collections. While Janie walks into the story—reminding her friends that she walked out of their town—Phoeby will walk from porch to porch to collect and pass on stories. In this miniature self-portrait, Hurston sketches her own porch migration, as well as her South-North, North-South, U.S.-Caribbean movements. Her entry into New York came at the end of the Great Migration. But she patterned her life as artist and scholar along migratory lines, asserting her right to explore her own allegiances and relationships. Thus the porch talk also resonates in multiple ways, conveying most slyly Hurston's critique of black academics and political leaders—"Negrotarians," she called them—who disapproved of her many aesthetic sides.

The "great rope of black hair swinging to her waist and unraveling in the wind" is remarked on once again as Janie passes the porch. This recurrence reminds readers of their place of witness with Phoeby; we are on the porch looking. It also suggests that in the community's view (also in Hurston's audiences' views) women's chosen migrations or journeys are shameful or arrogant or somehow both: erring women are troublesome and in the wrong. At this juncture, Hurston does not allow Janie to speak directly; instead, the narrating voice simply tells us that Janie "turned her face on the bander log and spoke" (11). Her silence is reiterated when she walks on to her house and the "gate slam[s] behind her" (11). Only when Phoeby speaks—as go-between or negotiating persona—do we hear Janie. What we hear first is more porch talk, talk that begins to construct Phoeby as a living and problematic link between Janie and the community. Before that hearing begins, however, Phoeby cautions the talkers, remarking that there may not be "anything to tell" and reminding the others that she is Janie's best friend "and *Ah* don't know." Lulu Moss cautions in return: "Tain't no use in your tryin' to cloak no ole woman lak Janie Starks, Phoeby, friend or no friend" (12). This exchange of cautions builds in narrative intensity since Lulu is warning Phoeby of her difficult position between Janie and the broader community. If "cloaking" is "no use," Phoeby will have to imagine another method of narrative movement. She initiates her response with the only definitive claim that the chapter plays out: "Ah'm bound to take her some supper" (13). Indeed, Phoeby *is* bound. Without her, the tale would never be told. As a go-between, her character occurs in combination with other characters, not independently. But if we take Phoeby as a conceit for the constructive center of the text, this "boundness" is neither peculiar to her nor despised by Hurston. Instead Phoeby's "boundness" is the very signature of Hurston's inventive sensibility.

Given the multiple women organized in this frame chapter, the implications of Phoeby's claim are several. If we begin at the further reaches of reference—the author's need for feeding—the claim signifies Mrs. Mason's literal feeding of Hurston while she gathered porch stories. If this was a feeding Hurston had to "wrassle" by keeping detailed accounts of all she spent,[31] the reference recurs as well to more liberal white and black women, like Fanny Hurst (who hired Hurston as companion) or to those, further back, who helped women like Nanny, Janie's grandmother, in their escape from slavery. Most dramatically, the author-narrator refers to her function as listener, since feeding and listening are metaphorically connected in Phoeby's role. At this level, black women's sympathetic nurture of one another is clearly conceived. But blackness itself, and even the category of black women, is not homogenized in this reference because Phoeby will leave the porch to take Janie her supper, refusing the offers of other black women to come along. And we can imagine that she will later share the story with men as well as women.

In the novel's frame as well as in her brief entrances in the central narration, Phoeby's identity is never individual and distinct but always borrowed and fabricated as she shifts from porch to porch. We see her, for example, "pick[ing] her way over to Janie's house like a hen to a neighbor's garden. [She s]topped and talked a little with everyone . . . turned aside momentarily to pause at a porch or two—going straight by walking crooked" (107). Phoeby is more troublesome—perhaps more compromised, more dually aligned, less *original*—than Janie. But she is also an occasion for interrogating an ideology of originality and separatism. As a woman identified through domestic roles, she nonetheless holds a mediating function in the town's life, relaying news, judging other people's stories, carrying information. In this position, she recurs to the black Mammy of slave plantation origins, who often acted as broker between the slave community and whites.[32] This often trivialized figure was actually an important character in southern history, extending the power base of black womanhood through a mixture of cooperation and resistance.

In fact, it is Phoeby's role as broker that lifts her from her secondary, passive role to her dramatic role as variegated audience. I have already pointed to the bowl of rice as metaphorical echo of her adjudicating function; the fact that Phoeby "covers" the bowl compounds its significance since *small* is actually *large* in the crossroads of the tale and *covering* is actually *telling*. The emblematic sharing of food gifts—and the self-effacement that accompanies the gesture—occurs in white and black women's writing. Hurston plays on the figure of the rice and the game of self-effacement to produce a negotiation of active/passive as well as physical/spiritual poles in the reader's imagination. The passage follows:

> "Ah knowed you'd be hungry. No time to be huntin' stove wood after dark. My mulatto rice ain't so good dis time. Not enough bacon grease, but Ah reckon it'll kill hongry."
>
> "Ah'll tell you in a minute," Janie said, lifting the cover. "Gal, it's *too* good! you switches a mean fanny round in a kitchen."
>
> "Aw, dat ain't much to eat, Janie. But Ah'm liable to have something sho nuff good tomorrow, 'cause you done come."
>
> Janie ate heartily and said nothing. The vari-colored cloud dust that the sun had stirred up in the sky was settling by slow degrees. (15)

This feminine interaction, unlike playing the dozens, includes self-effacement met by overstatement (it's *too* good) and a promise—not of more lethal insults but of more potent gifts. In writing Phoeby, Hurston plays with the domestic practice of swapping, a practice that ignores money and operates instead on the exercised belief that circulation multiplies the goods. Thus self-effacement may not empty the speaker but may operate as a discursive maneuver that activates a return on the part of the hearer. More simply put, active self-effacement may be chosen as a means of negotiating power and of gaining a more tangible relation to the text. This ploy puts Janie and Phoeby on the same *side* and alleviates the opposition—and hierarchy—we assume between speaker and listener, between voice and hearing. The imagistic play between light and dark, first initiated in the mulatto rice, is amplified here through the "vari-colored cloud dust" that settles as Janie is about to deliver her story. This imagery insists on the liminal and negotiating character of Hurston's delivery and serves as a metaphorical reminder of the multiple and contradictory relations within African-American letters.

Phoeby's rice, then, is less a figure for the black community or even black women than it is a complex and contradictory sign of negotiated relations among multicolored audiences, physical and spiritual demands, history and opportunity. Hurston cleverly amplifies Phoeby's rice by belittling it, the character's description—"ain't so good dis time" (15)—clearly encoding the woman-to-woman knowledge that the offering is excellent. Within the text, Phoeby's cooking appears to operate metonymically, merely designating her domestic (hear: secondary, feminine, acquiescent) identity. Within the frame of Hurston's novel, however, Phoeby's rice points metaphorically to Janie's mulatto history as well as to the dish she will serve, the food of her story. And beyond the text, the cooking signifies the transformation of history into myth. The itinerancy of slavery becomes a migrating word, a language stirring between Janie and Phoeby as well as between Phoeby and the reader. More than a mere receptacle of Janie's story, Phoeby's hearing activates the practice of swapping, presaging the negotiated *contents* of Janie's narrative. Shuttling between porches, between the community and Janie, between unheard and heard stories, Phoeby indicates Hurston's willingness to bet on some good hearings by many and diverse audiences. In marginalizing this second character, the writer mimics her own cultural marginality in both the place of her origin (now the place of her return) and the space of her formal education. Unlike the nomad-wanderer of mythic and biblical texts, however, the woman who swaps stories (here we are speaking of Phoeby and Hurston) positions herself close to and approximate with others. Phoeby is the critical relay who literally *makes known* the story, first in listening and communing and later in holding open this textual corridor for other self-critical female and feminist, even white and male readers.

Clearly Janie expects her friend to share her story rather than possess it; her soaking feet and chewing mouth suggest the peripatetic nature of her discourse. As we have seen, Phoeby's "moving . . . feet" are what convince Janie: "So [she] spoke" (7). Phoeby herself gives witness to her capacity for shifting or migratory knowledge when she says to Janie that "even wid dem overhalls on, you shows yo' womanhood" (4). While the people on the porch read Janie's overalls as resignifying Janie's slave status, Phoeby reads them differently: as advertising a powerful negotiation of cultural markers and an identity between fixed categories. In other words, Phoeby's "womanhood" refers not to an embrace of femininity or a cooption of masculinity but to an authoritative use of both categories in the performance of a speaking self.

Phoeby's hearing, then, announces the negotiated status of Janie's story: its modulations through multiple telling, its historical context in black/white interaction, and its secret relation to white as well as black women readers.

Janie's Crossings

From Phoeby's place in the novel, even Janie's story becomes a tale of successful negotiations, not one of consummate victories and subversions. A fictive contemporary of Hurston herself, Janie embodies both a history of white violence and a period of increased black migration. Recognizing Hurston's linking of mediation, mulatto, and migration, we turn our attention to the two stories of migration that the inset narrative tells: Nanny's story of coming "up from slavery," and Janie's journey south for love. What Phoeby first hears as Janie soaks her feet is a grandmother's narrative that begins with the Civil War. In 1865, at the war's end, Nanny was a freed slave, a released concubine, and a new mother. Her baby—Janie's mother—is a mulatto, conceived between Nanny and her previous owner. One of several white women sketched in Janie's telling is the white plantation mistress who threatens to flog Nanny for giving birth to her husband's child. Indeed, in Nanny's memory, this threat sets her in motion, leading her to hide—with her baby girl—in the swamp. Later in her story, she tells

Hurston's *Their Eyes Were Watching God*

of another white woman who helped her set up house and care for her daughter.

The oral narration of Nanny's liberation evokes the southern black movement from plantation slavery to sharecropping, but it also recommends remembrance of earlier movements. Nanny herself must have been born in the 1840s, three decades after the legal abolition of the Atlantic slave trade in 1808. Although illegal traffic in African slaves continued, the absence of a middle passage story (in Janie's narrative) suggests that Nanny was born on American soil and hence subjected to the possibility of domestic slave trade. Other significant migrations and movements are just beneath the surface of Nanny's story, for example, the Underground Railroad, slave women's short-term escapes from the farm, even escapes to neighboring plantations. These multiple movements indicate black women's agency, invention, and imagination in relation to migration—even in slavery—and not mere subjection. Among female slaves, who often ran off but then returned because of children and family, a number of social patterns developed. Such a woman might go, for example, to another white slave holder and beg for his intervention. Or she might ask a fellow slave to negotiate with a master in exchange for a promise of leniency. Sometimes a group of slaves would take to the woods in order to pressure an unpopular master into selling them. Thus they aimed at winning concessions within the system rather than challenging the system itself. But, as Eugene Genovese remarks, "Like strikes by free workers, they contained a germ of class consciousness and demonstrated the power of collective action. In both respects they combatted the sense of impotence that the slave holders worked so hard to instill in their slaves."[33] In the decades just after the war, mass Negro movements to Kansas (1870s) and to Oklahoma (1880s) would have provided other stories for Nanny's hearing.

The important point is that black migration provided new ways of telling stories and that these were, of necessity, negotiated narratives. What I mean is that the stories told were literally about social and political negotiations and, narratively, they imagined resistance but with plots that allowed for continuity. As for Janie, we can guess that she was born in 1882, in western Florida, since her birth resulted from her mother's rape by a schoolteacher in that part of the state when she was seventeen.[34] Thus Janie, like Hurston (born in Eatonville, Florida, in 1891), was born at a time of heightened black movement, both within the South and from the South to the North (where Hurston was to go). In the story, of course, Hurston imagines Janie undertaking her own migration and coming south to the fictive Eatonville. Rather than focusing on white-authorized Reconstruction, then, Hurston extrapolates on a history of movements, authorizing her own narrative negotiation of blackness and whiteness, female and male, African and European. In the novel's inset narrative, Janie's arranged marriage to Logan Killicks (insisted on by Nanny) is historically placed in the late 1890s and early 1900s, a time of economic depression that created severe problems for southern tenant farmers. Killicks's ownership of his farm is more significant than Janie ever guesses. But Nanny knows, as does Hurston. Later, Janie runs off with Joe Starks to central Florida; this move occurs around the turn of the century (or so I surmise) in the midst of depression. The Great Migration of blacks from rural to urban centers, from the South to the North (in some cases, from the North to the South, from the South to the West) was yet to come (1910–20). Anticipating the economically forced migration of blacks with Janie and Joe's voluntary move, Hurston insists on her power to renegotiate history and to develop zones of race, class, and gender contact according to her own vision. In other words, she does not wait for history; she recreates it according to a possible world view in which black characters can aspire to change without rejecting everything white.

Nanny's bifurcated picturing of whites—some helped her, some harmed her—is restaged with Janie. At her trial, for example, after commenting on the white women's "good clothes" and "pinky color" (274), the narrator intimates that Janie wants to "make *them* know how it was" (275). The wording here resonates with Janie's hope to give Phoeby the "understandin'" she needs. This textual migration between audiences creates a bridge between black and white listeners and results in a *conventional*—that is, enfolding and overlapping—rather than a subversive or separatist text. Even if the white women fail her, Janie wants them to understand. And as we have seen in the frame, most black women fail her too.

Nanny's *and* Janie's relations with white women are more complex—simultaneously more contentious and more coalitional—than Joe Starks's relations with whiteness. When Janie meets Joe (or Jody, as he is sometimes called), he tells her he's "been working for white folks" (47), but now he is on his way to Eatonville, a black town he will never leave. Jody's plan is to retire from working for whites or interacting with them in any way, though all of his plans are copied from white masculinist blueprints. He must, for example, form a committee (58), create a center (65), institute rank (66), mount the box-podium (73), direct others (78), and keep his wife from commoners (94). Finally, he erects the "gloaty, sparkly white" house (75). Copying whiteness in an all-black town, Jody becomes, of course, a caricature.

Jody's lack of self-consciousness about his plan's origins contrasts with Nanny's awareness of her mixed history and distinguishes Jody from Janie, who will borrow self-consciously even from him when it suits her purposes. For example, when she finally has enough of his lording, she takes the middle of the floor (122) and "thrusts" herself into the conversation (117). And when Jody is dying, she makes him listen, directing him not to talk back (131). But she will not occupy the center forever. Even as she indirectly directs Phoeby to talk and retell, she decentralizes herself in relation to the story. Since she shares Hurston's knowledge of porch banter, she knows that Phoeby's talk will not only be an original modification of the story she has heard; it will be a new story, taking on a life of its own. Each teller negotiates audience and *crosses* the story.

Janie also *borrows* Jody's money, banking most of it and—at Phoeby's suggestion—taking a few hundred dollars with her when she runs off with Tea Cake. In a plotting move to make Janie and Tea Cake equal, Hurston has him *borrow* Janie's money. But the reader never forgets that Janie has stored up savings. This material foundation is an important detail. It means, first of all, that Jody Starks does not operate only as Janie's *other*. Something of his offering is retained and valued by the text. Furthermore, *this store*—the money itself—means that Janie's migration to the "muck" (farmland in the Everglades) operates largely as play. In fact, some kinship exists between Janie's participation with blacks on the muck and white patrons' participation with black performers in Harlem. At first Janie looks on, and then she joins in. But she is never only one of them, as Mrs. Turner points out and as Hurston makes sure by setting aside Janie's inheritance. Money, then, creates freer play as much as love does. Hurston provides Janie with just what she herself needed and desired with Mrs. Mason. From the standpoint we have established in the story, this incidental detail gains significance as a revision of racial negotiations. Quite obviously, it suggests the need for economic redistribution of goods along racial lines. But it also—and just as significantly—suggests Hurston's cooption of some white values.

Finally, Janie's beauty—her "coffee and cream complexion" and her "luxurious hair" (208)—embodies her migrating consciousness and Hurston's negotiating text. As female mulatto, her body marks the space of forced intercourse between black and white. As we have seen, however, Hurston's novel seizes and reframes cultural negotiations in her narrative negotiations: Janie chooses to go south rather than being forced north; she keeps rather than distributes her dead husband's wealth. Repeatedly the novel produces an aesthetic and political sensibility that operates between opposite systems of value and identity. To make her point, Hurston textualizes narrative desire in terms of the porch, an interval space between private and public, female and male, day and night. At the story's beginning, Janie has taken a place on the porch; the novel itself will then come back around to this achievement, suggesting the preferability of flexible, open spaces of dialogue and debate. On the porch, swapping or lateral shifting (going to the horizon and back [183]) dramatizes knowledge gained between the binaries of domination and submission. By the time Janie moves with Tea Cake to south Florida (1920 or so—at the height of the Great Migration; Hurston herself had gone to Baltimore in 1917), Hurston is crafting black movement as a complex sign of cultural, discursive, and familial negotiations rather than forced migrations.

In time, Janie is the hyphen between slavery and freedom. Historically (in her grandmother's story), she marks a space between well-intentioned whites and the husband Nanny provides for her. In Joe Starks's store, she holds a place between working-class blacks and aspiring black capitalists. In the story's frame, however, she insinuates a textual space in which different women meet for the common cause of hearing about one another's struggle.

Indeed, by displaying her own migratory hearing in Phoeby's name, Hurston brings an alternate textual model into being. She celebrates the performance that is accomplished through interaction with multiple and even antagonistic audiences. This model is not apolitical. In other words, it does not operate through transcendence of race history. Instead, it invites diverse identities to share the same space—the frame, the porch—and to know the *other* (which is never the same because our reading *selves* are different) through the shared act of hearing. The inset story, then, is really the means for convening the frame or audience, meaning that Hurston's political text occurs in the biracial and bisexual *reading* or *hearing* of *Their Eyes Were Watching God*.

While Janie seems to have the world tied up (the horizon draped around her shoulders), Phoeby's character makes clear the always present *others* without whom one's story cannot be told. As a fabricator of the black social text, Hurston needs Phoeby in order to represent the social world of black speech. But Hurston also needed the white patronage and interest that would support (literally feed) her field work as well as a

Hurston's *Their Eyes Were Watching God*

broader American audience, white and black, to pass the novel to the future.

It is not so much speaking but hearing that keeps opening the window onto Janie's (and the author's) negotiations. Always facing the "hazards of writing within the institution"[35]—a situation now shared by many black and white, male and female feminists—Hurston *shows* through Phoeby's *ears* (my intentional metaphorical mixing) that aesthetic possibilities lie in the meeting of white and black technologies. The text produced in this negotiation provides not an aesthetic *home*, but a critical movement. As long as this negotiation is open, institutional hazards do not lead to absolute appropriation (of black by white; of feminism by patriarchy). As Michael Awkward has recently proposed, white readers can offer provocative analyses of black authored texts, and African-American critics can examine those readings in relation to the interpretive obstacle of white privilege that can shape white readings. This circulation and negotiation of texts avoids the essentializing of race, but it does not erase race and gender history. Instead, it allows us, Awkward writes, to "employ whichever hybrid combination of interpretive technologies we can access to create what will help us to illuminate precisely the many ways in which difference continues to matter at the end of the twentieth century."[36]

For Hurston to tell Janie's tale directly, to write *over* the mediator, would result in a purer story, or in a story that hides its mixed origins and negotiated relations. Instead, Hurston advertises her "return on a capital," her use of black folklore, female identity, and white resources in relation to powerful audiences, by dramatizing her own gathering of stories.

Phoeby's and Janie's porch locations function as a serendipitous icon for feminist debate. Hurston makes it clear that even these two—very similar women—are different. Each has her own complex subject position to elaborate. Just as important, each has different potentials as listeners, re-layers. We cannot always be certain ahead of time who will hear the tale best or relay it with the greatest authority. Although black feminists may be the most likely hearers of black women's creative projects, Phoeby's negotiating identity denies the absoluteness of this potential. By implication, of course, white feminists are also divested of their *natural* inheritance of white women writers. Black feminists can provide new hearings of Edith Wharton and Eudora Welty. These are hearings that white feminists can and should invite in planning conference panels and essay collections.

As Alice Parker and Elizabeth Meese write, "What matters most for feminist criticism is that we consider where we stand in relation to this law of borrowing as well as to that other law of the institution, always calculating our interest in these laws. We need to read our positions vigilantly through the tropes in which our speaking takes place, takes it place, to see what place that is and who is and is not here with us and why."[37] The only way to read Phoeby's text is to read through the swapping of identities that Hurston stages in both of her female characters. If our identities (black womanist; white feminist) keep us distinct and different, Hurston's audience accommodations, like Phoeby's bowl, do not; they insinuate a contact. By reading with Phoeby, Janie's narratee, we uncover feminist debts across color lines.

In contemporary feminism, practitioners cannot afford to continue a politics of distrust and absolutism. Feminist critics must take the risk of *cross-addressing* even though this double move means we risk rebuke. Actively swapping stories, theories, and locations in classrooms and conferences, reading lists and anthologies, feminist critics will enlarge the circle(s) of feminist listeners. I am often perplexed when my students will not vocalize an identity as feminist. But I wonder if it is a good first step that they *listen* to my feminist criticism even if they do not themselves *become* feminist critics, whatever that may mean. After all, their listening allows me to advance my arguments, provoke my own thought, problematize my own identity.

Returning to Hurston I might say that if white and male feminists are situated on the far porch and black female feminists are given the seat of favor next to Janie, white and male critics must learn to listen more intently. I am not a black feminist critic, but I can be an audience, part of the constructive center of black feminist work. On the other hand, I hope that black female feminists will recognize and theorize their need for white female and male as well as black male listeners. These turns in feminist criticism should lead to less emphasis on who is speaking and greater emphasis on who is listening. Our words really are not our own. For that reason, we are wise to be anxious about audience. But for the same reason, our words may truly be effective in changing hearts as well as minds.

4

The Character of Her Writing
Eudora Welty's *The Optimist's Daughter* and the Stories of Feminist Criticism

Like my teaching, my scholarship also oscillate[s] between the male-dominant tradition of canonical English literature and new feminist approaches.
—Judith K. Gardiner

Our generation of feminists has come of age—here we are in middle age, looking back, and forward, from the middle ground that society has taught us to dread and which we are trying to reassess.... As mid-life feminist activists and intellectuals, we are perhaps in the best position to negotiate the divide[s].
—Jerry Aline Flieger

For there is hate as well as love, [Laurel] supposed, in the coming together and continuing of our lives.
—Eudora Welty

THUS FAR I have demonstrated how two feminist-acclaimed novels yield tantalizing results when interpreted through the rubric of *negotiation*. Following the lead of Lily Bart and Phoeby Watson, our interpretation unfolded in the ambiguous position *between* positions. This go-between location sheds light on the contradictions of all identity while also demonstrating possible affinities between and among positions that have been viewed as purely oppositional. We have seen that accommodation to impure positions does not necessarily lead to compromise but can produce powerful—tensed—critiques of the status quo. To make my argument in relation to Wharton and Hurston, I appealed to their personal and writing histories. In this chapter, I appeal to certain vignettes from Eudora Welty's autobiography, but what I emphasize is the canny resemblance between her novel and American feminist criticism. Beginning here and in the remaining chapters, I read the fictive texts in relation to larger cultural and discursive histories, that is, the history of American feminist criticism, the African-American civil rights movement, and the feminist debates on mothering.

Although Kate Millet's *Sexual Politics* (1970) led the call for a dismantling of male literary power by feminist critics in the 1970s, in fact, the feminist critic of my opening vignette—the one struggling between obscurity and tenure—necessarily and sometimes heartily borrows from masculine authority in order to negotiate power.[1] Such critics oscillate between male-dominated institutions and the marginal spaces of female traditions, traditions that have been impressively chronicled by Elaine Showalter and Alice Walker.[2] Walker's *In Search of Our Mothers' Gardens* (1983) became nothing less than a mantra for feminist critics, but even so, in the 1980s many female graduate students writing dissertations on women writers were mentored by male professors, and most of them put male-oriented scholarship to work in textual, sexual, and political analyses.[3] Currently, and usually from well-established positions within academic walls, third stage feminist critics such as Spivak, Anzaldúa, Meese, and hooks are self-consciously reassessing relations with academic fathers and mothers, masculine and feminine traditions, heterosexual and homosexual economies. This reassessment of feminist histories proliferates genealogies at the same time that it cautions against absolute adoption of any one line. We are warned, for example, against essentializing women (privileging mothers) and, on the other hand, against embracing theoretical discourses (and fathers) that may mute women writers and readers.[4] At the same time, feminist *performances* (such as those offered by the writers just named) have begun to function as a new familial and sexual model for criticism. As Pat Mora writes in *Nepantla: Essays from the Land in the Middle*, "I am the middle woman, / not my mother, not my daughter."[5]

How can we describe the character of the "middle" feminist; to whom is she related and how? In this chapter, I suggest retelling the story of feminist criticism through a reconsideration of Mora's "middle woman." If, for example, Millet's text recommends a story of the daughter's rebellion (against fathers and male lovers) and Alice Walker's *In Search of Out Mothers' Gardens* tells the story of a daughter's reunion (with the mother and female lover), we can also tell the feminist story of midlife negotiations, of shifting sexualities and cross-gender identities. This story, to rewrite Edward Said, reconnects feminist analysis with many feminist critics' actuality.[6]

Welty's *The Optimist's Daughter*

Arguing the need for a mediating, critical, feminist position, Elizabeth Däumer invents such a midlife story in her essay "Queer Ethics." In the critical fiction she fashions, a woman named Cloe has moved from heterosexuality to lesbianism to bisexuality. Her last move is strongly resisted by her lesbian community. Nonetheless Cloe dreams "of somebody with whom she was not primarily a woman, a lesbian, or a misrecognized heterosexual. . . . Cloe dreamed not of instability or undecidability as much as of an intimacy not regulated through positionings in ostensibly stable sexual identities."[7] Although *lesbian* has represented the choice of the nondutiful feminist daughter for many critics, Däumer resists its universalizing force as the *opposite* of heterosexual. Instead she offers bisexuality as an epistemological position for feminist negotiations of sexuality and gender. In her view, bisexuality does not integrate heterosexual and homosexual operations but can serve as a political and intellectual bridge between communities and identifications. Because Cloe's bisexuality draws from two sexual identities and leaves the door open to both, it strengthens "our ability temporarily 'to forget' entrenched and seemingly inevitable differences—especially those of race, gender and sexuality—in order to focus on what we might have in common."[8]

I want to apply Däumer's theory of bisexual reason to a reading of what Eudora Welty has called her own authorial "third character." My purpose is to show how *The Optimist's Daughter* (1969) produces a familial "intimacy not regulated through positionings in ostensibly stable sexual identities." Although I will draw from *One Writer's Beginnings*, I am not seeking to establish Welty's actual world bisexuality. Neither will I raise that question in relation to Laurel Hand, the daughter-protagonist of the novel. Instead, I want to flesh out Welty's epistemological negotiation of narrative and gender in her writing of the novel. In Laurel Hand, Welty explores familially imparted intimacies and sexually inflected styles that do not adhere strictly to gender roles. Through her character, she makes palpable, as well, certain bodies of knowledge that do not always get read in heterosexual or homosexual plots, for example, the daughter's self-touching and the father's corporeality.

In "Writing and Analyzing a Story" (*The Eye of the Story*), Welty theorizes her writing of a short story in terms of a "third character"; her comments employ the strategy of feminine self-erasure since she both claims and denies the generative power of the middle player.[9] About herself as writer, Welty comments, "Once I'd escaped those characters' minds, I saw [the real point of view] was outside them—suspended, hung in the air between two people, fished alive from the surrounding scene. As I wrote further into the story, something more real, more essential, than the characters were on their own was revealing itself. In effect, though the characters numbered only two, there had come to be a sort of third character along on the ride—the presence of a relationship between the two."[10] Welty's description is rhetorically shaped through a series of contradictions: initially, the writer "escapes" her characters, but her consciousness is called "the presence of a relationship between the two." Furthermore, the "third character," who is the point of the entire description, is only "along on the ride," and yet she is more "real," more "essential" than the two characters "on their own." The point of view being described appears to be acted upon—suspended, hung—but, of course, the reader knows this middle character is Welty herself, hardly the backseat driver.

These contradictions go to the heart of my framing metaphor. As a trope for the personal, critical operations of feminist criticism, negotiation implies both distance and affiliation, separation and conjunction, aggression and effacement. Furthermore, negotiation as a critical trope confesses feminist imperfection, feminist criticism's profiting from its *others* and its complicity in binary constructs. Finally, it admits that we do our work in unlikely places and that our meanings are often carried through innuendo and inflection. "Along on the ride," for example, must be read for tone not literal meaning; self-effacement, as we witnessed with Hurston, may serve as a tactic for clearing authorial space. In a sly self-placement, Welty constructs a writerly persona who confesses both her dependence on others and her power to move them, the phrase "fished alive" suggesting the corporeal dimension of writing and Welty's agency in mediation, what I have earlier described as double or multiple siding. Through the witty negotiation of passive constructions ("was revealing itself"), she, like Hurston, actually expands her narrative possibilities. The result is a tensed awareness—especially significant for third stage feminist critics—that we are both masters and victims of narrative, both drivers and driven. Drafting an in-between position, Welty draws attention to a potent, dialogic middle.

Juxtaposed with the lexicon of feminist criticism, Welty's theory allows us to reread her most acclaimed novel as a story of the negotiating or epistemologically *bisexual* daughter.[11] Approached with this interest, Welty's essay and novel inform feminist criticism at the same time that recent feminism's deployment of negotiation amplifies Welty's text in new and compelling ways. Many feminist critics (especially white women, but Hurston also fits this pattern) began practicing the profession from the position of academic daughters; Welty's protagonist begins as a lawyer's daughter.[12] Such women inherited first the father's story (or imperative), which they sought both to emulate and dismantle, and then recuperated the mother's story, which they often mourned and embraced. Likewise, Laurel's father is destabilized and her mother's strength enhanced. In both Welty's novel and in American feminist criticism, *his* spaces are thought to include the traditional canon, critical language and theory, and the professorial life. The mother's field, on the other hand, includes domestic and maternal lexicons, critical vantage points from the margins, and actual instances of care. Laurel Hand, however, discovers a more complex rapprochement between her mother's and father's stories. Their fields become crossed and recrossed in her memory so that it is neither side, but rather her negotiation of both sides, that constructs *her* in-between character, making her a canny emblem for many American feminist critics.

Middle Age

In her story of daughterly negotiations, Welty simultaneously establishes and destabilizes the predictable categories of gender and sexuality. For example, she patterns Laurel's father and mother on two sets of opposing myths: the masculinist myths of male prerogative and female reception and the feminist revisions of masculine recalcitrance and feminine subversion.[13] Stirring up both of these paradigms in Laurel's memory, Welty trumps each mythology by allowing Laurel a cross-breeding of both.

The Optimist's Daughter is staged primarily in a family home, currently occupied by a second wife, but visited in the narrative by Laurel McKelva Hand, the daughter who grew up there. Welty points to her negotiating thematics through hyperbole and proliferation.[14] For example, the text recirculates the same key stories but with alterations so that we are never absolutely sure of how things were but only of how they might be reassembled. Here actual and possible worlds become hopelessly intertwined. In addition, both parental characters are exaggerated, the father in his defunct masculinity, the mother in her heroic resistance. Furthermore, by creating Fay (Judge McKelva's second wife) who blindly usurps Laurel's place, Welty pulls the "third" or in-between character (the daughter) from the backseat and puts her *out* figuratively. This ploy calls attention to Laurel's difference: her ability to critique and to forgive, to sympathize and appropriate from a non-ironic but judicious affiliation with opposing others. Fay, on the other hand, represents the daughter (the feminist?) who blithely sleeps with the father and then, in a fit of self-absorbed rage, kills him off: when Judge McKelva forgets her birthday—he is in the hospital recovering from surgery—Fay tries to pull him out of bed, an attack that precipitates his death.

Welty further develops the contrast between Fay and Laurel by representing "a superrational relationship" (Hemenway's phrase describing Hurston and Mason) between Laurel and Missouri, the McKelva family maid. When Laurel returns to the family home after her father's death, she is likened to Missouri rather than to the other white "daughter" Fay: "'Well, *I'm* here and *you're* here,' [says] Missouri," and the narrator comments that "it was the bargain [between them] to give and take comfort" (59). The comparison between Laurel and Missouri does not operate to gloss Laurel's southern politics—we are given no indication that the McKelva family resisted the economic structures that determine the position of black workers. Instead, this "bargain" suggests Missouri's moral superiority to Fay, the "daughter" who understands no debt. Missouri's ability to "give and take comfort" across race and class lines provides the ethical standpoint that guides Laurel later when she resists the temptation to stoop to Fay's level, that is, to act as if she has no debts.

The layering of Welty's novel creates a Chinese box effect: the first book narrating a father's death in the present, the second book his burial, the third remembering the mother's lingering death of years before, and finally, the fourth book drawing out the epistemological dividends of Laurel's mediating position. Reading the novel as an instance of scrambled autobiography,[15] I see in Laurel Hand a metafiction of Welty's negotiating feminism. I begin with the daughter's symbolic role as familial mediator, a role Welty claims for herself in *One Writer's Beginnings*. Through the *mise en abîme* or self-replicating structure of *The Optimist's Daughter*, the author replaces the myth of daughter as acquiescent receiver with a tale of the third character (a woman in middle age) as the generative intermediary of her own story.[16]

As the novel opens, Laurel has come south from Chicago to be with her father—Judge McKelva—who has begun to lose his eyesight. From the beginning, this crisis recurs to Laurel's mother's death since her passing too was precipitated by loss of vision. Closing both parents' eyes, Welty closes the door to any direct course for Laurel. Her character will not be constructed through a direct merger with or rejection of either parental line.

According to the narrator, Judge McKelva's "admission of self-concern was as new as anything wrong with his health, and Laurel had come flying," literally (7). Laurel's father has a new wife, though in her silliness and self-indulgence Fay might better be understood as a spoiled daughter.

Welty slyly points out that "she was forty, and so younger than Laurel" (26). As I suggested earlier, the resemblance with and displacement of Laurel that Fay's youth creates instigates a narrative that must, above all, redefine the daughter's identity. None of the singular or stable designations fits Laurel; she is neither wife, daughter, nor mother.

Chapter 1 exemplifies Welty's hyperbole. According to Judge McKelva, he scratched his eye while pruning his former wife's rose bushes, which he calls "Becky's Climber." This naming already insinuates the mother's gender transgressions, her assertiveness within the family. McKelva's account of the accident—witnessed by the characterologically diminutive Fay, the family doctor, and Laurel—offers an instance of Welty's fabulist style. The dead wife, the wife's impostor, the rose bush, the injured eye—all add up to an instance of male blindness. When Laurel asks about the location of the tear, the doctor replies that it is "close to central" (8).

By the end of the chapter, the patriarch has been rendered merely human. Looking through Laurel's eyes, we see him "in his creamy panama. But though his paunch [is] bigger, he look[s] less ruddy, look[s] thinner in the face" (11). This description is reminiscent of Janie's view of the aging Joe Starks. He too became simultaneously larger and weaker in her eyes. This story, like that one, stages the father-patriarch's death in narrative relation to his spacial and linguistic demands. Always the town lawyer—the man with the biggest voice—McKelva has now become "a man admitting to . . . uncertainty in his bearings" (12).

But Welty's demonstration of Judge McKelva's weakness is less subversive than negotiating. Destabilizing patriarchal power in her opening chapter, Welty will still make use of the judge's epistemology, one practiced through distancing and judgment. The affiliation Welty writes between daughter and father, then, avoids representing maleness as "irredeemably condemnable" and encourages instead an ongoing examination of masculinist strategies and personas.[17]

Laurel is clearly conceived by the author as a mediating character. Welty hints in the opening paragraphs that Laurel is "between." In the novel's first sentences, for example, readers see a "nurse [hold] the door open . . . Judge McKelva [went] first, then his daughter Laurel, then his wife Fay." This brief staging of characters in the threshold is reminiscent of Wharton's strategy. But Welty's tactic is to overstate her case: Laurel is described as "in her middle forties" (3) and "in the middle of her present job" (19). Welty has done away with Laurel's husband in the novel's foreground so that the daughter is returned to a preadolescent middle position: "there had only been the three of them" (19). Even the mythic female

The Character of Her Writing

go-between—Persephone—can be detected in the opening paragraph of chapter 2, as Laurel "[stands] in the doorway" waiting for her father to be brought out of surgery.

In the New Orleans hospital, Laurel attends her father, "setting her inner chronology with his" (19). In "his unnatural reticence" (22) and the "uncertainty in his bearings" (12), she detects his need, and though she considers her presence "useless" (19), she choreographs her actions and her father's thinking. This narration produces a daughter-father intimacy that appears to make Laurel a passive vehicle. But a careful reading demonstrates how Welty is already reworking the subject of female mediation. Here the "setting of inner chronologies" effects an elongated symbiosis, suggesting, in fact, an almost uterine symbolism. The fuller passage reads: "she was conscious of time along with him, setting her inner chronology with his, more or less as if they needed to keep in step for a long walk ahead of them" (19–20). Later, Laurel will think of her father's upper lip as "short and soft as a child's" and of his smile as "the smile of a child who is hiding in the dark" (34). Thus Laurel's attendance with her father is turned outside in: timing is feminized and maternalized and the daughter's thinking becomes not only his, but *our* narrative guide.[18]

Outside her father's hospital room, as Fay sleeps and her father rests, Laurel sees a "bridge—it stood out there dull in the distance, its function hardly evident" (14). Later Laurel will look out the same window and see "the whole Mississippi River bridge in lights" (33). In her usual iconographic way, Welty shows and then emphasizes her meaning, Laurel's nocturnal viewing of the lighted bridge dramatically underscoring her mediating agency. As Judge McKelva lies perfectly still, Laurel acts as his eyes and mouth, interpreting, amending, and providing connection with the past. A conscious watcher, Laurel achieves almost Crone status, integrating daughterly sympathy with critical distance.

As Judge McKelva's condition worsens, he is joined in his hospital room by another patient, Mr. Danzell, who mistakes the judge for his "long-lost son Archie Lee" (21). The fantastic humor of this mistaken identity further deflates the father figure even as Laurel becomes more and more his linguistic medium, reading to him, communicating with his doctors, sharing with him memories from the past. Thus Welty insists that the daughter's mediating role is not the complement to a father's power but rather that she is appropriating his former powers of endurance and wry humor: "Now it was she who was offering [optimism] to him" (29). Though Laurel demurs—"[the optimism] might be false" (29)—the doubt functions as a negotiation of paternal guises, not as a rejection of them.

Laurel knows that she has adopted a necessary, though not necessarily *true* posture as she hopes against her father's impending death.

To explore Welty's representation of a father-daughter rapprochement, it is useful to go ahead in the novel's chronology to discover the origin of McKelva's "optimism." During Laurel's mother's illness, at least as Laurel remembers it, her mother sought comfort in complaint. With only the power of her voice left, she showered on her husband the unanswerable demands of dying. Unable to comfort her—his words could make no headway against Becky's—McKelva would put on his hat and go to his office, leaving Laurel with her mother. The father's walking out with his hat is a trope for (white) masculine prerogative and indicates the falseness of his optimism for Becky. But a picture Laurel discovers after his death retrieves his prerogative and optimism—what we come to see as a kind of willed stoicism—as an available stance *for her*. In it, "he [is] slender as a wand, his foot on a milepost, swinging his straw hat" (136). The clearly phallic imagery establishes McKelva's sexuality, his autonomy, and his narrative choice. Wand, foot, milepost, and hat draw to the reader's attention the culturally inscribed tools of masculine culture. Thus the picture reiterates the sexual mythology of patriarchal power. But in the novel—as Welty tells it—the images now rest in Laurel's hands; her name is *Hand*. Like McKelva's optimism, his "choice" is also available to Laurel as a tool for negotiating self-composure. This textual maneuver recalls Gayatri Spivak's suggestion that feminism can negotiate with patriarchal structures, giving assent to masculinist histories and texts in order to open them toward a new horizon of possibility. Without excusing Judge McKelva's complicity with masculine privilege, Welty provides a "peculiar affirmation" (Spivak) between daughter and father, bequeathing to Laurel his methods and personas and requiring of her an understanding "on his side." At the end of the novel, Laurel travels back to Chicago alone, returning to her job as a designer. In other words, she, childless and unmarried, gains the prerogatives of self-interest, of distance and choice. At the same time, Welty critiques the father through a full demonstration of his imaginative and social limits.[19] After all, he married Fay.

In book 2, Welty makes it clear that the process of inner negotiation, of becoming the middle woman, requires the daughter's revision of her father. At Judge McKelva's funeral, friends exaggerate stories from the past, leading Laurel to insist that "they're misrepresenting . . . falsifying" (83). Laurel "tr[ies] to testify . . . for her father's sake" (83). In this move, Laurel lays claim to McKelva's lexicon. She thinks he has been "put on trial," as elsewhere she believes the "facts" of Fay's blundering to be "a verdict" and her actions in relation to Fay to be "justified" (130–31). But her motivation is misguided since she believes *herself* to be upholding the truth. A family friend, Miss Adele, reminds Laurel that even her father would lie "[i]f the truth hurt the wrong person" (83). Thus Welty deepens the daughter's understanding on McKelva's side, demonstrating that even the father cannot be categorized as *one* thing. His law and language are pliable—if not perfectable. As Judith Butler writes, "The possibility of multiple identifications . . . suggests that the Law is not deterministic and that 'the' law may not even be singular."[20] Thus McKelva's language is usable but is opened up to a new feminist horizon. His legacy becomes the negotiated one of justice, choice, *and* the sympathetic lie.

Structurally, Welty situates the story of mother and daughter (book 3) within the frame of the father's death. Alone in the Mississippi house after the funeral, Laurel revisits Becky McKelva. This thematic crossing of parental legacies operates in the novel in two ways, each of which can best be described metaphorically. On the one hand, the father's dying recurs, from the beginning, to the mother's life and death. Thus a shuttle effect is established even in the novel's first two books which deal primarily with Judge McKelva and Laurel Hand. On the other hand, the father's story opens onto the mother's story, creating, as I have indicated, a Chinese box effect. Both of these structurings create in the reader a sense of oscillation, of back and forth movement, rather than of forward progression.

Becky's death is remembered in a chapter that begins with a storm. Laurel, along with a chimney swift, seeks shelter indoors, and the scene unfolds as the two circle through the house. Thematically, this inset narrative serves to further postulate the dynamism of an in-between position, the symbol of the bridge being exchanged for a number of bird images. In Welty's fantastic narration, however, Laurel actually seeks retreat from the swift, *backing into* the spaces that are key to her self-knowledge. In this doubtful, "backwards" search for her past, Laurel becomes intimately reacquainted with her mother's double legacy. She winds up in the sewing room, a small space off from her parents'—now Fay's—bedroom, and begins to look through her mother's cast-off treasures.

As "windows and doors alike . . . [sing], buffeted by the storm" (130), Laurel searches through her mother's desk. Having diminished the father in order to negotiate his power, Welty first portrays Becky as a female figure of startling proportions. In this case, Welty's hyperbole is necessitated by Becky's domestication. So far, readers have seen her only through the instrument of the rose bush and as the dead—and fantastically replaced—

wife. But Becky McKelva, who must have been born in the first decade of the twentieth century, was not herself confined to one position or role.[21] Coming of age just after the first American women's movement, she is remembered by Laurel as a daring experimenter. Looking at a photograph of a young Becky, Laurel conjures the roles of teacher, seamstress, and photographer, the last a particularly potent professional identity at the turn of the century: "How daring and vain she was when she was young, Laurel thought now. She'd made the blouse [she was wearing]—and developed the picture too, for why couldn't she?" (136–37). Placing the mother in the picture and making her its developer as well, Laurel interrupts the unilateral operations of the male gaze. Becky can be looked at, and she can look. Through Laurel's internalized vignettes or narrative memories, Welty continues to draw a woman larger than life. Sharing the daughter's consciousness, we see *Becky* as a daughter who took a daring journey to Baltimore with her sick father, fording a river filled with ice, and guiding him to a hospital full of strangers, where he dies, and she is left alone.

Welty's description of the desk itself is not left to chance but is cunningly designed to suggest an erotic torsion between women and language, between mother and daughter. Laurel has looked for a key to the desk but discovers it is "keyless," a detail suggesting the irrelevance here of phallic control of borders. In the daughter's thought, Becky "had assumed her privacy." While Laurel seems unintentional in entering the sewing room, she is not unintentional as she approaches the desk: she did not "hesitat[e] here—not now. She touched the doors where they met, and they swung open together" (134). The image of the absent key and the intimation of privacy prepare the reader for the extended metaphor of door as vulva, desk as womb. In the apparently domestic space of the sewing room, then, Welty produces her own feminist version of *l'écriture*.[22] Here the daughter reads the sexual/textual body of her mother, touching—by analogy—her own female organ.

In the desk itself, Laurel finds all manner of writing: letters, recipes, a gardening diary, and diagrams of *Paradise Lost* from a class notebook—perhaps her mother's own figuring of the Milton-colored Eden myth.[23] But she also discovers that her mother has evolved her own discursive system: "Laurel opened out the writing lid, and reaching up she drew down the letters and papers from one pigeonhole at a time. There were twenty-six pigeonholes, but her mother had stored things according to their time and place, she discovered, not by ABC" (135). Becky McKelva's use of the

The Character of Her Writing

"twenty-six pigeonholes" provocatively suggests feminist critics' "discovery" of a maternal language. The holes have also become letters (a language) which the mother manipulates to record her story.

Laurel's memories of her young mother offer a fictive analogue for Alice Walker's theory of female artistic genealogy—for recovering inspirational mothers who pull gardens out of clay. Her powers—and her choices—recommend her as every bit Judge McKelva's equal. But Laurel's memories are not only of her mother's youth; they assemble also her mother's long illness and her parents' hurtful language toward one another. The resulting collage requires more daughterly negotiation of Becky than direct emulation.

Likewise, the feminist search for women's writing—gynocriticism—is certainly evoked by Laurel's find. But what the daughter discovers is a mixed text. The love letters were written by her father, the garden diary and the bread recipe by her mother. Furthermore Becky's use of the alphabet and her notes on *Paradise Lost* suggest a negotiation with the father's law since Becky worked within the symbol system at hand. Her scrambling of alphabetic order alerts us to the fiction of alphabets but does not subvert language and time as cultural tools. Instead, Becky seized her allotted spaces and filled them differently, finding a new order within the old. Finally, and as I have already suggested, Becky McKelva's powers most certainly assumed the assistance of black servants like Missouri. Thus her own heroic resistance to a prescribed femininity hinges on a mediating presence that her writing does not acknowledge.

The authorial insistence upon the mother's linguistic agency and the obvious contradiction in the passage—Laurel is remembering her mother's *death*—demonstrates once again Welty's modulation on the subject of female intermediaries: Laurel mediates memory here on her own behalf. Furthermore, this passage demonstrates Welty's argument elsewhere (especially in *One Writer's Beginnings*) that language is the property of father and mother. The peculiar gift of the imperfect but still inspiring mother lies in her penchant for scrambling the code and writing something of and for herself. Like a box within a box, then, this memory compresses and elaborates the novel's thematization of Laurel's midlife negotiations and makes palpable, I believe, a primary operation among feminist critics. We have always been thinking in just this manner—between cultural stories, between genders, races, histories, and family markers—and on our own behalf. We "cross the bar, the divide, making a connection that manages to include . . . both [terms], even while gaining in force from a maintained tension between the terms."[24] The more self-conscious we become about these operations the more honest we can be about the hidden or silenced negotiations—like Missouri's—that underwrite feminist work.

The further back Laurel goes in memory, the more she understands the significance of her middle positioning for herself. She recollects a trip taken with her mother to West Virginia. Vivid in Laurel's imagination is an image of pigeons eating from each others' beaks. In this particular vignette—one that echoes Becky's pigeonholes—Welty makes it clear that the middle character must be more than the vehicle for the other two.

> Flying in from over the mountain, over the roof and a child's head, high up in blue air, pigeons had formed a cluster and twinkled as one body.... Laurel had kept the pigeons under eye ... and had already seen a pair of them sticking their beaks down each other's throats, gagging each other, ... swallowing down ... what had been swallowed before.... They convinced her that they could not escape each other and could not themselves be escaped from. So when the pigeons flew down, she tried to position herself behind her grandmother's skirt.
>
> [The] pigeons were waiting to pluck each other's tongues out. (140)

The birds are not threatening far off, but together and close up, their embeddedness is shocking as they "swallow ... what had been swallowed before," blindly accepting the loss of tongues. The presence of the grandmother behind whose skirt Laurel hides suggests the familial significance of this representation—the birds as Laurel's parents—as well as Laurel's reluctance to see the truth.[25] As much as she would like to believe in family romance, in fact, she is repeatedly disallowed the essential pairing that that romance circulates. Her father is not so fatherly and her mother not so motherly. But the loss of this romance is not equivalent to the loss of genealogy. Instead, it becomes the occasion for the daughter's choice to draw from both sides.

Laurel is neither unified nor singly divided between masculinity and femininity but is the consciousness that shuttles between gendered positions in language, continually refining and reopening identity. Within the tale, Welty figures this negotiation by placing Laurel close to nature but with open eyes. Through her character, the writer divines a sociopoetic space between the dichotomous choices of masculine assertion and feminine reticence, a composing space in which the daughter's tongue is not "plucked," where her voice is "a little different."

Using this passage as an authorial gloss on *The Optimist's Daughter*, we recognize that the pigeon tale cautions the loss of the third character, of the narrative epistemology of a woman-authorized *in-between*. Far from a constraining reality, the familial "regression" that Laurel travels is represented as an occasion for her self-composure.[26]

For example, Laurel's agency as a mediating subjectivity is clearly depicted in this narrative commentary on her mother's death: "When someone lies sick and troubled for five years and is beloved, unforeseen partisanship can spring up among the well. During her mother's long trial in bed, Laurel, young and recently widowed, had somehow turned for a while against her father. [Then] Laurel battled against them both, each for the other's sake. She loyally reproached her mother for yielding to the storms that began coming to her out of her darkness of vision. . . . As for her father, he apparently needed guidance in order to see the tragic" (145).

Welty makes explicit Laurel's dual siding. Revising the myth of daughter as bearer of language, this vignette (which emphasizes Laurel's place between parents; she is "recently widowed"), represents Laurel as coming into her own speech by way of her position between mother and father. She "reproaches" and "guides," active verbs revising the myths of daughterly constraint and silence.

In Laurel's memory, her father's "domestic gentleness" occasioned the mother's grief. Unable to bear "any sort of private clash" and "reach[ing] a loss," he chose, as we have seen, the prerogative of walking out (146). But this parental breach is difficult to lament because it allows the daughter more textual room. At the level of memory, the father's voicelessness gives place to the mother's voice (her recitation), which—in narration—fishes from the air Laurel's "essential" character.

In Laurel's memory of her mother's death, Welty achieves the "third character" that she hints at in the novel's opening sequences. Narratively, Laurel's thinking is relayed to us from a position "hung in the air" between mother and daughter. For example, we read that "Laurel's own mother, . . . lay in bed in the big room reciting to herself sometimes as she had done on horseback at sixteen to make the long ride over the mountain go faster. She did not like being read to, *she* preferred to do the reading" (142). This indirect realizing of the daughter's memory comes to us as something, someone, other than Laurel or Becky. The "character" riding between those two—Welty as author—represents the memory of one and the figure of another.

In my reading and at the level of writing, *Laurel is the character of Welty's feminist writing*. The middle-aged female character—no longer daughter—serves as a feminist relation between the author, her text, and her reader. Laurel's mediations between parents dramatize the plasticity of the writer's voice and represent the dramatic field of fiction that readers are invited to enter. Composing Laurel's life in personal negotiations and narrative inlays, Welty offers another myth of the female subject: as hybridized, transitional, and appropriating. Shuttling between contradictory voices, the third character generates a layered narrative that accommodates and critiques more than one view and in which any *pure* voice is lost. As the subject of the text, Laurel can be described as the negotiating identity that "move[s] inside working contraries" to "disrupt . . . [her own] univocal posturing."[27]

Not only Laurel's gender position but the sexual analogues for her knowing are set in motion in Welty's novel. Recentering the family economy around the daughter's choice and constraint, Welty offers an alternate pattern in which succession is replaced with patterns of oscillation and heartfelt bargain. Between Judge McKelva and Becky McKelva, between past and present, youth and age, marriage and celibacy, Laurel marks the possibility of a negotiating—but not homogeneous—women's knowing, of a bodily intimacy that reissues choice within limits.

Negotiating Distance and Love

As the middle-aged daughter goes back and forth in memory between father and mother, she exercises an epistemology that disrupts the dominant sex/gender system by making use of both sides of the divide. In this sense, all of her postures are *untrue* because inessential; in another sense, the only thing that is "essential" or "real" in the novel is this movement, this negotiation of family and gender in composing a loving and critical self. Gloria Anzaldúa says that the *mestiza* first "take[s] inventory," asking what she inherited from her ancestors. Then she "puts history through a sieve," a process that gives her new perspectives toward many "others."[28] The metaphor of the sieve clarifies the relation between the female negotiator, from a feminist perspective, and the female negotiator or mediator, from a patriarchal perspective, where her in-between status is imposed by and for the male. Anzaldúa's *mestiza* holds the sieve, just as Laurel holds her father's photographs and her mother's letters. In both instances, women's agency in family histories is represented in their hands (Laurel *Hand*), a likely metaphor for Welty-as-writer.

In the last quarter of the novel, Welty offers a parabolic summary of her poetics. I draw these closing scenes to our attention because they demonstrate the difference between critical negotiation and normalizing synthesis. In a dream scene that occurs while Laurel sleeps in the sewing room, Welty represents a journey Laurel took with her husband, Philip

The Character of Her Writing

Hand, when she was a young bride. The dream motif should *awaken* Welty's readers who are accustomed to her fabulist style and frequent use of reversal. Laurel remembers the dream after she wakes up, in fact, and what she remembers is a particular point in her passage, the moment when her train crossed over the Mississippi and Ohio Rivers and she and Philip looked together "at the whole morning world" (160). Welty appears to endorse this scene since she repeats it in *One Writer's Beginnings*, literally reading from the novel. But if Welty favors this narrative moment, I suggest that her preference for this place in the story is more complex than we might at first expect. The passage features the metaphor of confluence, of rivers and characters merging one with the other. But closer attention to Welty's narration leads us to reconsider this appearance. There is, after all, a spacial distance between the Laurel who looks and the scene below, between the train and the river. Not only this, but the train must, at some point, cross the river, and not always run confluently. The passage in the novel reads

> There were two rivers. Here was where they came together. This was the confluence of the waters, the Ohio and the Mississippi.
> They were looking down from a great elevation and all they saw was at the point of coming together, . . . as he touched her arm she looked up with him and saw . . . sky, water, birds, light, and confluence. It was the whole morning world.
> And they themselves were a part of the confluence. . . . They were riding as one with it. (159–60)

Welty presents the same confluent imagery earlier in the novel when she writes of Laurel's memory of her parents' voices coming up the stairs at night, lulling her to sleep (really, of course, according to this myth, into feminine consciousness):

> When Laurel was a child, in this room and in this bed . . . she closed her eyes like this and the rhythmic, nighttime sound of the two beloved reading voices came rising in turn up the stairs every night to reach her. She could hardly fall asleep, she tried to keep awake, for pleasure. She cared for her own books, but she cared more for theirs, which meant their voices . . . their two voices reading to each other where she could hear them, never letting a silence divide or interrupt them, combined into one unceasing voice and wrapped her around as she listened, . . . She was sent to sleep under a velvety cloak of words, richly patterned and stitched with gold, straight out of a fairy tale. (57–58)

This "fairy tale" acts as an epigraph to "Listening" in *One Writer's Beginnings*. There, Welty remembers her parents' platonic voices arising in similar "duet" and surrounding her in song. The voices "running between them" are apparently preferred to the artificial sound of the Victrola.[29] In the passage from the novel, the young Laurel prefers her parents' voices to her books, apparently to her own voice. In both "confluent" vignettes, the active verbs belong to someone besides the daughter: "He touched her arm"; "the voices came rising" and "wrapped her around." But what if this excessive deactivation of the daughter is the writer's device for turning our attention to *the narrative lie in the daughter's passivity*? For example, Welty tells us that the story is a fairy tale. Unlike a possible world, a fairy tale operates to reinstate boundaries and dispel danger. But Welty's *writing* of the daughter's generative power *as a reception* conceives a possible world in which receptivity is active. In this case, Welty claims the power to turn mediation from passive feminine attributes to "'world'-travelling" skills.[30] This possibility calls into question the installation of feminine identity and claims instead the usefulness of crossing back and forth, of establishing a self in the controversial, shifting sidings with more than one identity and place. Given the distance between the fairy tale and Welty's writing life, her representation of a receptive feminine role should be thought of as a resource for imaginative play, not as a regulatory plot.

Indeed, if we continue to examine these authorially preferred passages (preferred through several tellings), we find a breach. Not only has Welty amplified the representation of Sleeping Beauty through numerous retellings and self-quotations, a strategy that can be read as masquerade and satire,[31] but she also inscribes the story's undoing by contradicting her character. In Laurel's dream of journeying with Phil, Laurel thinks that she and he "were a part of the confluence." But Welty's narration insists otherwise. Laurel and Phil are bridging the confluence: "They had ridden together over a long bridge" (159). Between these two claims is a struggle with myth that Welty's writing negotiates rather than synthesizes. On the one hand, for Laurel to be a part of the confluence is for her to be feminine (and silent) nature. On the other hand, her placement on the bridge (with Phil) suggests the masculine position of mastery and metaphor. In writing both sentences—"They themselves were a part of the confluence"; "They had ridden together over a long bridge"—Welty as narrator shuttles between positions, alternately valorizing and deconstructing her own emblematic tale. Her voice comes to us in the "double-crossing" of her own metaphor.[32]

The crucial narrative point in these representations is that a distance is figured in the telling of love stories. For example, in Laurel's dream, she looks from a bridge to the river below. This spacial distance is redefined in the dream, itself a looking back. Finally Welty's telling through third person narration implies the linguistic distance between word and thing. Just as Laurel's bridge crosses (rather than joins) the confluence, Welty's text repeatedly crosses representational myths with her own manipulation of the story's events. In bricolage fashion, she works within a set of narrative conventions to imagine a textual identity that is neither daughter's nor parents', neither *man's* nor *woman's*, but which is instead all of these in turns. I would say that her textual logic is both/and/yet, the *yet* naming an inconclusive, though connected self living in the torsion of mythic divides. This "character," as Judith Butler claims, invites a new beginning. "If identities were no longer fixed as the premises of a political syllogism, and politics no longer understood as a set of practices derived from the alleged interests that belong to a set of ready-made subjects, a new configuration of politics would surely emerge."[33]

If we could move into the other *bisexually*, identifying with more than one difference and resisting the impulse to make only our difference count: then we would have cause for a true optimism. Welty's method of identifying and negotiating gender difference seems to shed light on such a possibility. For the first time in my professional career, I wonder if we should reconsider *feminist* criticism. What name would move both ways—toward a new femininity and a new masculinity, a new mother and a new father? What name might call to mind the middle woman, the one who is neither daughter nor mother but both and more than both—also related to the father and the son? *Gender criticism* is an option some have chosen but the term seems too neutral, not specifically aimed toward the inside/outside of a woman's position in relation to family dramas and critical histories. Elizabeth Meese calls for "feminist criticism*s*," with an emphasis on the many positions within our field. Perhaps *feminist-gender criticism* is as close as I can get at the moment. It may be time for a hyphenated name.

5

Sifting through Bags and Bones
Practical Negotiations in Toni Morrison's *Song of Solomon*

Conflict, competition, stress, struggle, etc., within the narrative conceived as carrier bag/belly/box/house/medicine bundle, may be seen as necessary elements of a whole which itself cannot be characterized either as conflict or as harmony, since its purpose is neither resolution nor stasis but continuing process.
—Ursula K. Le Guin

I characterize different feminist theories according to their ability to comprehend and represent conceptually a mediational and formational view of social practice. Their ability to accomplish a less one-sided social analysis and interpretation, I claim, depends on their understanding and handling of mediation.
—Himani Bannerji

IN TONI MORRISON'S *Song of Solomon* (1977) I find my most successful instance yet of a negotiating womanist subject. The ancestress, Pilate Dead, represents the negotiations of identity that I have come to associate with a certain kind of leading character. The difference in Morrison's text is the degree to which Pilate exercises her internal negotiations outwardly, making her a skilled intermediary in the actual world she inhabits. More than Lily, Phoeby, or Laurel, Pilate becomes an active and open negotiator among and between the people she knows and loves.

Morrison develops her character through three levels of representation. First, she shows us Pilate's actual maneuvers among white and black communities in the period of Reconstruction. Pilate's wanderings after her father's death demonstrate the same black migrations that Hurston represents in *Their Eyes Were Watching God*.[1] In addition, Morrison develops extended metaphors to demonstrate Pilate's negotiating subjectivity in her present life, her heartfelt attachment to oppositionally situated people, places, and ideas. This is the sort of representation that has structured our discussion thus far. Finally—and most important to my discussion here—Morrison brings Pilate out as an active intermediary in other people's conflicts.

The cultural horizon of my reading shifts in this chapter to the civil rights movement of the 1960s. I focus in particular on the historical figure of Fannie Lou Hamer, a woman from the South who actualized a negotiating sensibility in both her speech and actions. This horizon moves the text away from the assimilation/resistance binary that structures the Martin Luther King versus Malcolm X debate and toward a lived sensibility that I and others associate with feminist negotiations.

In her essay "The Social Construction of Black Feminist Thought," Patricia Hill Collins argues that black women's thinking is more than the sum of a multiplicity of frameworks. It is thinking conceived through ongoing processes of *movement* across ideological and cultural divides. This knowledge standpoint is conceived in "the act of being simultaneously a member of a group and yet standing apart from it." Collins's description refines the concept of negotiation by reminding us that not all margins are equidistant from the center(s). Some feminist workers have further to travel in moving between Nancy K. Miller's island and mainland.[2]

Mae Gwendolyn Henderson observes this point while remaining optimistic about the sorts of knowledge that are produced by black women writers' "dialogics" and "dialectics."[3] These women, she argues, write "simultaneously [out of] homogeneous and heterogeneous social and discursive domains."[4] Her essay, "Speaking in Tongues," demonstrates how African-American women writers enunciate the other within (dialogics) and *"the same within"* (dialectics). Her framework speaks to my conceptualization of feminist critical negotiation as a practice that allows discursive common grounds as well as actual, political differences. Along these lines, Collins claims that a black feminist epistemology does not choose between African-based thought and female-based thought. "Rather than being restrained by their 'both/and' status of marginality, these women make creative use of their outsider-within status and produce innovative black feminist thought. The difficulties these women face lie less in demonstrating the technical components of white male epistemologies than in resisting the hegemonic nature of these patterns of thought in order to see, value, and use existing alternative Afrocentric feminist ways of knowing."[5] Collins's words remind us that different feminist workers negotiate different sets of thought, but she reiterates the possibility of feminist knowledge gained at the intersections of interpretive frameworks.

In his essay "Theorizing Signifyin(g) and the Role of the Reader," William Spurlin urges African-American and other critics to exhibit a negotiating sensibility in professional literary endeavors: "I submit that readings based on multiple frames of reference need to be shared and intersubjectively negotiated within and among specific interpretive communities; the space for this negotiation of knowledge could be our classrooms, professional meetings and conferences, university departments . . . and the pages of our scholarly journals."[6] Spurlin's call for actual world practices of intersubjective negotiation suggests a bridge to Morrison's novel. Pilate's house and yard become Milkman's (her nephew's) school, and her dialogic interactions with various people demonstrate the power of intellectual negotiations to move us morally and epistemologically.

Collins's and Spurlin's essays show what Mary Hawkesworth says monadic conceptions of reason fail to grasp, namely, "the complexity of the interaction between traditional assumptions, social norms, theoretical conceptions, disciplinary strictures, linguistic possibilities, emotional dispositions, and creative impositions in every act of cognition."[7] This complex interaction—this negotiation of sources, norms, emotions—is, in Hawkesworth's argument, the essence of feminist knowledge. This interactive knowing is exactly the sourcebook that Morrison develops in Pilate Dead, making her the most knowledgeable and the most interpersonally effective character in *Song of Solomon*.

Fannie Lou Hamer and the Civil Rights Movement

Melissa Walker's contextualization of *Song of Solomon* in the civil rights movement is a valuable correction to ahistorical readings of the novel.[8] But Walker sets the novel's political debate in the bipolar framework of Martin Luther King and Malcolm X, thus focusing her reading on the novel's young black men, Milkman and his friend, later nemesis, Guitar Baines. Black women's political action and thought during the movement may offer a more promising historical and epistemological position for reading Morrison's celebrated female character, Pilate Dead.

We might, for example, consider Morrison's text in relation to the Mississippi organizer, Fanny Lou Hamer. Her call to educated black women of the 1960s demonstrates her negotiating logic: "A few years ago throughout the country the middle class Black women—I used to say not really Black women, but the middle class colored women, didn't respect the kind of work that I was doing. But you see now baby, whether you have a ph.d., dd, or no d, we're in this bag together. And whether you are from Morehouse or Nohouse, we're still in this bag together."[9] Here and elsewhere, Hamer argues for common concerns among differently situated women as well as among blacks and whites. Though she never excused white or middle-class hegemony, she operated as though intersubjective negotiations across color lines would improve the land of America.

A look at Hamer's life suggests the difference between negotiations that are no more than forced compromises and the political standpoint of negotiation expressed by her self-authorizing claim that "we're in this bag together." Born October 6, 1917, in Montgomery County, Mississippi, Fannie Lou Hamer was the youngest of twenty children, a daughter of sharecroppers. Essentially trapped by the dominant economy, she suffered from inadequate clothing and food, never moving in her formal education beyond the sixth grade. In a chilling vignette, she explains, "One day when I was about six, I was playing beside a gravel road . . . and the landowner came and asked me could I pick cotton, I told him I didn't know. He told me if I picked 30 pounds of cotton that week that they would carry me to a commissary store . . . and I could get Cracker Jacks. . . . Then the next week I was tasked to 60 because what he was really doing, was trapping me into work."[10] From the white landowner's perspective at the time, Hamer represents exploitable labor. What are her choices? But Hamer tells this story during the civil rights movement in order to negotiate a system of representation that she desires: the democratic process. In other words, Hamer, like Gayatri Spivak, says "yes" to the system that excluded her. The difference between Spivak and Hamer is that Hamer says "yes" from the position of Spivak's subaltern. She is the woman often named in feminist academic discourse. The contact Hamer initiates between her personal history and the promises of the Constitution vividly demonstrates the effectiveness of actual world negotiations in formulating a more inclusive feminist sensibility.

As a civil rights worker in the 1950s and 1960s, Hamer bargained her way to speech, thus negotiating the economic trapping of her youth. When forced to choose between her job and her right to vote, she chose to vote in order to have more choices about work. And when she attended the Democratic Convention in 1964 as a member of the Mississippi Freedom Democratic party, she turned down the compromise forged by Hubert Humphrey and Walter Mondale—to seat the regular all-white delegation and give the MFDP two seats at-large—and gained instead an opportunity to speak. As the leader of the group, Hamer drew Humphrey into a debate on the question of representation: "Well Mr. Humphrey, do you mean to tell me that your position is more important to you than 400,000 Black lives?"[11]

Refusing compromise, Hamer nevertheless depended on strategies of negotiation and dialogue. Her commitment to voting rights provides the material example par excellence. Even though Hamer expressly rejected the white feminist notion of "equality" with white men, she coveted the principle and reality of democratic decision making. To her mind, equality with white men signified the right to rule. Committed to improving black lives, she did not envision liberation through irresponsible power. Thus, she reasonably rejected equality with men and simultaneously embraced the right to vote. This logic provides an instance of feminist negotiation since it borrows from and discriminates within the common store, illustrating the "both/and" positionality of one who is part of a community and apart from it.

Hamer's rhetoric—in speech, interview, and song—evokes her negotiating reason, demonstrating beyond any doubt that the woman who mediates cultural divides is not bound to serve the status quo. In her speech on the floor of the Democratic Convention, for example, she interfaced the lives of black Americans with the rhetoric of white America. "If the Democratic Party is not seated now, I question America.... Is this America? The land of the free and the home of the brave? Where we have to sleep with our telephone off the hook, because our lives be threatened daily?"[12] Mixing emotion with idealist "American" rhetoric and concrete references to the material conditions of poverty within the democratic process, Hamer created a negotiating, not a compromised, "book." The "we" of her testimony shifts back and forth from a black identity to a more heterogeneous American community as Hamer oscillates between loyalty to a marginalized past and faith in a more equitable future.

Speaking in Mississippi in 1963, Hamer borrowed presidential rhetoric, promising that "a house divided against itself cannot stand. America is divided against itself and without they considering us as human beings one day America will crumble."[13] Arguing in affiliation with black Americans, Hamer simultaneously enfolds many displaced others. Employing a rhetorical crescendo, she cautions those who threaten to "force every Negro out of the state of Mississippi." In her words, "after they have sent the Chinese back to China, the Jews back to Jerusalem, and give the Indians their land back; they take the *Mayflower* back from where they came, the Negro will still be in Mississippi!"[14] The dialectal mix formalistically frames Hamer's negotiating reason—the "high standard" presidential phrasing discursively joined with idioms from Black English ("without they considering," for example). Collins writes about the difficulty of translating Black English to Standard English. For example, passive constructions are nearly impossible in Black English. Rather than translate, Hamer negotiates dialect through quoting, borrowing, and juxtaposing. Her listing of Americans—like Walt Whitman's in "Song of Myself"—offers another level of formalistic negotiating. Evoking a number of positions while preferring one (the Negro's), Hamer illustrates her political commitment and her willingness to accommodate other voices.

In an interview in 1965, Hamer explicitly critiqued the "pure" identity of white America: "But this white man who wants to stay *white*, and to think for the Negro, he is not only destroying the Negro, he is destroying himself." [15] Narratively and analytically, Hamer points out the flawed reasoning of those who forget the complex interaction of histories, emotions, and sources that produce their knowledge; in essence, Hamer tells whites how black they are. In her account of an American purging of others, quoted earlier, those who would be required to leave are the very ones whose logic requires the displacement of all others. Hamer's claim, resting on the residence of Negroes in Mississippi, resists the separatist framework of origins and insists instead on a black place in America, indeed, on the blackness in whiteness. Not just Negro identity, but white identity in America can never be other than negotiated, sorted and pieced from the mixed bag of independence and dependence, nobility and barbarity, African and European.

Taking her mother's life as her point of political departure, Hamer practiced a knowledge beyond the either/or dichotomy that often directed black male leadership: "I do agree with the late Dr. King's non-violent approach in some cases, but in other cases one has to take a more militant approach," she reasoned. [16]

Bernice Johnson Reagon, a young coworker in the movement, articulates Hamer's role as "cultural carrier," a naming that suggests a potent mediating and negotiating subjectivity, one kin to the fictive Laurel Hand's. Reagon's assessment of Hamer's reasoning process is especially telling. Fannie Lou Hamer "believed that the movement was an unmistakable door that the people had opened in their own lives and now must be fortified to walk through. Whenever she talked, you felt that she was processing material that had come to her and was analyzing it and blending it with the challenges of the day." [17]

Locating Hamer in the transitional doorway and building on the trope of movement ("opening" and "walking"), Reagon describes Hamer's daily epistemology in a way that echoes Henderson's and Collins's descriptions of black feminist knowledge. Unlike liberal pluralism, which welcomes difference to a containing center, Hamer meets the material that comes to her across a number of borders. She analyzes it and "blend[s] it with the challenges of the day" to establish a decentered and yet synthesizing (not synthesized) knowledge.

Hamer was not free from social limitation, demanding relationships, or even debt. But neither was she wholly determined by these realities. Instead, she made her life out of the real circumstances of kinship and history—out of conflict, change, and contradiction—a practice that yielded a negotiated way of knowing. In turn, her adept handling of this process makes her a negotiating model for feminist criticism, the sort of model we need in rereading Pilate Dead.

Pilate's Knowledge and Practice

Song of Solomon tells the story of two families: on the one hand, Macon and Ruth Dead and their offspring: Magdalene and First Corinthians and their son Macon Dead II, called Milkman; and, on the other, Pilate, her daughter Reba, and her daughter Hagar.[18] Macon and Pilate Dead are the children of Sing, the mother who died when Pilate was born, and Jake, the father who visits Pilate from the dead after being killed by white poachers. But these two families occupy different classes, Macon's worth being measured in keys and money, Pilate's in loyalties and necessary cares: for the dead, for example. Macon's middle-class dream of American success and its pure antecedent—princely African ancestors—is juxtaposed, then, with Pilate's shameless mixing of inheritances and patrimonies. She claims vital links to her father, her brother, and the white man she and Macon killed, as well as with her fatherless female offspring. Unlike Macon, she does not kowtow to dividing lines: between past and present, legitimate and illegitimate, for example. She would, we learn, welcome Macon's cultural fathering of her granddaughter.[19] But as the purist that he thinks he is, Macon retreats into silence and assumes the goodness of hierarchy and division. As a negotiator, Pilate speaks to and among all of the novel's opposites, assuming that respectful and discriminating contacts can be established across class and gender divides.

And yet, the negotiating subject of Morrison's text is not so much the knower—Pilate as supreme intermediary—or the known—an irrefutable body of knowledge. Instead, the crucial difference in Pilate is her learning—until the very end—*through the process of negotiating*. Her methods include caring for her sources, even when they contradict one another, inventing from reclaimed materials, and mixing the denominations of unfaltering loyalty and flexible commitment. She lives out the intermediate position where differences rub up against each other, sometimes in anger and hate, sometimes in love and compassion.

Despite Pilate's textual centrality—she begins the story with her singing; she narrates her history in the middle of the novel, and the story ends with her death—*Song of Solomon* has been read as "center[ing] on Milkman Dead's unwitting search for identity."[20] In this interpretive framework, the novel investigates the history of the Deads, recurring to a number of ancestors who lead Milkman from a middle-class complacency to a revitalized knowledge of black American history. Certainly, the novel does feature Milkman's growth into manhood through the device of his, at first reluctant, recovery of the past. But the novel also tells the story of Pilate Dead, who already knows who she is. What pertains in a reading alongside her character is a reconstitution of the intermediary's work. Along these lines, Genevieve Fabre calls Pilate "the depository: 'She who heard the voice and sang the song.'"[21] The discriminating use of known stories, rather than the discovery of a hidden past unfolds as Pilate's text. In relation to the interests of this book, her mixed knowledge—coming from black folk tradition, an African heritage, American geographies, and domestic practice—becomes a source for her negotiating actions.

Indeed, Morrison's primary agent for resistance *and* connection is Pilate. In the text's opening chapters, Morrison shifts the textual focus from the "deadlock" of Milkman's parents toward a third parental and familial figure: Pilate Dead. A carrier of bones and geographical remnants, Pilate is the active conduit not only of Milkman's discovery but of the reader's. The negotiating alternative she offers is, like Hamer's, more than a centrist position between extremes. She is neither the androgyne nor the trickster, neither a union of opposites nor a subversive change agent. Instead, Pilate is a knower who listens and sorts bits of information to determine the course of her action, a negotiating agent inside and out. In this sense, she is a model for the reader. Her story—which is narrated in the middle of the novel—operates as a hinge, just as she does, turning Milkman from the exclusive reason of Macon Dead toward the more inclusive—but still discriminating—reason of the engaged mediator. For example, Morrison tells us that when Pilate began to head home, having been ostracized from yet another community because of her mysteriously missing navel, she faced a choice. "Right there she knew she must decide on whether to get to

Virginia or settle in a town where she would probably have to wear shoes. So she did both—the latter to make the former possible."[22] This brief narration makes clear Pilate's preferences (going home and not wearing shoes) and her logic (some accommodations get you further down the road). This mixed or impure thinking discriminates between likes and unlikes but also forges connections between opportunities and requirements. Macon mistakes this thinking as indiscriminate, believing that Pilate has no logic or standard. Predictably, she is, in his mind, a witch and a sorceress. But Pilate's history makes it clear that she thinks through her options and her desires and fastens on courses that will move her along with the people she loves. As other readers have noted, she is more spiritual guide than siren.

Morrison has Pilate follow her birth narrative with stories of her early geographic mobility. Her only school experience awakens her love of geography, and when she runs off as a girl, she takes the geography book with her. Her present collection of rocks signifies this early itinerancy.[23] She made her way with help from other blacks, but she was also shunned by them when they learned about her physical deformity. Pilate tells Ruth that after twenty-some years of wandering, she took stock of her situation. Though she discarded everything she had learned to date, her method of personal recreation is that of the *bricoleur*, the transfer-artist, who takes up old patterns, fragments, used bits of knowledge and convenes a multi-situated, nonoppositional self: "When am I happy and when am I sad [she asked] and what is the difference? What do I need to know to stay alive? What is true in the world? Her mind traveled crooked streets and aimless goat paths, arriving sometimes at profundity, other times at the revelations of a three-year-old. . . . Her alien's compassion for troubled people ripened her and—the consequence of the knowledge she had made up or acquired—kept her just barely within the boundaries of the elaborately socialized world of black people" (149). Perhaps the most important aspect of this description is what Morrison leaves out. Pilate's mixed-bag identity is presented in terms of self-pleasing discriminations, not wholesale rejections. Furthermore, although she may be "just barely within the boundaries" defined by "black people," she is also described in terms of her "*alien's* compassion" (emphasis added). Pilate is really between worlds—inside and out—more than she is a member of one.

Making up knowledge out of history and land, Pilate is both stable and changing. Her negotiating intelligence methodically selects, conjoins, and mixes habits, loyalties, identities, that society holds in opposition. Thus, for example, she stares into other people's eyes ("among black people the height of rudeness") but is simultaneously a gracious provider of food to anyone who visits her home (149). She gives up all interest in table manners but "acquire[s] a deep concern for and about human relationships" (149). She stands out, from the beginning, because of her inattention to dress; in the opening scene she wears a quilt instead of a coat. And yet her character is most distinguished by her attention to people.

Metaphorically, Morrison evokes Pilate's internal negotiations in Macon's and Milkman's responses to her house. Genevieve Fabre remarks that the house "symbolically . . . is for Milkman the threshold, both margin and *limen*."[24] But Fabre reads this space as representing a phase in Milkman's life; I read it as establishing a central philosophical concept of the novel—the notion that the self is composed of many souls.[25] Pilate's windows are open and welcoming; even Macon cannot resist looking in one night and listening to the singing. Looking over his shoulder, readers see what Macon at first hears: melodious interchanges among Pilate—the leader—with Reba and Hagar. While Pilate stirs "something in a pot," Hagar braids her mother's hair. All three are mixing and relaying sound: "They were singing some melody *that Pilate was leading*. A phrase that the other two were taking up and building on" (29, emphasis added). Pilate's window is really a window onto a relaying, negotiating subjectivity that momentarily reconnects Macon with his love for her. She is without a doubt the reader's "leader" and teacher, the subject position that makes the others known.

When he first visits his Aunt Pilate, Milkman observes her open posture and large frame: "On the front steps, [she was] sitting wide-legged in a long-sleeved, long-skirted black dress. Her hair was wrapped in black too, and from a distance, all they could really see beneath her face was the bright orange she was peeling. . . . One foot pointed east and one pointed west" (36). Here and elsewhere, the isomorphism of the scene flows into descriptions of Pilate, and she flows back into the geography. With feet pointing east and west, Pilate is a map of the American soul that Hamer postulated in her "bag." Her body signifies the interactive space of meetings and crossroads, her feet a sign of the transnational movements distilled into her character. The orange, which she works with her hands, serves as a stylized signifier for Pilate's orality. Its color speaks a wisdom beyond the overworked tropes of blackness and whiteness. But Pilate's mixing hardly makes her indiscriminate, and her loving nature does not make her obsequious. Her house is open *and* she critiques her nephew aggressively, challenging his youthful pride and his poor English.

When Milkman enters Pilate's house, he sees a "large sunny room that looked both barren and cluttered" (39), a description uncannily suggestive of a schoolroom. Like his father, he will observe odd collections: of fruit, old pieces of furniture, bottles, and newspaper articles. At this juncture, neither man recognizes Pilate's wisdom. Her capacities and her thinking are—like Hamer's—too large for the narrowly constructed knowledge of middle-class America (black or white). Unlike the Deads' house, Pilate's domicile is expanded through more than one economy—for example, wine making, lovemaking, song, linguistic analysis, and cultural negotiation. Her wisdom is determined not by a trial of strength but rather by a dream of meeting, collaborating, and nurturing. Her last words confirm this association of love and knowledge: "If I'd a *knowed* more [people], I would a loved more" (336, emphasis added).

Because her mother died before she was born, Pilate emerged without a navel. While this physical sign is certainly open to interpretation, I read its absence as signifying another presence in the text's possible world—the metaphysical world beyond Macon's world of tangible evidence. Born after her mother's death, Pilate appears without the umbilicus. While we might at first understand this significant detail as pointing to Pilate's lack of a mother, her lack of a navel also suggests the absence of cutting. In birth and life, Pilate remains both separate and attached, merged and yet distinct.

Signified by the absence of an umbilicus, Pilate operates as textual placenta, a vital connector which is neither of mother nor child but a third relating entity, a living, breathing intermediary. In relation to Ruth and Milkman, Pilate is a transmitter of both life and intelligence, a characterization that furthers an epistemological distinction between achieved or essential identity and negotiated knowledge. Whereas the navel operates as noun and is simultaneous with the separation of the individual, the placenta operates as verb or process. To offer another distinction, we might say that the navel—like the period at the end of a sentence—announces an end and a separation, whereas the placenta—like a comma—announces overlap, adjustment, and expansion. As a figure for negotiated knowing, the placenta is other than individual or communal, notifying us of the many sides and origins of Pilate's wisdom.

In a published conversation, Luce Irigaray and Helene Rouch retell the story of the placenta. "Although [it] is a formation of the embryo, [the placenta] behaves like an organ that is practically independent of it. It plays a mediating role on two levels. On the one hand, it's the mediating space between mother and fetus, . . . On the other hand, it constitutes a system regulating exchanges between the two organisms."[26] A number of critics have commented on Pilate's critical role in Milkman's conception. Recognizing Ruth's loneliness, she concocted the brew that awakened

Macon Dead's sexual desire and brought him to Ruth's bed. After the conception, she stood between Macon's threat to abort the fetus and Ruth's fecund body. Reading Pilate as placental figure, however, we bring to life the mediated space between father and fetus, between mother and son, between aunt and niece. This interpretive adjustment makes it possible for us to imagine a multihinged and, at the same time, free-floating subjectivity. Like the placenta, Pilate is anchored in relations with others (her father, her daughter, her nephew), but she is also an alchemist possessing the lode of familial and cultural knowledge, moving beyond and ahead of the other characters.[27]

Textually speaking, "placental" knowledge may be likened to oral transmission and to the generative activity of retelling. Bernice Johnson Reagon remarks that "when you are a part of an [oral] environment the experiences that are passed in that space become forever a part of who you are."[28] At the same time, "You walk out of that space with responsibility for the stories you now carry."[29]

Pilate's placental *nous* amends a competing view of the relation between maternity, subjectivity, and writing popularized by Hélène Cixous and widely embraced by white American feminism. Cixous likens women's writing to giving away, rhetorically questioning whether "the woman, who has experienced the not-me within me, [could] not have a particular relationship to the written? To writing as giving itself away (cutting itself off) from the source?"[30] But cutting herself off (or being cut off) is precisely what Pilate does not do and what Morrison's possible world warns against. As ancestress, Pilate is the one Hagar and Milkman should not be cut off from. At the same time, she is not identified with the mother but with the mediating figures of midwife and placenta. Culturally and literarily, black women authors, like many white women writers and academics, may not conceive of themselves as separate and can hardly afford to give themselves, their offspring, or their books "away." Mae Gwendolyn Henderson's description of black women writers' situations is instructive. "In negotiating the discursive dilemma of their characters, these writers accomplish two objectives: the self-inscription of black womanhood, and the establishment of a dialogue of discourses with the other(s). The self-inscription of black women requires disruption, rereading and rewriting the conventional and canonical stories, as well as revising the conventional generic forms that convey these stories."[31] Henderson fashions a model that recognizes the black woman writer's betweenness, a model that neither cuts her off nor requires her absolute giving. Indeed, Henderson's description of epistemological "negotiating" sounds much like Collins's and is exactly what Pilate practices when she tutors listeners (or readers) in how to enter stories from other sides and to learn to discern one's own equivocal and contradictory movement in the world. Through this process, one can claim *"the same within"* while continuing to discriminate. Structurally and intellectually, this move allows us to annex epistemological locations without conceding to dominant mentalities.

The logic of such a model is contradictory as the passage from Irigaray implies: Pilate is "practically independent," but also "mediating," always maneuvering between. As Henderson makes clear in her feminist criticism, black women writers both disrupt and revise—and they do so in relation to both hegemonic (white) and nonhegemonic (black) discourses. Their work, then, constitutes a negotiated knowledge, but not a fixed or separate one.

According to Morrison, "Pilate is the apogee of [male/female relating]: of the best of that which is female and the best of that which is male, and that balance is disturbed if it is not nurtured, . . . if it is not reproduced."[32] Key to Morrison's description are the verbs "nurtured" and "reproduced." Unlike the static androgyne, Pilate as conceived by Morrison is the "apogee" of what must be an ongoing process, a process that yields a subject both "fierce" and "loving." What is interesting in this characterization is how Pilate both critically engages and selectively appropriates various positions. And although Morrison's description might be seen as assuming gender designations, the question is moot with Pilate's own practice, which scrambles and recirculates the various gender roles she assumes. Indeed, Pilate as "apogee" might be best understood in relation to the word's first (rather than the more predictable second) meaning: "The point in the orbit of a satellite of the earth or of a vehicle orbiting the earth that is at the greatest distance from the center of the earth" (*Webster's New Collegiate Dictionary*). In this definition, the subject's relational but decentered movement is stressed. *Apogee* as "culmination" or "highest point," on the other hand, suggests static achievement, hierarchy, and an essential nature, all of which characterize Macon Dead's subjectivity, not Pilate's.

Pilate's negotiated knowing is emblematized in her instructions to Milkman in the preparation of boiled eggs. Speaking to her nephew, she remarks, "Now, the water and the egg have to meet each other on a kind of equal standing. One can't get the upper hand over the other. So the temperature has to be the same for both. I knock the chill off the water first. Just the chill. I don't let it get warm because the egg is room temperature, you see. Now then, the real secret is right here in the boiling. When the tiny bubbles come to the surface, when they as big as peas and just before they get big as marbles. Well, right then you take the pot off the fire" (39). Of course, the water and the egg are not on equal standing; Pilate makes them "kind of equal" in order for them to meet, perform, and yield the "perfect soft-boiled egg" (40). Her recipe includes the doing of a "small obligation" while the egg sits: "generally," she tells Milkman, "[I] go to the toilet . . . for a [short] stay" (40). This interfacing of tasks or relaying of "obligations" parabolically evokes one form of negotiating knowledge: attending to alternate duties.[33] Telling about it, Pilate not only concocts a story of personal maneuvers; she also digests the results, a move that suggests the sustenance rather than sterility of a negotiating "attitude."

Morrison, more than any of our authors thus far, declares Pilate's intermediate function: "She was a natural healer, and among quarreling drunks and fighting women she could hold her own, and sometimes mediated a peace that lasted a good bit longer than it should have because it was administered by someone not like them" (150). Morrison's narrative association of Pilate's difference—she is not "like them"—with her community caretaking and commitment to peace suggests the feminist negotiations I am defining in this book. She is both related and apart; her lack of a navel attests to this, as we have already seen. What makes her a potent figure for current feminisms is how she seems to decide each case through compassionate affiliation *and* critical distance.

Pilate's negotiating sensibility surfaces most powerfully in passages that have been underread in Morrison criticism. Her one act of violence, for example, offers an illustration of Morrison's character's politics and demonstrates what I would call Pilate's "discriminating inclusiveness," her practical, this-world negotiations. Using a knife and her tongue, she attacks a neighborhood man who has been abusing her daughter Reba: "Now I'm not going to kill you, honey. Don't you worry none. Just be still a minute, the heart's right here, but I'm not going to stick it any deeper. Cause if I stick it in any deeper, it'll go straight through your heart. . . . If you're real still, honey, I can get it . . . out without no mistake. But before I do that, I thought we'd have a little talk" (93–94). Reasoning with the man, she continues, "You see, darlin, that there is the only child I got. . . . Women are foolish, you know, and mamas are the most foolish of all. . . . You got a mama, ain't you? . . . I'd hate to push [the knife] in more and have your mama feel like I do now" (94). Employing common knowledge and irony, Pilate clearly satirizes gender stereotyping at the same time that she makes use of it. This double stance toward her own familial identity—at once undermining accepted knowledge about mothers and employing it—distinguishes Pilate's negotiating character from a subversive one. Her use of gendered knowledge is straight from the heart *and* performative—not solely ironic or essentializing—as she deftly picks her way back and forth across a motherly compassion that verges on madness and a fatherly certitude that plays with phallic symbolism ("I'd hate to push it in more"). Her logic creates multiple and contradictory connections: between self and daughter; self and another mother; even Reba and this man: both have mothers.

Pilate makes it clear that the common good calls for nonviolence even as she temporarily employs violence and promises not to ("You might lose about two tablespoons of blood but no more" [94]). Furthermore, Pilate's rhetoric—which is ironically self-deprecating ("mamas are the most foolish")—also establishes motherhood as the crucial vantage point in this negotiation, a position that makes clear the limits of Pilate's bargaining. She will not give Reba up.

In another key passage, exactly halfway through the novel, we find further rendering of Pilate's intercessionist negotiations. Fearful of Hagar's attempts on Milkman's life, Ruth has come to Pilate's house to confront her niece. The encounter becomes one of mutual threats, each woman vowing to kill the other. Pilate enters as mediator between her granddaughter Hagar and her sister-in-law Ruth, breaking up the conflict. For readers, her character becomes an intermediate space for reasoning through conflict. Pilate's tools are analogy, oscillation—from one perspective to another—as well as self-disclosing narration. Declaring that Milkman "wouldn't give a pile of swan shit for either one of you" (137), she gains the other women's attention and requires both to sit down. Directly to Ruth and within Hagar's hearing, Pilate draws connections between the women to illustrate their "contradictory common ground." "You won't never be able to forgive her. For just tryin to [kill him] you won't never be able to forgive her. But it looks to me like you ought to be able to understand her. Think on it a minute" (139). Separating "forgiveness" from "understanding," Pilate recommends the second over the first, an intriguing inversion of Christian doctrine. Where forgiveness is not humanly plausible, perhaps shared comprehension is. This is certainly what Ruth has asked of Milkman and what Macon absolutely refuses to give.

Pilate goes on: "You ready now to kill her—well, maim her anyway—because she's tryin to take him away from you. She's the enemy to you because she wants to take him out of your life. Well, in her eyes there's somebody who wants to take him out of her life too—him. So he's her enemy. He's the one who's tryin to take himself out of her life. And she'll kill him before she lets him do that. What I'm sayin is that you both got the same idea" (139). Articulating their differences and situating them in the same psychological space, Pilate's thinking likens, not only Ruth and Hagar, but the relations between each woman and Milkman, as well as his likeness to Hagar: both are someone's "enemy." This reasoning introduces a third character—Milkman—to disrupt the simple dualism scripted by mother and lover. Thus Pilate offers recognition of similarities as well as new antagonisms. Now Ruth must recognize her son's callousness in relation to another woman. Pilate understands that Ruth cannot forget and forgive, certainly not Hagar, perhaps not Milkman.[34] Neither can Pilate forget or forgive her father's murder. But understanding may lead to a future, whereas forgiveness without understanding, and violence as a consequence, will not. In Morrison's novel, the biblical names—Hagar and Pilate—recall the disastrous outcomes of stance/counterstance and suggest, through their novelistic mixing, the more livable option of political and textual negotiations.

Focusing on Ruth and Hagar's "idea," Pilate makes explicit the relation between thought and action, suggesting that understanding one another's thinking processes is crucial. From Hagar's perspective, her violence makes immanent sense, while from Ruth's, it only makes sense if she reenters the story on Hagar's side. Indeed, Pilate forcefully illustrates the possibility for learned sympathy with others' perspectives, an interpretive movement that is something besides appropriation or forgiveness since the purpose is not merely self or other enhancement but self/other survival. Going one step further, Pilate makes it clear that Ruth and Hagar's contradictory connection—their psychological likeness—is also the reason for redirecting their energy. Otherwise, either (or both)—in a rhetorical play invented by Morrison for *her* uses—ends up merely killing (or saving) a dead man.

Even before this address by Pilate, Ruth registers her sister-in-law's "equilibrium," a balance in Pilate that "overshadow[s] all her eccentricities" (138). As we have seen, however, this "balancing" occurs in movements—like stirring something in a pot and talking over the day's struggles—not in an achieved equipoise. Insisting on the openness of her character's intermediate status, Morrison does not enforce Pilate's tutelage. The narration offers no evidence that Hagar hears her grandmother, for example; instead she remains fixed on her one love object, Milkman.

Milkman, on the other hand, though reluctant at first, seems to store Pilate's wisdom for later flowering. In one of her early "lessons," for example, Pilate tutors her nephew in "blackness," intimating that there are several shades of "dark": "You think [it's] just one color, but it ain't. There're five or six kinds of black. Some silky, some woolly. Some just empty. Some like fingers. And it don't stay still. It moves and changes from one kind of black to another" (40–41). Whereas Guitar Baines bets his life on the cultural overdetermination of black/white conflict, Pilate's signifying on blackness makes clear the shifting nature of cultural identity, calling to mind Cornel West's notion of "dynamic changing, revisable historical legacies."[35] Guitar believes in a system of equivalences that is quite different from Pilate's "balance." For every black killed, the Seven Days—a vigilante group of local black men—evens the score by randomly killing a white. This reductive logic mimics zero-sum negotiations in which a finite win on one side must be matched by an equal loss on the other. The critical difference in Pilate's and Guitar's reasoning is that more can be gained through affiliation and criticism than through either of those modalities alone. In this case, Hamer is a better historical model for reading the novel than is Malcolm X or Martin Luther King. Pilate will safeguard relationships through dialogue and even discriminating violence, but Guitar safeguards an identity and a quota through violence alone.

In Morrison's text, complicity is not the crucial flaw; some complicities are necessary. Instead moral failure is devised as an unawareness of the multiple webs that sustain and enliven identity and history. Pilate openly negotiates the tension between black and black, male and female, middle class and working class. Macon, on the other hand, jealously controls his son, fearful that he will be seduced by Pilate's indiscrimination and mixings. In Macon's thinking, Pilate's duplicity, like Eve's, can only mean her fecklessness, just as Ruth's love of her father can only mean "slut." Both women are witches in Macon's mind, trafficking out of control. But Pilate's thinking reveals a subjectivity that traffics in open interchange and fierce loyalty, in movement back and forth across options that foster the lives she holds dear.

With Macon and Pilate, then, Morrison negotiates blackness. But she does so by mixing their families rather than through rigid adherence to the binary opposition they seem to suggest. Thus Macon Dead (Milkman's father) and Hagar (Pilate's granddaughter) are likened in their strict adherence to one economy; neither can live without the pure acquisition of a single love object. And Pilate Dead (Macon's sister and Milkman's aunt) and Milkman (Macon's son, Pilate's nephew, and Hagar's lover) are likened in their learning. Pilate's mediating practices yield her negotiating reason, the reason that ultimately becomes Milkman's saving grace. In the words of Fannie Lou Hamer, "You can kill a man, but you can't kill ideas. 'Cause the ideas going to be transferred from one generation [to the next]."[36]

Pilate's Bag

Patricia Sharpe, F. E. Mascia-Lees, and C. B. Cohen connect black men's and white women's positive response to black women's creative writing with black female writers' textualizing of liminality. In their argument, black women's texts intensify liminal symbols through multiple uses of transitional spaces and rituals, undermining "the idea that structure is inevitable and unchanging" and providing "a mechanism for conceiving of women as not fixed in otherness."[37] This perspective allows us to theorize the strength and vitality of more porous, more negotiating narratives like Morrison's. Like Pilate's house, Morrison's novel corrects the claims of identity and ownership and redirects our energy toward the practices of cultural negotiation. Even though much of Pilate's knowledge is flawed or mistaken, her practices work. If she was supposed to remember her mother "Sing" (147), her singing instead works to relieve her gloom. Indeed, Morrison suggests that Pilate's *processing* of information is as important—if not more—than is its "accuracy." Although Morrison identifies Pilate as ancestress, this characterization is not grounded in canonical wisdom. Instead, her daily capacity to negotiate (people, ideas, materials) is what makes her a cultural carrier. The process of Pilate's wisdom—not an identifiable body of knowledge that can be handed down like gold, either to daughters or sons—makes her worthy of remembering.

We are educated to this perspective through Pilate's "bag," the tarp she hangs from her ceiling, the very one that Milkman and Guitar try to steal, mistaking it for gold.

For most of her life, Pilate has carried the bones of the white man she and Macon killed when they were hiding out in Pennsylvania as children. After separating from Macon, who wanted to take the gold, Pilate is visited by her father. He gives her two messages—"Sing. Sing," and "You just can't fly on off and leave a body" (147). The first she understands as "To sing, which she did beautifully, reliev[ing] her gloom immediately" (147). The second she understands as a message to go back to Pennsylvania "and collect what was left of the man she and Macon had murdered. (The fact that she had struck no blow was irrelevant. She was part of her brother's act, because, then, she and he were one)" (147). In Pilate's understanding, connected identities are not determined through a legalist assessment of guilt but through desire for the same things: she and Macon were "one" because they were trying to stay alive together. What she hears is a requirement to "own" and "carry" the lives you take; not just one's past but one's future includes a partial merger with the other. This practice makes one remember, and it shapes one's other choices and actions. Carrying a bag of bones (or a daughter and granddaughter, or twenty-one children, like Ryna, Milkman's great grandmother, did), one will make some choices and not others. One will choose in relation to those others. And so the white man's bones, along with the geography book, the rocks, and two spools of thread constitute Pilate's "inheritance" which she suspends from her ceiling in the coveted tarp; she lives in relation to these signifying objects, objects that belong to her and to which she simultaneously belongs. In a postmodern move, Morrison does not have Pilate's inheritance *come down* to her but, instead, represents her ancestress as *picking up and chosing* her legacy.

When Milkman and Guitar attempt the theft, they fail, of course, to find any gold. But theirs is not the only misreading of the tarp's interior. As Milkman learns, the bones Pilate carries are her father's, not an anonymous white man's. She has misread them, then, just as she misheard her father's clue "Sing." With her nephew at the novel's end, Pilate buries the bones on Solomon's Leap. But Pilate *thinks* throughout the novel that she is holding a white body. The uncanniness in both mistakes—the body and the name—is that Pilate's interpretations worked for her. If singing kept her cheerful, carrying the white man's bones saved her from an ossifying hatred, the hatred that makes Macon so dead and Guitar so deadly. Whether the bones are black or white, Pilate is *"the same within"* in her choice not to leave them.

Morrison's "correction" of Pilate's thinking, far from undermining it, actually reinforces it since Pilate acts the same in relation to the bones whether they are white or black. In both instances, her actions signify "identities in dialogue" since she affiliates with the bones in any case. Like Hamer, she seems to understand the logic of "not leaving." In Hamer's rhetoric, the Negro will not leave Mississippi. Pilate, in an inverse way that is still the same, knows that she cannot just go off and leave a body. In burying her father's bones, she clearly demonstrates discrimination: some lives are valued more than others. But none are despised or "left." Morrison's revising of the bones can be compared with Wharton's revision of the dream scenes in *The House of Mirth* and Welty's revision of the bridge in *The Optimist's Daughter*. All three authors negotiate the objects that identify their characters. By revising, they indicate a certain plasticity in their materials, their world views, their politics and poetics. In Morrison's case, the bones seem to become clarified in revision: as black bones. But bones do not show color. Or if they do, they are white. Thus Morrison seems to suggest that all Americans are in this bag together. This does not mean that she urges historical forgetfulness. Instead it suggests that historical memory can only be fruitfully mined by those who see themselves as related to the whole mix of the past. Beyond the predetermined organizing structures—white/black; victimizer/victim; speech/silence—Pilate invents a possible world for an identity that claims a productive relation even to a past of violence. Thus Morrison's replacement of Pilate's missing navel is textually signified with bags, and they, in turn, signify her mediating reason, one that is always "non-innocent," "reinvented," and "obligated to its enabling sources."[38]

As we near the twenty-first century, feminist criticisms can be directed by Hamer's and Pilate's "bags." Not only are we in them together; our mining of them requires love as much as anger, goodwill as much as accuracy, intellectual relationship as much as intellectual identity. Claiming a relation even to the other who excludes us, feminist readers can invent for ourselves a more productive sourcebook. If someone else writes us out, we do not have to leave them. Like Hamer, we can refuse to leave. Writing them in—guided by Hamer and Pilate—we enlarge our bag, our vision, our history. At this juncture in feminist reading, perhaps "insidership," imagined as a series of relays between positions, should be the metaphor of choice. If feminist critics are only "out," who exactly is their audience? Who are feminist critics teaching? And whose models are at the heart of feminist critique?

6

Negotiated Motherhood
Contradictory Leanings in Marge Piercy's *Woman on the Edge of Time*

The difficulty, in general, has been the lack of a space where . . . two modes could meet, negotiate, and generate through their mutual asymmetry an effective but a progressively complex and mediated sense of "history" and "reality."
—R. Radhakrishnan

We need . . . to use others' methods and others' meeting places, in others' neighborhoods and not only our own. We need to recognize the humanity of those whose labors support us, be they woman, man, or child, of whatever color, religion, culture, or state of "normality." We need to recognize their humanity in their terms, not simply our own. Even with the backbreaking burdens of an academic career, the challenge to academic feminists is to find a humble, effective way to do these things. The first step lies in knowing ourselves.
—Kathryn Pyne Addelson

MARGE PIERCY'S *Woman on the Edge of Time* (1976) seems a fitting conclusion-as-beginning for this study of feminist criticism and American women's fiction on the edge of the twenty-first century. In the last stages of revision, I have realized that all of the characters organizing this book are "older"—as I am older since I began this project—and in a sense poised on the divide of youthful dream and mature vision. Lily is twenty-nine, Janie and Laurel in their forties, Pilate and Connie Ramos—Piercy's heroine—older than that. But in another sense, these characters provoke a new and New Age feminist criticism: one that takes responsibility for its theoretical centrality—its academic insidership—while retaining its ties with the political margin, whether lesbian, black, or working-class scenes of struggle.

Negotiated Motherhood

This chapter operates by opening the novel, circling through the feminist debate on mothering, and then analyzing Piercy's narrative as a negotiation of biological maternity and technological "brooding." A subject of heart and mind, motherhood remains, as Tillie Olsen has written, "the least understood, the most tormentingly complex experience to wrest to truth," not the least of all in feminist criticism.[1] This is true because, among other things, most mothers are working class, not privileged writers.

Piercy selects a mother as the most likely candidate for time travel in her realistic and utopian novel, *Woman on the Edge of Time*.[2] Visiting the village of Mattapoisett, Massachusetts, in the twenty-second century, Connie Ramos hears a language both familiar and strange. Her future companions speak of "inknowing and outknowing," of "feel[ing] with other beings. . . . [of] coning, going down, . . . reach[ing] nevel, . . . [of] slow[ing] at will." When Connie asks for a translation ("What is all that stuff?") and her guide, Luciente, complies (inknowing and outknowing, coning, and reaching nevel are learned "states of consciousness," "types of feeling"), Piercy's time-traveler replies in anger. "How can you teach somebody to feel? From a book you can learn the multiplication tables. But how can you teach love?" The New Age answer: "But every mother always has. Or failed to."[3] Later, Connie learns that "mothers" are not necessarily female; indeed, the old tags—male and female—have about as much significance as height or hair color among future Mattapoisetts. Even in the reproductive arena, embryos grow in a mechanical "brooder" and are ceremonially delivered to adoptive mothers—male and female—at the end of gestation.

And yet Piercy's severing of the tie between the female body and biological reproduction (cutting the umbilicus that Morrison symbolically sustains) seems to up the theoretical ante rather than to neutralize the maternal issue, since Piercy models parenting on social and biological performances that readers associate with mothers. Thus Piercy relies on readers' memories of female mothers just as her future society relies on Connie Ramos for its historical, textual projection. Piercy seems to honor this debt in retaining the *mother* word, that tantalizing, devastating sign. How then are we to read Piercy's use of mechanical gestation when she sustains the taxonomical name and historical memories of mothering? Connie's political oppression, as witnessed again and again in the novel, has less to do with pregnancy and birth than with other medical and legal technologies of the twentieth century, such as sterilization and drug "therapy."[4] I answer that Piercy's choice operates narratively rather than thematically. Her novel does not, in other words, offer a unidirectional revision of mothering. Instead, the textual negotiation conceptually represented between Connie's memories of maternity and a nongendered reproductive practice in the possible future of Mattapoisett creates in readers a difficult adjudication of motherhood.

Most of Piercy's critics interpret her novel thematically. In these receptions, her text deplores Connie's present condition—as indigent, woman, Chicana, mother—and advocates the political, social transformations possible in Luciente's future, among them nongendered, technological reproduction.[5] Where Piercy is assumed to be writing utopian fiction, critics conclude that she writes Connie's past only to dispose of it. In other words, Piercy affiliates politically with only one side of her story. Along these lines, Angelika Bammer writes that Piercy's text is "at once more conventional and less hopeful than [Joanna Russ's] *The Female Man*.... There is not . . . a whole range of possibilities; the options, as Piercy presents them, are starkly either/or." To my mind, Bammer's claim misses the distinctive feature of Piercy's narration because it does not address the issue of how Luciente's utopia is always mediated through Connie's present and her dream of a possible past; in other words, how it is paid for narratively. Composing a text in which the plot operates through characters' intrusions in simultaneous actual and possible worlds, Piercy situates the reader in narrative spaces that look in both directions. Connie Ramos is *our* intermediary, and thus Piercy's plotting suggests an indebtedness to Connie's personal history as well as to the dream of Luciente's future. This positioning and plotting confesses a theoretical and political relatedness to several positions, narratively refusing the either/or thinking that critics have wanted to attribute to the novel. I will show that Piercy's novel "hears" at least three positions on mothering: the omniscient critique of Connie's actual world where she is sentenced to mothering; Luciente's possible communalizing of a maternal persona and technology; and Connie's first person memory of maternal love enunciated in the future. Luciente's world is not, as Bammer claims it is, "everything that Connie's is not" because Connie's thinking is the means of negotiating that other world, and her intelligence is often organized around the memory of biological birth and her dreams of a possible past, memories Luciente must be supplied with.[6]

Motherhood and *reproduction* (like *woman* and *Chicana*) always operate metaphorically, in other words, as ciphers or bridges for multiple human values and stories. Thus the textual suspension or interruption of prebirth maternity in *Woman on the Edge of Time* actually *brings to hearing* the very stories and concepts that flow through the word *mother*. When we approach the novel from the kind of negotiating framework that I recommend, Piercy provides a hearing on motherhood that is far from conclusive. The future option of nongendered maternity offers Connie room for rethinking several maternal histories (her mother's, her own, her niece's), histories characterized by physical violence as well as expressions of passionate care. Narratively considered, then, Piercy's "brooder" reproduction becomes an axis for negotiating motherhood on both sides of the historical and textual border.

The critical travails of contemporary feminism are nowhere more evident than in discussions of mothering. The controversy recurs to the question of an essential feminine nature. Are women different because of biology or because of the culture of motherhood? Is it desirable—even in fantasy—to posit a link between feminist politics and a mothering body? Even when the theorist's work is not limited to the subject of mothering, her conclusions can be attacked for suggesting a female, maternal tie.

Response to Carol Gilligan's *In a Different Voice* serves as a familiar case in contemporary feminist theoretical politics.[7] Gilligan leans toward a cultural understanding of women as caretakers and inventive sympathizers, but her methodological association of mothers' bodies and morality—among other things, she investigates women's response to their own abortions—hints at material bedrock. This essentialist nod bodes badly for her among readers who fear the rebinding of maternal ties.[8] In response to my own work, a leading and influential critic has argued that feminist energy might be better spent in establishing woman's *human* nature, not her maternal nature.[9] Raquel Portillo Bauman's remark to Susan R. Suleiman about her article on mothering—"it stirred a series of uncomfortable feelings"—flags another concern: that most research situates itself with white middle-class women, ignoring other maternal histories and complexes.[10] If some consensus is emerging about "the extent to which a largely white, Western, middle class ideal of mothering has literally and figuratively overwritten the many voices, experiences, and interpretations of women," feminist theory continues to be stymied by *mothering*.[11]

Michelle Stanworth argues that the feminist divide on technology and mothering is primarily about motherhood.

> The depth of feeling among feminists about conceptive technologies has partly to do with their links, not to medical technology, but to the diffi-

cult terrain of motherhood. In some accounts, conceptive technologies have been used to delineate a boundary between "good" motherhood and "bad." On one side of the boundary is empowering motherhood, the motherhood that represents a positive counterpart to masculinity. On the other side of the boundary, where creating or sustaining a pregnancy depends upon medical assistance, lies coercive motherhood that locks women into subordination.[12]

In this passage, Stanworth conceives of two antithetical positions stationed on either side of the "boundary." Fleshing out her analysis, she claims that some feminists, like Sara Ruddick (or Carol Gilligan), see maternal practices as generating alternative values. Other feminists link motherhood with women's cultural and economic subordination as well as their inferior place in symbolic systems. About the time that Piercy was writing *Woman on the Edge of Time*, Shulamith Firestone was representing motherhood along these lines; in her words, "The nature of [the] bond [between women and children] is no more than shared oppression." Indeed, "the heart of woman's oppression is her childbearing."[13] In recent feminist theory, Catharine MacKinnon's work compellingly reiterates the political tie between the dictates of motherhood and sexual exploitation. In "Reflections on Sex Equality under Law," for example, she creates a poetic litany linking reproduction and the oppression of gender: "Reproduction is socially gendered. Women are raped and coerced into sex. When conception results . . . it is a girl or a woman who was violated, . . . When miscarriage results from physical assault, it is a woman who was beaten. When there is not enough money . . . for an abortion, it is a woman who is forced to have a child."[14]

Sara Ruddick, on the other hand, while distancing herself from the essentialist arguments of biology (she downplays gestation and birth), builds her theory of peace making on women's practices of maternity. Risking faith in women's historical practices with children, Ruddick's recent work recalls Tillie Olsen's fiction of the 1950s and 1960s in which mothers build "safe enough" worlds.[15] Based in children's requirements for holding, maternal care provides Ruddick with a feminist standpoint "produced by the political conditions and distinctive work of women."[16] Ruddick calls maternal nonviolence "a reality in the making," in other words, an ideal human posture encouraged by the kind of work that women do as mothers. For example, she argues that "there are maternal practices in which ideals of nonviolence actually govern. Mothers can, and often do, renounce the violence to which they are tempted, fight back against the violence done to them and their children, name and insist on responsibility for damages done, yet forswear a scarring hatred in favor of a peace in which they can love and work."[17]

Even while she locates her argument in social practices, Ruddick argues against male birth parents or mechanical embryos, finding "this vision of shared, genderless birth unfounded and dangerous. It is increasingly clear that the envy that lies behind the minimalization of birth fuels a technocratic and legal apparatus able to intrude on and exploit *women's* bodies in unprecedented ways." Moreover, she writes, "so long as we fear and deny the distinctly female character of birth, we risk losing the symbolic, emotional, and ultimately political significance of birth itself."[18] For political reasons, Ruddick wants to value what women *know* as mothers without essentializing *or* intruding upon female birth parents.

For my purposes in reading *Woman on the Edge of Time*, Ruddick's theory—"a reality in the making"—can be critically linked with the literary strategy of utopian fiction. Even though Ruddick does not favor mechanical reproduction or male birth parents, her theory expresses faith in human ability to extrapolate a nonviolent politics out of known patterns of maternal behavior. This means that, for her, *mother* operates as an organizing metaphor for the peace-loving people we can become and thus leans into the axis of possible worlds. MacKinnon's rhetoric, on the other hand, can be linked to the strategies of literary realism. She aims at verisimilitude in her description of women's lives and assumes the theoretical proposition that words are vitally linked to physical actualities. In her analysis, then, *mother* designates real histories, political positions, and enforced behaviors. What interests me in this chapter is how Piercy's novel "hears" the feminist debate about mothering by speaking in both of these genres, negotiating bipolar feminist views on mothering and words through a plot that "sides" with both perspectives.

The Chicana myth of La Malinche which permeates Piercy's text serves as a negotiated construct for reading MacKinnon and Ruddick together. Readers will remember that La Malinche, lover and adviser to Hernando Cortez, was traded away by her mother and is considered to be the creator of the *mestizo* race. Among Chicana feminists, her figure—though with differing accents—summarizes the controversial subject of mothering as well as the body politics of masculinity and femininity. Her story seems to advertise woman's actual, physical pawnability (MacKinnon). But recent feminist work on La Malinche has also argued that her intermediate role is productive of transworld knowledge and hybrid subjectivities (Ruddick). As Sandra Messinger Cypess writes, "The problem for feminists . . . has been how to balance the idea of La Malinche as slave on the one hand, obeying her master, and as independent, active translator on the other, who searched for the right words to bridge the gap between cultures, who served as a link for two cultures, becoming the mother of the new race of mestizos."[19]

The theoretical feminist negotiation of motherhood in Chicana-Latin American studies of La Malinche can be fruitfully compared with the work of some African-American feminist theorists. In "Outcast Mothers and Surrogates," for example, Angela Davis reviews a history of forced surrogacy in African-American history, that is, black women's mothering of white children. But she also remembers the chosen practice of "play mothering" prominent in the black community. This practice, in which an aunt or friend acts as mother for a niece or nephew, coexists with the economic and social demands of actual or biological mothering and enforced surrogacy. Thus Davis's discourse on maternity offers the space that R. Radhakrishnan says we need in order to "negotiate subject positions in an uneven world." We need a "space where . . . two modes"—here a critique of enforced surrogacy and a celebration of "play mothering"—can "meet, negotiate, and generate through their mutual asymmetry an effective but a progressively complex and mediated sense of 'history' and 'reality.'"[20]

In just such a way, *Woman on the Edge of Time* offers a space for two modes of feminist thought "to use others' methods and others' meeting places" first, to come to terms with our own interest in *motherhood* and, second, to begin to recognize those many mothers "whose labors support us" as Kathryn Pyne Addelson suggests.[21] By sympathetically siding with Connie's memory of motherhood while theoretically preferring the option of technological birth among future "Americans," Piercy's text narratively links feminist arguments that have often been conceived as absolutely distinct and antithetical. Both of these vantage points are admitted as loci of feminist value so that the apparent absolutes of oppressive individual motherhood (MacKinnon's vantage point) and liberated social maternity (Ruddick's and Davis's vantage points, though with different emphases) are each intruded upon by the other. Piercy's device for this "intrusion" is the possibility of time travel enacted by Connie and Luciente. Each enters the other, learns from the other, and gives some knowledge back.

Readers who accompany Connie on her journey move, like the primary characters, through in-between locations, witnessing discordant ways of thinking about a common subject. Piercy's plot, then, alternately sides with oppositional voices, making her novel our most fully developed instance of "negotiation our text" and placing us always in "anxious space[s] where

Negotiated Motherhood

decisions and choices are not easy."[22] For though the story of Connie's present includes physical torture, it also harbors the protagonist's longing to hold and touch her daughter, Angie. Likewise, Piercy often enunciates Connie's maternal history in *future* conversations, so that the logic of social mothering is interrupted by a once silenced, but now heard personal history which we value despite its pain and limitations. The plot, then, allows agendas and subjectivities to intrude upon one another—like Luciente and Connie—creating a figural-political instance of the negotiating practices that are at the very heart of feminist criticism. Neither side alone will do—not even the side of utopia.

The Mothering Sentence

I have already alluded to Piercy's simultaneous centuries, narrated from geographical positions in the northeastern United States. In the twentieth century, a poor Chicana—Connie Ramos—is falsely accused of instigating violence against her niece's pimp, Geraldo, and punished through institutionalization and medication: her brother, Luis, agrees that she is "sick."

As Piercy demonstrates, Connie's actual world enforces the narrative sentence linking female to *mother*. Because a woman *can* mother, she is made one: subsequently, the scenes of her life include the physical violence of rape, coerced abortion, and unelected hysterectomy as well as the political equivalents: silence and invisibility. In this world—one very much like the world described by Catharine MacKinnon—maternal words are spoken from an unlocatable position above Connie. In the Catch-22 of enforced maternal labor, *mother* is exactly the word Connie must *be* but cannot *tell*. This is the quandary that Spivak recognizes and deplores in theorizing the subaltern. In a linear illogic, this poor Chicana's capacity to bear children is literally erased (through hysterectomy), her living child taken (through "lawful" intervention), and *then* her maternal failure advertised: "old bitch" she is called. This "stamp[ed] . . . value"[23] literally imprisons Connie despite the physical exorcising of her maternal "markings" of ovaries and womb. Thus social scripting of motherhood actuates Connie's life, working on her literally to inscribe both the authority of an educated elite and the subordination of the maternal body.[24]

Connie Ramos recommends herself to the future because, as Luciente, her futuristic companion and/or alter consciousness,[25] informs her, she is a "catcher," one "wide open" to others' feelings and needs. As Luciente puts it, "catcher" describes "a person whose mind and nervous system are open, receptive, to an unusual extent" (42). Connie, however, receives this intended compliment in the context of her present culture; here "wide open" denotes a sexual and political posture of subservience, a placement that institutes physical devaluations of the mother.[26] Why Connie "reads" as she does is clear to us when we consider the novel's first scene, one marked by a number of forced openings and Connie's subsequent incarceration.

That scene begins with Connie in her sparse apartment, her stirring from a dream to a pleading at the door, and her recognition of a beloved voice. Communication with the future is foreclosed as Connie attends to her badly beaten niece, Dolly, undressing her "tenderly as a baby" (11). The action, and Piercy's description, achieves double valence when Connie recognizes Dolly's endangered pregnancy.[27] Within moments, pimp and hired abortionist force their entry into the apartment. Thus, the chronology of the passage enacts a double signing of maternity and a double enclosure as Geraldo beats Connie and with uninterrupted ease has her committed for instigating the attack. In a second, physical duplication, "pimp and [licensed] doctor discuss . . . [Connie's] condition" (18) while pimp and hired hand likewise plan to abort Dolly's fetus. According to Norma Alarcón, the first reading of woman in a male rendering of La Malinche is "woman as sexually passive and hence at all times open to potential use."[28] Clearly, it is within a literally inscribed sexual-maternal wording that Connie hears Luciente's intended praise. From this opening scene, then, Piercy builds a narrative case for a feminist analysis of motherhood as literally imprisoning. Connie (and reader) cannot yet give positive naming to the narrative opening she offers as a bridge to possible worlds.

Both of Connie's institutionalizations stem from her mothering, the physical treatment she receives each time designed to cure her of her words. "They trapped you into saying something," Connie thinks, "and then they'd bring out their interpretations that made your life over. To make your life into a pattern of disease" (26). Her first commitment, occurring before the novel's beginning, resulted when Connie hit her daughter and broke her wrist. Though multiple economic and familial crises led to the event, Connie is not allowed to explain. Instead her "dysfunctional" mothering, already a sentence of judgment, becomes the canopy for a diseased life. "You have a recurrent disease, like someone who has a recurrent malaria" (373), she is told. Later committed for her sheltering of Dolly, Connie is "hauled . . . along the hall like a bag of garbage" (20). She has entered a space "where all who were not desired, who caught like rough teeth in the cogwheels, who had no place or fit crosswise the one they were hammered into, were carted to repent of their contrariness or to pursue their mad vision down to the pit of terror" (31). Whether Connie hits her daughter or shelters her niece, she is "hammered into" a word ("mother") so overdetermined that her own historical contingencies—personal psychology, language, economics—are refused admittance. Indeed, the mother metaphor has lost all connection with the material base—this mother—who bears it. Because she is unfit, she is *not* a mother and because she is not a mother, she is unfit. Angela Davis's analysis of African-American women's forced surrogacy of white children bears remarkable resemblance to Piercy's representation. Although black women provided the actual care (including nursing) of white infants, only white women were assumed to share the moral sensibility requisite to the cult of motherhood. Thus women who performed the physical labor of mothering—in Davis's history, African-American women—were scripted as maternal workers but could not claim for themselves the "higher" wording of white domestic morality. As Diana Fuss writes about colonized persons, these women—and Connie—are forced to occupy "the static ontological space of the timeless 'primitive.'"[29]

Piercy further illustrates the unilateral sentencing and double binding of mothers in the present through the characters' experiences of abortions. Connie suffered a cheap abortion after being beaten by her husband, and then an unelected hysterectomy. She remembers that her mother, who bore seven children in poverty and then "[had] her womb [taken] in the hospital" (45), "died when Connie was twenty, the year of [Connie's] first abortion" (47). As we have seen, Dolly is beaten and physically coerced into an abortion. This tracing of maternal history through abortion sculpts the political reality that can neuter and silence Connie in her actual world. Those with cultural power—doctors, social workers, psychiatrists (including the white educated women who assist such social agents), and even pimps—may decide when and how Connie and Dolly will mother and when they will not. For example, an authoritative voice can at one and the same time declare that Connie willfully abused her child and that she is "not responsible for her actions" (60). Formalistic verbal plays overlook Connie, reifying the "good mother" (Connie has been told that "as a mother" her "actions are disgraceful and uncontrolled" [60]), while actually seizing this mother's biological and social capacities to mother when she does not behave.

This side of Piercy's tale clearly privileges MacKinnon's claim that "women are prevented from having children they do want and forced to have children they do not want because they are not in a position responsibly to take care of them."[30] Among feminist theorists, MacKinnon has provided the most convincing account of the reality of women's sexual and cultural oppression. As this passage indicates, the female sex and motherhood—as words and as practices—exist in the bonds of subordination. In the novel's actual world, motherhood exists as an enclosed and guarded field, one without an outlet.

At Rockover, the state mental hospital to which she is committed, Connie must fulfill the basest definitions of femininity, volunteering to clean up after incontinent patients and waiting passively in line to make a single phone call. To intimate self-knowledge here is to challenge the official diagnosis: as a site of maternal dysfunction, Connie—not her circumstances—*is* the problem; as depleted social labor (without a fecund body and the requisite social skills to mother within the lines), she is reduced to the status of polluting substance.

In the twentieth century, then, Connie's mothering leads from one physical abuse to another, although each violence is rhetorically masked as therapy. "All those experts lined up against her . . . all those cool knowing faces had caught her and bound her in their *rhetoric of jargon hung all with tiny barbed hooks that stuck in her flesh and leaked a slow weakening poison*" (60, emphasis added). Piercy's rhetoric insists on the powerful connection between words and physical suffering. Even in the most mundane exercises of mothering, this potent tie constructs Connie's experience. She remembers, for example, "long maze[s] of conversations" (62) required merely to secure a cheap pair of shoes for her daughter.

As "a bad girl" (60), poor, and separated from her family, the institutionalized Connie seems especially vulnerable to the experiments of her doctors. At first, they merely "paw . . . through the rags of her life like people going through cast-off clothes at a rummage sale" (92). Finally, however, they inscribe their rhetorical power in the most dehumanizing of physical interventions: unelected brain surgery. "First Dr. Redding drilled on her skull. It did not hurt; it was merely horrifying. She could feel the pressure, she could feel the bone giving way, she could hear the drill entering. Then she saw them take up a needle to insert something. She did not understand what it was, because she felt nothing" (281). Thus Piercy's twentieth century begins and closes with violent openings that recontain—and waste—the mother. When Connie fights back—poisoning her doctors—she fulfills the sentence that was written for her. Siding with this perspective, Piercy's text listens to the horror of coerced or closed-field maternity. Connie's clear thinking about her situation—"They would rape her body, her brain, her self" (179)—indicates her own good (that is, accurate) reading of her actual world. Only Connie's oppressors have the wonderful option of movement, of coming and going.

Alarcón writes that "woman [in the La Malinche myth] is seen as highly pawnable, [and thus] nothing she does is perceived as a choice." Within the rhetoric of Connie's present, this perspective is written in her flesh. As "other" or poor mother, Connie becomes the isolated space or territory for rhetorical and surgical practice, which in the end reduces mothering to socially policed behavior. In Connie's actual world, "the enemy [would only] press on and violate her frontiers again as soon as they chose their next advance" (337). Alarcón's description of La Malinche makes clear how much this side of Piercy's story remembers that myth: "As long as [women] continue to be seen [as sexually open] we are earmarked to be abusable matter . . . by . . . all cultures . . . that [breed] us."[31]

Piercy's angry representation of Connie's physical maternal body assures our hearing of a political analysis that believes words matter. Only through this partisan hearing are we engaged enough to negotiate the textual opening provided by Luciente's future and Connie's passage to it. Indeed, Piercy's passionate scripting of this first position illustrates how potent feminist analyses of mothering are, how partisan, how "interested."

Social Mothering

Though Connie is an invisible person in her actual world, though she speaks and no one hears, in the novel's opening paragraphs, she is being visited by a character from a future world.[32] We later learn that this presence is Luciente, a character we can read as actually intruding on Connie's world or as Connie's dream of a powerful self in possible worlds. When Connie travels to the twenty-second century, readers are reintroduced to "America." On the other side of a nuclear disaster, citizens of Mattapoisett, Luciente's community, advance technologies that are ecologically sound and communally acceptable. Thus, they ride bicycles, grow their own broccoli, *and* reproduce in a laboratory.

In the alternative world of her text, Piercy sides with theorists who, like Angela Davis, speak for social mothering, and those like Ruddick, who describe and advocate a maternal philosophy.

On this side of the historical, textual boundary, the author reinstates *mother* as a sign of empowering care. Every child is shuttled among three mothers, so that the word *mother* connotes the human work that gives us a future, not the body that gives birth. Thus motherhood maps a communal social geography; as one character boasts, "we all became mothers" (105). This thematic leverage—between word and body—is crucial to a utopian mothering. In Mattapoisett, one is never too old, too male, too poor, or too smart for giving and receiving care. Indeed, a discourse of care modulates human interaction even if a member chooses *not* to mother. As a sign of the community's self-understanding, mothering seldom provides an individual with "per" identity ("per" = his or her), but instead serves as an informing and flexible role for gaining knowledge, insight, and feeling. In this future—one very much like that "dreamed" in Ruddick's philosophy—a community expresses anger but seldom resorts to violence.

Connecting every child with three mothers, Piercy emphatically resists the defining maternal nexus father/mother/child (usually son) of contemporary theory and myth.[33] Although the residents of Piercy's novel appear to talk less *about* their children and their individual mothering, they speak more often *in* a maternal way, by which I mean their speech is patterned in relation to daily bodily cares. This utopian representation of mothering sides with Sara Ruddick's "reality in the making," her analysis of mothers and peace: "Out of their failures as well as successes, mothers develop a conception of relationships that undermines the paranoid conception of individuality that fuels conquest. . . . They not only modify aggression in the interest of connection but develop connections that limit aggression before it arises. The self who *desires* other selves to persist in their own lively being is a self at least capable of respecting the lives and life-connections of quite different others."[34]

Ruddick's critique of "paranoid . . . individuality" is very much like Luciente's criticism of Connie's "fastening" on women's biological maternity. The maternal rhetoric on this side of the feminist debate valorizes maternal logic ("respecting . . . lives and life-connections of quite different others") but prefers not to locate this logic in biology. In Mattapoisett, mothers are encouraged to develop several identities so that mothering is not essentialized as one's sole identity. Social productions—including mothering—are thought to be enhanced and enhancing when different gifts and potentialities are rotated, shared, borrowed. The fortunate child, whose call for "mother" brings three, will also be expected to give back.[35] At "end-of-mothering," the young adult becomes a co-nurturer in the community.

In Piercy's future, maternal words are no longer confined to the inner spaces of women's wombs. Nor are they policed by a transcendent authority. Rather they provide nodes of meaning among maternal practitioners, mapping the social and moral landscape of Luciente's society. Luciente's observation—"We grow up closest to our mothers, but we swim close to all our mems" (113)—visually indicates a fluid connection between mothers, children, and landscapes. She goes on to say, "It's hard for me to inknow what it would feel like to love only *one*" (113). In Mattapoisett, then, maternal rhetoric functions as a device for envisioning a harmonized world. This language operates to move people out into the community as mothering laborers, not as a rhetoric for keeping people in their isolated neighborhoods. When Luciente, for example, says that she and Connie must "suck patience" in order to speak to and hear each other, she opens the metaphor of nursing toward a new horizon of political undertakings. Similarly, adoptive "birthing" choreographs community receptivity, a kind of receptivity that Connie also witnesses in Mattapoisett's community debates. While mothers no longer "bear" children, all Mattapoisett mothers "nurse," and "holding" emerges as familiar interhuman posture: "everybody who feels like it lugs [children] around" (135).

The possible world of Piercy's novel imagines motherhood as the basis of philosophical and medical knowledge. Thus we hear Luciente remark—again in language strange and familiar—"We suspect loving and sensual enjoyment are rooted in being held and sucking and cuddling" (135). In her sentence, maternal rocking operates as the root metaphor, in onomatopoetic sounds—"sucking"—and reduplicative wording—"sucking and cuddling." Maternal rocking and shuttling gain narrative amplification in young people's naming. When one reaches adolescence, one chooses a new name and becomes a full member of the community. But often new adults change their names several times, "playing" back and forth with themselves and with others to sound out their identities. This approach to mothering—almost poststructuralist in its preference for difference—favors such "play" over the essential roles that biological reproduction seems to secure.

The balancing that Luciente recommends in mothering—that mothers give "enough" love, food, and attention without spoiling children; that mothers not be consumed with mothering—extends the possible maternal logic of Piercy's future world. What excesses are allowed (costumes, jewels, paintings) are circulated (much as children and stories are), so that pleasure (in the text; in Luciente's world) breaks the mold of ownership (the assimilated novel; the owned child; the identity of "Mother").

To dramatize a rhetorical practice that shares rather than hoards (or polices) its persuasive metaphors, Piercy depicts men's bodies as literally becoming more maternal. Visiting the nursery, Connie sees a man come in, scoop up a baby, and suckle it: "He had breasts.... Small... like a flat-chested woman... swollen with milk.... he began to nurse.... An expression of serene enjoyment spread over [the man's] intellectual school-master's face" (134). The scene (and "seen" of this passage) scrambles a number of binaries, not merely male/female, paternal/maternal, nature/culture, but text/reader as well. While Connie looks at the nursing (male) mother, the reader watches her looking. Thus reader, Connie, Luciente, (male) mother are all situated in relation to a maternal event that moves us beyond Connie's present and beyond our present knowledge of what maternal rhetoric can do. This moment provides a salient connection with Davis's analysis of surrogacy and her argument for more "open"—less female and heterosexually bound—discussions of reproduction. In addition, it calls for a radical readjustment of vision, as well as hearing, in readers. "Seeing" a male mother nursing his child, *we* are entered by a scene that challenges our sexual, maternal ideologies.

In talking about mothering as well as other relationships, characters speak of breaking "the old one-to-one bind" (132), the belief in separate fields and essential roles, and of "root[ing the] forebrain back into a net of connecting" (140). Paradoxically to Connie's way of thinking, the significance of bodily difference dims at the same time that mothering is culturally centralized, and both moves are made in order to create more equitable dispersals of power. A multivocal maternity ("So we all became mothers") replaces private ownership (and authorship) of mothers.

Visiting the static equation of female body-maternal condition with the flexible role of adoptive mother, Piercy's rhetorical invention of the mothering subject on this side of the divide radically revises our conception of the site of nurturance and of the words that describe "her."

At several moments in the novel, characters from the future compare other activities to mothering, thus, as I suggested, resuscitating *mother* as metaphor: "To be a chef is like mothering, you must volunteer" (173). Such moments challenge our certainty about the "fastening" power of words, suggesting instead human choice in relation to all roles and performances, even perhaps, physical birthing and physicality itself. Indeed, a part of the restructuring of mothering was the changing of genetic makeup so that racism could never recur: "At... grand council... decisions were made... to breed a high proportion of darker-skinned people and to mix the genes well through the population" (103–4).

Thus Piercy's future citizens can choose to hold onto cultural identities. Based in the traditions of the Wamponaug Indians, Luciente's twenty-second-century village has "limited resources." "We plan cooperatively," Luciente explains, "We can afford to waste . . . nothing. You might say our—you'd say religion?—ideas make us see ourselves as partners with water, air, birds, fish, trees" (125). Like Alice Walker, who also prefers maternal circulations—she claims that her stories are really her mother's—Piercy's possible world practices maternal revisions that are not bound to repeat the past although they are required to recycle.[36] At a funeral, Mattapoisetts sing, "Only in us do the dead live. Water flows downhill through us. The sun cools in our bones. We are joined with all living in one singing web of energy. In us live the dead who made us. In us live the children unborn. Breathing each other's air, drinking each other's water, eating each other's flesh, we grow like a tree from the earth" (322–23). The stunning phrase "eating each other's flesh" alludes to the shared work of nursing human infants. It also resonates metaphorically with the concept of power as transformation. The utopian link between mothers and an interdependent cultural organization reinvests bodily sacrifice with thinking and choice. Connie's present allows her only one side of the metaphorical pole (bodily sacrifice), whereas Luciente's future argues that mothers are wise.

Between Actual and Possible Worlds

The negotiating voice or perspective scripted and heard in Piercy's text is the dissenting, contradictory voice of the time-traveler. In Luciente's possible world, Connie can speak back, express her maternal desire, and remember her personal history—her possible past. Thus the suspension of prebirth maternity in that realm actually creates a space for the physical mother. This "both/and" logic distinguishes Piercy's text from the contentious feminist debate on mothering, making it more than the sum of its parts. For example, Connie expresses a visceral "no" to contraceptive technologies, but she also dreams of handing her daughter Angelina to the future, in other words, assenting to surrogacy. This complex voice marks out a third logic in relation to the subject of motherhood and carries readers back and forth across the divide of feminist debate. Donna Haraway's description of a "cyborg narrative" offers a construct for thinking about Piercy's text. Haraway says that "cyborg politics is the struggle for language and the struggle against perfect communication, against the one code that translates all meaning perfectly, . . . That is why cyborg politics insist on noise and advocate pollution, rejoicing in the illegitimate fusions of animal and machine."[37] If, as I suggest, the novel's future suspension of biological gestation creates a space for Connie to express her physical maternal desire, then it invites dissent and negotiation, in other words, empathetic feminist debate on the subject of motherhood. Rather than choosing "perfect communication" or "the one code that translates . . . perfectly," Piercy advocates the "noisy," incongruent, voice of Connie Ramos. Her body-based desire and maternal history intrude upon the technological option of mechanical birth. Rather than resolve this narrative tension, Piercy's text negotiates it. This rhetorical strategy commits writer and reader to "keeping the window open," so to speak, on the maternal question. Like Pilate's house, Piercy's novel never closes.

Thus, for example, in Piercy's textual future or possible world, *mother* suggests a variety of voices and styles, including Connie's defense of the body that births and Luciente's defense of the machine that broods. Piercy's creation of excessive social mothering and her interruption of biological reproduction amplifies rather than minimizes the material history of mothering. As I have remarked, we hear most of *Connie's* story of mothering *in the future*, where biological reproduction is suspended. That is, the reproductive "idea" in Piercy's future forecloses biological birth, but Piercy's scripting of that future includes Connie's voice of longing, her desire for a different past in which she might possibly have given her daughter better care. In Piercy's "cyborg narrative," mothering remains polyphonically alive rather than monologically ossified, always in a "state of becoming, amid agreement, disagreement, conflict, encounters, understandings, and misunderstandings."[38] We might say that Connie's incarceration *represents* the mothering sentence (it shows us that words matter), while her encounter with future mothers *enacts* a maternal philosophy, offering a new hearing of the subject. But these sites and discourses intrude upon each other, making Woman on the Edge of Time a textual corridor in which mobility across positions is allowed and the efficacy of separate spheres or politics is called into question.

Planting Connie's memory in the future, Piercy interrupts "play" motherhood with the desires of Connie's history, requiring that we consider what is lost and what is gained through contraceptive technologies. The aware reader will understand that Luciente's knowledge of maternity always runs back through Connie's physical maternity. Connie wonders, for example, "How . . . anyone [could] know what being a mother means who has never carried a child nine months heavy under her heart, who has never borne a baby in blood and pain" (106). Luciente explains why her culture developed this form of reproduction: "It was part of women's long revolution. When we were breaking all the old hierarchies. Finally, there was that one thing we had to give up too, the only power we ever had, in return for no more power for anyone. The original production: the power to give birth. Cause as long as we were biologically enchained, we'd never be equal. And males never would be humanized to be loving and tender. So we all became mothers" (105). But Connie is never entirely convinced, so that her question and Luciente's answer coexist as noisy debate, not as rhetorical question and monological resolution. Connie's voice—not the omniscient narrator's—recalls her biologically carried child: "Angelina, child of my sore and bleeding body" (105).

Connie's witness of a future birthing occurs in a narrative corridor in which she moves in and out of the future. Having escaped from the hospital ward, Connie dreams of the possible delivery, witnessing herself with two other mothers as they receive a child in the birthing chamber. In this moment, she also hears Luciente caution her against "fastening" (251) on mothering. The coeval narration of the dream of desire—Connie wants to hold her own child—and the dream of surrogacy demonstrates Piercy's narrative negotiation of maternity: making sense by witnessing both perspectives, by knowing from more than one position. The dream scene recalls Welty's use of dreams. In both cases, this motif acts as a hinge for imagining a world founded on the possibilities between oppositions, in the case of Piercy's novel: the (feminist) positions of loyalty to historical mothers or the deconstruction of motherhood as institution and identity.

Neither representational nor utopian readings alone register the narrative empathy in Piercy's storytelling, where the thematization of biological birth *and* adoptive mothering is mimicked in the plot itself. Intruding on the future, Connie is adopted as a member of Mattapoisett. Simultaneously, we as readers are witness to her voice, her longing. Thus the triangulation of relations in Mattapoisett (where each person is born between three mothers) reflects and deepens the interpretive relation of the reader to author, narrating persona, and character. This resemblance between thematics and narrative structure makes our reading of the novel an instance of negotiations coming out of the text. Not only does Connie think and act through internalized and actualized negotiations; the novel negotiates our expectations by becoming more than representation. It becomes action as responding readers must negotiate knowledge of Connie's past (her desire for a lost daughter, Angelina, and her physical abuses) and Luciente's future (her desire for a world in which individual mothering matters less and is communally practiced more), and Piercy's responsible witness to both.

Narratively speaking, what Piercy's novel trades *in* is not biological mothering but absolute positions. This trade[39] suggests an arbitration between feminist discourses that have been imagined as exclusive terrains: the critique of mothering and the valorization of mothering. Piercy's plotting, then, provides the story of a world characterized by a "non-synchronous and multi-temporal development: a world animated by plural subject positions that are simultaneous but not synchronic."[40] Heard and viewed this way, the subject of mothering in Piercy's text becomes more interesting to a number of feminist readers. We can imagine, for example, a meeting of cultural feminists and poststructuralists, of "motherists" and lesbians within this story because Piercy choreographs a subjectivity that is all of these at different moments. Luciente, for example, who chooses a more androgynous persona, and who practices lesbianism some of the time, owes her cultural memory to Connie, who is heterosexual, a mother, and Chicana. None of these markers is entirely "covered" by any other, but all of them overlap in the text.

The reader, visiting both worlds, coincides fully with neither of these maternal positions but finds herself or himself inside and outside both, enjoying and profiting from the dialogue rather than being coerced into sympathy with one. This pattern, of course, is true at the level of the entire novel, since the reader is always leaning both toward Connie's past and her future, toward her history and her dream. The reader who writes back (in critical essay, other fictions, shared journal entries, letters) gives life to the conversation, collaborating in the construction of this text's meanings and keeping its maternal genealogy alive.

Thus Piercy "crits" (the word for speaking criticism in "Mouth of Mattapoisett," 210) the totalizing of the mother-child relation while her fictive maternal option—technological birth—begins new narrative negotiations: between Connie's possible memory, Luciente's telling, and the reader's position. This instance of triangulated dialogue allows Piercy to rewrite the maternal body as a potential agent, not a pawn, in the negotiated work of love and care. This narrative choice returns us to the question of the name—*mother*—and Piercy's retention of that sign. Although her text circulates the name among many, the *mother* word remains tied to Connie's historical identity. In a "both/and" logic, then, Piercy's text acknowledges that words matter and that words are interchangeable.

Paula Gunn Allen offers a cultural history that may illuminate Piercy's use of *mother*. She reminds us that among pre-Conquest Indian women, "bearing, like bleeding, was a transformative ritual act. Through their own bodies [women] could bring vital beings into the world. . . . They were mothers, and that word implied the highest degree of status in ritual cultures."[41] It is important to pay close attention to what Allen says. In the mythic panoply she describes, biological mothering is understood as a human point of contact with a divine power. This description functions as metaphor: inherent in the action of mothering is the power of transformation. The two potentialities—birth and transformation—are not collapsed into one. Rather, a nonsynchronous relation is established so that human/divine actions "touch" in the performance of birth. Piercy's retention of *mother* may act in just this way, reminding the reader of the metaphorical tension in the word. In other words, by erasing the marks of motherhood (blood and birth), Piercy creates an absence that reminds us that "mother" always names someone or something more than the individual mother. This erasing-reminding maneuver by Piercy recurs to Pilate's navel. In both instances, the narrative effect is akin to cultural liminality. Interpretation requires negotiating the two (or more) realities that interact in the metaphor. Piercy raises the question of how we will reinvest the individual mother with an empowering identity. This new fiction, then, recognizes the significance—to women—of the historical identity of mother at the same time that it argues that we associate the transformative work of care with more androgynous human features: the embrace, for example. Thus the negotiation of surrogacy (or a heterogeneously conceived mothering) and biological mothering (which may be understood as woman's difference) is not a zero-sum game in which one must be given up in order for the other to win. Instead, Piercy visits each site, always relating the "truth" of one position to the "truth" of the other.

In this light, Connie's "assenting . . . to Angelina in Mattapoisett," her "giving" the daughter up to the future can be fruitfully reread. The passage may appear as a resignation, and we may wonder at Piercy's cynicism in repeating the myth of La Malinche, given up by her mother to Cortez's future. But in my reading, Angelina travels with me back to my actual world. Because she is never placed within the text—we never actually see her except in Connie's memory and dream—she exceeds the cultural options that compete for her: abandonment or adoption. Thus readers receive Angelina in our futures but *as Connie's living daughter*, as her mother's dangerous (that is, potent) memory and material history. As feminist theologians note, such "dangerous memories" not only keep the past alive but open the way for a different future.[42] For feminist critics, Angelina becomes another node in the overlapping fields of mothering debate, interrupting, polluting, and scrambling the theoretical landscape, quickly filling in the narrative gap offered through "brooder" technology. In a way, Angelina is a reborn La Malinche, a regenerated third woman who walks out of the text but through the context of her mother's history of struggle.

Thus the open maternal rhetoric in Mattapoisett acts as a seduction but not to full identification with the future. Instead, Piercy insists on a dialogic and dialectical exchange that pulls the reader into heartfelt, double-visioned relation with Connie *and* Luciente, daughter and mother, past and future, identity and multiple positioning. This negotiating plot allows us to hold an identity (say, mother) while also exploring undecidable or multisituated identities (Luciente's gender- flexible persona). Without *one* slot to slip into, readers are recruited for the more difficult work of negotiating on behalf of (at least) two positions, voices, visions.[43] This personal/textual action fully realizes my view of feminist critical reading as a practice that takes contradiction to heart.

In Piercy's text mothering is spoken and *heard* through contradictory stories. As a negotiating text, *Woman on the Edge of Time* cannot be commodified (its argument will not support any *one* feminist position), and, as memory, it cannot be abstracted from the specifics of Connie's material longing. Rather than an exchange of mothering bodies (from fathers to sons), Piercy's novel practices an interchange of mothering actions (and the words for them, such as nursing, birthing, holding) and Connie's maternal identity, revising our debate by showing us points of contact.

Piercy offers an instance of Haraway's situated knowledge, a form of knowing that is responsible to (re)vision: "The topography of subjectivity is multi-dimensional; so, therefore, is vision. The knowing self is partial in all its guises, never finished, whole, simply there and original; it is always constructed and stitched together imperfectly, and *therefore* able to join with another, to see together without claiming to be another."[44] Connie and Luciente together look back and forth from variable locations to account for their competing sense of motherhood and value. Rather than collapsing into mere relativism, this cross-plotting of views and voices seeks to establish what is known in each location. This is not the same as claiming that every location is equally valid. Certainly Piercy does not commend much of Connie's present experience. But in my personal reading, nothing in the text has greater claim or makes more sense than her unprovisional longing for the particular, physical touch of her daughter:

"Worse, finally, than never to be loved again was never to hold a child next to her body. Her child. Her flesh" (125).

Piercy's negotiation of biology and surrogacy, identity and multiplicity, clarifies but does not lessen our difficult work. As feminists, we sift oppressive histories through utopian hopes and reconnect faith with material life. This means we are always thinking negotiation. Our intermediate—not indeterminate—identity is exactly what distinguishes our thought, providing the basis for our ongoing energy. In reading and writing, we work through faith and caution, anger and love.

EPILOGUE

Riparian Corridors and Other Progressive Middles
New Directions for Feminist Criticism?

> *There is no purity of heart.*
> —Kathryn Pyne Addelson
>
> *So I have decided to hark back to the great American lesson that it is valuable, and a great advantage, to be bilingual and bicultural. It is better to see and hear the world in stereophonic wide wrap-around sound, than in mono. If one has been placed in the middle of everything that is going on, why not enjoy it? And I do.... I embrace all the treasures that [my] two cultures offer me. Why choose less, when one could have more?*
> —Judy Scales-Trent

IF MEMBERS OF my family get as far in this book as this last epigraph, they will laugh. I have always believed that one should not "choose less, when one could have more." Recently I was at the funeral of an old, dear friend and gathered there were family friends, some from my child-of-missionaries days in Nigeria. One, an "aunt," recounted the anecdote of my coming over to her house in the morning, still in my nightgown, and asking, in my three-year old voice, for the center piece of coffee cake; never mind that she had to cut it out since she had already begun slicing from one end.

When Judy Scales-Trent writes, in *Notes of a White Black Woman*, of "being placed in the middle of everything that is going on" and argues for more instead of less, she is certainly not arguing that African-American women give up their distinct heritage and critical perspective *for* a place in the center with whites. She is not even assuming that whites have a monopoly on the center. She is assuming instead, and, yes, with more optimism than is fashionable, that there are middle positions from which one can fashion a critical self and contribute to a bicultural world.

What I have been arguing in this book is that we view feminist critics in in-between positions in order to theorize a criticism not from the margins but from the middles. "We don't have to glorify the borders and the margins," writes Scales-Trent.[1] By choosing the "more" of middles, Scales-Trent and I do not imagine a mere inversion of textual/sexual/racial politics. Such a scheme depends on monolithic views of center and margin as well as on essentializing notions of what is female and what male, what black and what white. Instead, we argue, like Gloria Anzaldúa, for strategic "leanings" into more than one world, heartfelt "hearings" of more than one story. These leanings and hearings are not mere homogenizations of everything that we are in the middle of, however. Almost everything we see and hear is filtered through the critical sieves of many feminist, ethnic, and postcolonial theories, identities, what I might call "hearts of knowledge." This negotiation is a difficult art that becomes a second nature.

Writing this book in the middle of third stage feminist criticism—and in the middle of my life—I am drawing to consciousness a critical process that is, in my view, feminist criticism's second nature. I have attempted to give a language and a tropological analysis to what is perhaps our very best feature *though we have overlooked it in our own words*. Like my name, "Elaine," which I found homely and awkward growing up, *negotiation* is a term that has enjoyed a lowly status at best. But it is time to bring negotiation out, to extrapolate the middle grounds that feminist critics live in and draw from. This will not be easy work because such a project admits impurity to begin with. Many will suspect this as a poetics of naiveté at best and cooption at worst. In the first several years that I worked my way toward writing this manuscript, I found myself often accused of imprecision, of using methods I did not understand, of "carelessness." Perhaps my early attempts were awkward; perhaps they will still appear awkward to some. But I also think that "carelessness" was a code word for "impure." I was criss-crossing terms and muddying theories, bringing together pieces of a puzzle that, to me at lest, spelled *feminist negotiation*. I was less concerned with difference than with similarity, obviously out of step with the times. Thus I lumped together sentences from Gloria Anzaldúa, Gayatri Spivak, Elizabeth Meese, bell hooks. Before I could define, I needed a substance to knead, a clay to sculpt.

To make my meanings clear—perhaps dangerously clear—I chiseled an outline of the negotiations that would shape this study. Setting up my argument in chapter 1, I observed that we can trace a certain progress in

Riparian Corridors and Other Progressive Middles

rhetorical and thematic negotiations in American women's fictions as we move through the century. But I made this argument, of course, in relation to the representative texts I have chosen: two novels from the first half of the century; three novels published between 1969 and 1977. If I were to imagine a second book along the critical lines of this one, I would locate it in American women's fiction of the 1980s and 1990s and read widely in this period to see what progress—and what difference—is discernible in this contemporary literature. Would Louise Erdrich's novels, for example, fit the typology that I outlined in chapter 1? And what differences would I find in the broad field of contemporary African-American women's fiction? I have a sense that Erdrich's novels can be fruitfully approached by way of my negotiating critical model and, in fact, her novel *Tracks* emphasizes the contentious middle grounds that I have been mapping in this book. *Tracks* might be a good place to begin a second book since it so vividly represents the difference between forced compromise and the feminist-narrative-epistemological negotiations that I describe and develop in the preceding chapters. Erdrich's own placement in two worlds—German-American and Native American—and her practice of writing collaboratively with her spouse also recommend her text to a negotiating feminist criticism. In addition, her choice of a male lead and hinge character (in Nanapush, one of her narrators) suggests a redirection and renegotiation of my emphasis in this book on female characters who occupy that position.[2]

Unable to fall asleep one evening a few weeks ago, I found myself watching Henry Louis Gates and Cornel West on a late-night television show. The commentator asked Gates how he and West were different. Without much hesitation, Gates responded, "I'm a centrist. I'm the murky, muddy middle." Now anyone who knows Gates knows that he is nothing if not critical and selective; hard working and black identified. What Gates meant, I believe, is that he can negotiate with just about anyone, anywhere. He can find something of use. He can make things work. I was thrilled with his confession and his claim, "I'm the murky, muddy middle." And so, to my mind, is the heart of feminist criticism. From this rich loam, our genius flowers.

Finally, it is time to stop apologizing. In this world at least, impurity is preferable to purity, negotiation to victory. I make a bid for the in-betweens, not as a place I pass through, but as a place I live. Like the riparian corridor of conservation biology, feminist criticism literally keeps many of us alive—connecting the world of discipline and the world of empathy, the category of gender and the category of literature, above all, connecting heart and mind.[3] If we first found ourselves in this middle location as a result of patriarchal bias or U.S. race history or the odd peregrinations of a colonialist childhood, we can live here and thrive because we choose the "more" of diversity and identities in dialogue. And who knows who "we" will be here? Our last names are still in the future.

Notes

Preface

1. At the time (early to mid-1980s), I did not think of the status quo as "white," a confession that reveals my own "whiteness"; now I do, hence the parenthesis around "white."

2. This trend is demonstrated in recent programs from the yearly meetings of the Modern Language Association and the American Studies Association. Toril Moi's *Sexual/Textual Politics: Feminist Literary Theory* (London: Routledge, 1985) provided an earlier instance of how feminist criticism has preferred "self-consciousness" since the mid-1980s.

3. I am thinking of a number of differences that locate these critics: different cultural backgrounds (white, African-American, Chicana), different university locations (public and private, the North and South), different canons (including different commitments to theory and other genres), different subjects (race, sexuality, language, genre).

4. I found Carrie Menkel-Meadow's work very useful, especially in the early stages of my work. She is interested, as am I, in reimagining negotiation. See "Toward Another View of Legal Negotiation," *UCLA Law Review* 31 (1984): 754–842.

5. See Judith Butler, *Gender Trouble: Feminism and the Subversion of Identity* (New York: Routledge, 1990), 143. I find Butler's book useful though we differ in our emphases since her theory extends a subversive poetics. Other cultural critics who influence my definition of negotiation but who are not named in the text are Henry A. Giroux, *Border Crossings* (New York: Routledge, 1991), José David Saldívar, *The Dialectics of Our America* (Durham NC: Duke Univ. Press, 1991), and Ross Chambers, *Room for Maneuver* (Chicago: Univ. of Chicago Press, 1991).

6. Michael de Certeau's *The Practice of Everyday Life* influences my thinking here (Berkeley: Univ. of California Press, 1988). See p. 18 especially.

7. Laurie A. Finke, *Feminist Theory, Women's Writing* (Ithaca: Cornell Univ. Press, 1992), 5.

8. Michael Awkward, *Negotiating Difference: Race, Gender, and the Politics of Positionality* (Chicago: Univ. of Chicago Press, 1995).

9. Lauren Berlant and Michael Warner, "What Does Queer Theory Teach Us about X?" *PMLA* 110 (1995): 348.

1. Negotiated Homelands

1. Elaine Showalter, "A Criticism of Our Own: Autonomy and Assimilation in Afro-American and Feminist Literary Theory," in *Feminisms: An Anthology of*

Literary Theory and Criticism, ed. Robyn R. Warhol and Diane Price Herndl (New Brunswick: Rutgers Univ. Press, 1991), 170. I hope it is clear here and elsewhere that I hope to negotiate with the feminist practitioners who precede me, not merely to counter them.

The most self-conscious use of negotiation as a critical topoi is in Shakespearean studies. See Stephen Greenblatt, *Shakespearean Negotiations* (Los Angeles: Univ. of California Press, 1988), and Theodore B. Leinwand, "Negotiation and New Historicism," *PMLA* 105 (1990): 477–90.

2. Judith Fetterley, *The Resisting Reader: A Feminist Approach to American Fiction* (Bloomington: Indiana Univ. Press, 1981). Alicia Ostriker, *Stealing the Language: The Emergence of Women's Poetry in America* (Boston: Beacon, 1986).

3. See Donna Haraway's "Situated Knowledges" for a similar fiction of vision, in *Simians, Cyborgs, and Women: The Reinvention of Nature* (New York: Routledge, 1991): 183–201. Karla Holloway illustrates the limitations of some "purer" feminisms in chapter 1 of *Moorings and Metaphors* (New Brunswick: Rutgers Univ. Press, 1992), see pp. 26–31 especially.

4. Gloria Anzaldúa, "La conciencia de la mestiza: Towards a New Consciousness," in *American Feminist Thought at Century's End: A Reader*, ed. Linda S. Kauffman (Cambridge: Blackwell, 1993), 428. Elizabeth A. Meese, *(Ex)tensions: Re-figuring Feminist Criticism* (Urbana: Univ. of Illinois Press, 1990), 14. Meese criticizes the feminism of a largely white female academic constituency for excluding differences within feminism and for discouraging engagements across critical boundaries.

5. Adrienne Rich, *A Wild Patience Has Taken Me This Far* (New York: Norton, 1981).

6. Jerry Aline Flieger, "Growing Up Theoretical: Across the Divide," in *Changing Subjects: The Making of Feminist Literary Criticism*, ed. Gayle Greene and Coppélia Kahn (London: Routledge, 1993), 253.

7. I unfold these "stories" more fully in chapter 4, where I read *The Optimist's Daughter* in relation to the history of American feminist criticism. Julia Kristeva elucidates the stages of feminist criticism in "Women's Time," *Signs* 7 (1981): 13–35, though I am not strictly reproducing her descriptions. Elaine Showalter gives a different accounting of the first two stages of feminist criticism in "A Criticism of Our Own."

8. Meese, *(Ex)tensions*, 98.

9. Ibid., 156 and 163. Nancy K. Miller, *Getting Personal: Feminist Occasions and Other Autobiographical Acts* (New York: Routledge, 1991), 117.

10. Meese, *(Ex)tensions*, 11.

11. Ann Snitow, "A Gender Diary," in *Conflicts in Feminism*, ed. Marianne Hirsch and Evelyn Fox Keller (New York: Routledge, 1990), 9.

12. Sara Ruddick, *Maternal Thinking: Toward a Politics of Peace* (Boston: Beacon, 1989), 78.

13. Gayatri Spivak, "Feminism and Deconstruction, Again," in *Between Feminism and Psychoanalysis* (London: Routledge, 1989), 206.

14. Ibid., 206.

15. Ibid., 211.

16. Ibid., 212.

17. Meese, *(Ex)tensions*, 98.

18. Ibid.
19. Flieger, "Growing Up Theoretical," 264.
20. Haraway, *Simians, Cyborgs, and Women*, 191.
21. By not insisting on the irony of feminist negotiations, these critics fashion a modality somewhat different from "poaching," "tricksterism," or "maneuver." See Ross Chambers, *Room for Maneuver*, for descriptions of these textual modes.
22. Spivak, "Feminism and Deconstruction," 220.
23. Anzaldúa, "La conciencia," 434.
24. Ibid., 430.
25. bell hooks, *Yearning: Race, Gender, and Cultural Politics* (Boston: South End Press, 1990), 90.
26. Anzaldúa, "La consciencia," 428.
27. Ibid., 434–35.
28. Elisabeth D. Däumer, "Queer Ethics; or, the Challenge of Bisexuality to Lesbian Ethics," *Hypatia* 7.4 (1992): 103.
29. Although I often distinguish in this book between women, female authors, and feminist readers and workers, I see these categories overlapping in the practice of "negotiation" that I am outlining. Whenever I refer to women writing or female authors I mean individual performers writing with a consciousness of male privilege in their social worlds.
30. See, for example, Rey Chow, "'It's You and Not Me': Domination and 'Othering' in Theorizing the 'Third World,'" in *American Feminist Thought at Century's End*, 95–106.
31. Homi Bhabha cites mimicry as a form of "civil disobedience within the discipline of civility: signs of spectacular resistance." "Signs Taken for Words," *Critical Inquiry* 12 (1985): 162.
32. Meese, *(Ex)tensions*, 159.
33. Ursula K. Le Guin, "The Carrier Bag Theory of Fiction," *Dancing at the Edge of the World* (New York: Harper & Row, 1989): 169.
34. Miller, *Getting Personal*, 126.

2. Negotiation Our Text

1. My chapter title is a play on Lillian Robinson's "Treason our Text: Feminist Challenges to the Literary Canon" *Tulsa Studies in Women's Literature* 2 (1983): rpt. in *Feminisms*, 212–26.
2. My method in this chapter is fostered by Catherine Belsey's "Constructing the Subject: Deconstructing the Text," in *Feminist Criticism and Social Change*, ed. J. Newton and D. Rosenfelt (London: Methuen, 1985): 45–64; Susan Lanser's "Toward a Feminist Narratology," in *Feminisms*, 610–29; and Diane Freedman's "Border Crossing as Method and Motif in Contemporary American Writing, or, How Freud Helped Me Case the Joint," in *The Intimate Critique*, ed. Diane P. Freedman, Olivia Frey, and Frances Murphy Zauhar (Durham: Duke Univ. Press, 1993), 13–22.
3. Elaine Showalter, "The Death of the Lady (Novelist): Wharton's *House of Mirth*," in *Sister's Choice: Tradition and Change in American Women's Writing* (Oxford: Clarendon Press, 1991).

4. Wai-Chee Dimock, "Debasing Exchange: Edith Wharton's *The House of Mirth*," *PMLA* 100 (1985): 791 and 783.

5. Ibid., 783, emphasis added.

6. Nancy Topping Bazin, "The Deconstruction of Lily Bart: Capitalism, Christianity, and Male Chauvinism," *Denver Quarterly* 17.2 (1983): 97; Roslyn Dixon, "Reflecting Vision in *The House of Mirth*," *Twentieth Century Literature* 33 (1987): 218; Robin Beaty, "Lilies that Fester: Sentimentality in *The House of Mirth*," *College Literature* 14 (1987): 271; Elizabeth Ammons, *Edith Wharton's Argument with America* (Athens: Univ. of Georgia Press, 1980), 37.

7. Edith Wharton, *The House of Mirth* (New York: Charles Scribner's Sons, 1905), 113 and 86. Further citations in the text refer to this edition.

8. Susan Goodman, *Edith Wharton's Women: Friends & Rivals* (Hanover NH: Univ. Press of New England, 1990), 2.

9. Amy Kaplan, *The Social Construction of American Realism* (Chicago: Univ. of Chicago Press, 1988). See chapter 3 especially.

10. Ibid., 103.

11. Marie-Laure Ryan, *Possible Worlds, Artificial Intelligence, and Narrative Theory* (Bloomington: Indiana Univ. Press, 1991), 22. Providing the vocabulary of actual and possible worlds, Marie-Laure Ryan writes, "For the duration of our immersion in a work of fiction, the realm of possibilities is . . . recentered around the sphere which the narrator presents as the 'actual' world. This recentering pushes the reader into a new system of actuality and possibility. As a traveler to this system, the reader of fiction discovers not only a new 'actual' world, but a variety of A[ctual] P[ossible] W[orld]s revolving around it."

In the rest of the book, I use "actual" and "possible" worlds as Ryan theorizes the terms, though I avoid quotation marks except when I need to refresh the reader's memory.

12. R. W. B. Lewis, *Edith Wharton: A Biography* (New York: Harper & Row, 1975), 149.

13. Kaplan, *Social Construction*, 77.

14. Ibid., 80.

15. See Carroll Smith-Rosenberg's "The Female World of Love and Ritual," *Disorderly Conduct: Visions of Gender in Victorian America* (New York: Oxford Univ. Press, 1985). Smith-Rosenberg describes a female paradigm of love and friendship which Wharton deploys in relation to, or "alongside," male models, rather than "against" them.

16. This is what feminist critics need, if my experience is any indication.

17. Early feminist critics might have translated "without women writers, male mentors, or tenure."

18. Edith Wharton, *A Backward Glance* (New York: Charles Scribner's Sons, 1933), 114.

19. This is Henry Louis Gates's phrase. See "Beyond the Culture Wars: Identities in Dialogue," *Profession* (1993): 6–11.

20. *The Woman's Encyclopedia of Myths and Secrets*, ed. Barbara G. Walker. New York: Harper & Row, 1983.

21. See Victor Turner, "Liminality and Communitas," *The Ritual Process: Structure and Anti-Structure* (Ithaca: Cornell Univ. Press, 1969).

22. Goodman makes a similar argument about Wharton's short story "Friends" (*Edith Wharton's Women*, 7).
23. Ibid., 7.
24. See my discussion of Gayatri Spivak in chapter 1.
25. Beaty, "Lilies that Fester," 272 and 274, for example, says that Lily is "reduc[ed] to a sentimental heroine"; she wonders if Wharton hasn't "compromised her usual commitment to 'high art'" in these scenes.
26. Goodman, *Edith Wharton's Women*, 60.

3. Our Confounded Identities

1. "Confounded identities" is Hortense Spiller's phrase. See "Mama's Baby, Papa's Maybe: An American Grammar Book," *Diacritics* 17.2 (1987): 65.
2. Here I revise "anxiety of influence" and "anxiety of authorship." See Sandra Gilbert and Susan Gubar's discussion of both concepts in *The Madwoman in the Attic* (New Haven: Yale Univ. Press, 1979), chapter 2 especially.
3. See Shelley Fisher Fishkin, "Interrogating 'Whiteness,' Complicating 'Blackness': Remapping American Culture," *American Quarterly* 47 (1995): 428–66.
4. Awkward, *Negotiating Difference*, 4.
5. Sandra Harding, "Reinventing Ourselves as Other," in *American Feminist Thought at Century's End*, 145. Michele Wallace, "Variations on Negation," in *Reading Black, Reading Feminist* (New York: Penguin, 1990), 53.
6. A number of feminist readings have focused on the black womanist identification and subversion of whiteness represented in *Their Eyes*. Gay Wilenz, for example, writes that Hurston creates a folktale "of the white man as a false 'god' who must eventually be defeated." See Wilenz, "Defeating the False God: Janie's Self-Determination in Zora Neale Hurston's *Their Eyes Were Watching God*," in *Faith of a (Woman) Writer*, ed. Alice Kessler-Harris and William McBrien (New York: Greenwood Press, 1988), 285. See also Henry Louis Gates Jr., "Zora Neale Hurston and the Speakerly Text," *The Signifying Monkey: A Theory of African-American Literary Criticism* (New York: Oxford Univ. Press, 1988). Alice Walker's criticism is also influential in this regard. See "Zora Neale Hurston: A Cautionary Tale and a Partisan View" and "Looking for Zora," *In Search of Our Mothers' Gardens* (San Diego: Harcourt Brace, 1983).
7. bell hooks, *Yearning*, 147, 66, and 6.
8. Françoise Lionnet, "Autoethnography: The An-Archic Style of *Dust Tracks on a Road*," in *Reading Black, Reading Feminist*, 386.
9. Lionnet, "Autoethnography," 385. Karla Holloway offers a similar description of black women's writing: "Ironically, it is the subordination of the opposition between the subject and the object that is a hallmark within the black woman's text. This literature reconstructs the schismatic pair by insisting upon the collaborative nature of the enterprise—the communication between . . . author and character, reader and text (subject and object)—a clear challenge to the Western (Hegelian) notion of their polarity" (*Moorings and Metaphors*, 30–31). Jacqueline Bobo has recently theorized black women's reception in terms of the specifics of the context and the complexity of their negotiated reason: "Although

they were very vocal in their praise of the film [*The Color Purple*], fuller examination of these women's responses revealed that their seeming conflation of the film with the novel was due to a complex process of negotiation. Black women sifted through the incongruent parts of the film and reacted favorably to elements with which they could identify and that resonated with their experiences." *Black Women as Cultural Readers* (New York: Columbia Univ. Press, 1995), 3.

10. The literary tactic of "signifying," with which Henry Louis Gates builds his theory of African-American criticism, is as much a negotiating tactic as a subversive one, since the speaker enters into the (dominant) other's terrain, redirecting and reallocating "his" discursive goods. Such a move must result in an impure, at times collaborating, sometimes resisting subject.

11. Françoise Lionnett makes this point. See "Autoethnography," 382–414.

12. Zora Neale Hurston, *Dust Tracks on a Road* (New York: Harper, 1991), 23 (originally published in 1942).

13. Robert Hemenway, *Zora Neale Hurston* (Urbana: Univ. of Illinois Press, 1977), 27.

14. Ibid., 92.

15. Alice Walker, "Searching for Zora," *In Search of Our Mothers' Gardens*, 110. Dianne F. Sadoff argues that Walker's need for a model leads her to misread Hurston in crucial ways. See "Black Matrilineage: The Case of Alice Walker and Zora Neale Hurston," *Signs* 11.1 (1985): 4–26.

16. Mary Helen Washington, in *I Love Myself When I Am Laughing: A Zora Neale Hurston Reader*, ed. Alice Walker, intro. Mary Helen Washington (New York: Feminist Press, 1979), 13.

17. Hemenway, *Zora Neale Hurston*, 108.

18. Ibid., 109.

19. Hurston, *Dust Tracks*, 151, 136, 135, and 129.

20. See Gates, *The Signifying Monkey*.

21. Though the coercive nature of black migration makes it a politically charged subject, black literature has exploited the idea of black movement, articulating identity in relation to intermediate geographies, "found" relations, and processes of change. Beginning with slave narratives—for example, Harriet Jacobs's *Incidents in the Life of a Slave Girl* (1861)—African-American letters have often symbolized the hazards and skills of *being* black in America through the representation of a "migrating character" whose consciousness is born through multiple movements across antagonistic territories. This "migratory character" has often been grafted with the mulatto to explore and amplify the view from in-between or corridor locations (in Jacobs, the attic is such a space). James Weldon Johnson's *The Autobiography of an Ex-Colored Man* (1912) and Nella Larsen's *Passing* (1929) stand as important examples, though their stories emphasize the tragic dimension of this character's experience.

22. A number of critics mention Phoeby as the ideal listener but none that I know of has read her function as a convening of biracial female listeners. Holloway says, for example, that "while [Phoeby] participates as an observer, and does extract some benefit from her vicarious posture, [her] gain is finally, merely residual," *Moorings and Metaphors*, 134. The only essay I know that focuses primarily on Phoeby is Alice Reich's "Phoeby's Hungry Listening," *Women's Studies* 13 (1986): 163–69. Michael Awkward criticizes the romanticizing of Janie's "voice" but does

not give sustained attention to Phoeby's hearing. See his *Inspiriting Influences* (New York: Columbia Univ. Press, 1989).

23. Lionnet, "Autoethnography," 387.

24. Lorraine O'Grady, "Olympia's Maid: Reclaiming Black Female Subjectivity," in *New Feminist Criticism: Art Identity Action*, ed. Joanna Frueh, Cassandra L. Langer, and Arlene Raven (New York: HarperCollins, 1994), 164.

25. Zora Neale Hurston, *Their Eyes Were Watching God* (Urbana: Univ. of Illinois Press, 1978), 169. References in the text are to this edition, which retains the pagination of the original Lippincott edition published in 1937.

26. I focus in this essay on black and white women's questioning of the other's sincerity. In the novel's reception, however, the question of Hurston's sincerity was forcefully raised by Richard Wright, who deplored the novel's "romance." For a recent review of Hurston's and Wright's theories of black voice see Gates, *The Signifying Monkey*, 180–91.

27. This thought is influenced by O'Grady, "Olympia's Maid," p. 157 especially.

28. Readers may compare my reading with Gates's. He too sees Hurston as "negotiating": "Hurston's very rhetorical strategy, her invention of what I have chosen to call the speakerly text, seems designed to mediate between . . . a profoundly lyrical, densely metaphorical, quasi-musical, privileged black oral tradition . . . and a received but not yet fully appropriated standard English literary tradition. . . . The quandary for the writer was to find a third term, a bold and novel signifier" (*The Signifying Monkey*, 174). Our approaches differ in that I focus on Phoeby and Hurston's audience assembly, while Gates, like most of Hurston's critics, focuses on Janie and her voice.

29. Hurston, *Dust Tracks*, 155.

30. Hemenway notes that Hughes and Hurston sat on footstools at Mrs. Mason's feet; *Zora Neale Hurston*, 107.

31. "I shall wrassle me up a future or die trying," wrote Hurston to Mason in a letter. From *I Love Myself When I Am Laughing*, 14.

32. See Paula Giddings, *When and Where I Enter: The Impact of Black Women on Race and Sex in America* (Toronto: Bantam, 1984), 58.

33. Eugene Genovese, *Roll, Jordan, Roll: The World the Slaves Made* (New York: Random House, 1974), 656. My summary of strategies is drawn from Genovese.

34. The text does not specify the teacher's race, but Janie's "lighter" characteristics suggest his whiteness.

35. Alice A. Parker and Elizabeth A. Meese, *Feminist Critical Negotiations* (Amsterdam: J. Benjamins, 1992), 86.

36. Awkward, *Negotiating Difference*, 192.

37. Parker and Meese, *Feminist Critical Negotiations*, 97.

4. The Character of Her Writing

1. Kate Millet, *Sexual Politics* (Garden City: Doubleday, 1970).

2. See Elaine Showalter, *A Literature of Their Own: British Women Novelists from Brontë to Lessing* (Princeton: Princeton Univ. Press, 1977), and Walker, *In Search of Our Mothers' Gardens*.

3. I was one whose dissertation became a first book on a woman author: Elaine Orr, *Tillie Olsen and a Feminist Spiritual Vision* (Jackson: Univ. of Mississippi Press, 1987). A wonderful example of feminist criticism derived from male and female models is Mae Gwendolyn Henderson's "Speaking in Tongues: Dialogics, Dialectics, and the Black Woman Writer's Literary Tradition," in *Reading Black, Reading Feminist*, 116–42. Some favored male theorists in interdisciplinary work were Sigmund Freud, Roland Barthes, Paul Tillich, Claude Lévi-Strauss, and Clifford Gertz; more recently, Jacques Derrida and Jacques Lacan.

4. See Linda Alcoff, "Cultural Feminism Versus Post-Structuralism: The Identity Crisis in Feminist Theory," *Signs* 13 (1988): 405–36; also Teresa de Lauretis, "Eccentric Subjects: Feminist Theory and Historical Consciousness," *Feminist Studies* 16.1 (1990): 138.

5. Pat Mora, *Nepantla: Essays from the Land in the Middle* (Albuquerque: Univ. of New Mexico Press, 1993), 5.

6. Edward Said, *Culture and Imperialism* (New York: Knopf, 1993), 14.

7. Däumer, "Queer Ethics," 94.

8. Ibid., 99.

9. Eudora Welty, "Writing and Analyzing a Story," *The Eye of the Story: Selected Essays and Reviews* (New York: Random House, 1972).

10. Ibid., 111–12.

11. Eudora Welty, *The Optimist's Daughter* (New York: Random House, 1972). Further citations in the text refer to this edition. A shorter and different version appeared in March 1969 in the *New Yorker*.

12. A comparison with Edith Wharton's *Summer* might disclose interesting results (New York: McClure, 1917). Charity Royall's father is also a lawyer: Lawyer Royall.

13. I am indebted to Margaret Homans (*Bearing the Word* [Chicago: Univ. of Chicago Press, 1986]) for her expansive illustration of the difference these myths make in women's writing.

14. Patricia Yeager also reads Welty's representation of gender in terms of hyperbole. See "The Case of the Dangling Signifier: Phallic Imagery in Eudora Welty's 'Moon Lake,'" in *Faith of a (Woman) Writer*, 253–91.

15. The phrase "scrambled autobiography" was suggested to me by Nicole Ward Jouve, who reads criticism this way. See "*Ananas*/pineapple," *White Woman Speaks with Forked Tongue: Criticism as Autobiography* (London: Routledge, 1991). Welty critics are familiar with the autobiographical elements of the novel. Welty went north to study as a young woman and returned south to attend her sick mother. The primary revision in the novel, then, is the father's illness as Laurel's call to return and her eventual return north. Welty has remained in Jackson, Mississippi, for her entire writing career and still lives in the family home.

16. Eudora Welty, *One Writer's Beginnings* (New York: Warner Books, 1983).

17. Paul Smith, "Vas," in *Feminisms*, 1012.

18. This pattern reminds us of Wharton's method of turning gendered discourses and fields inside out.

19. A comparison with Charlotte Brontë's *Jane Eyre* seems promising.

20. Butler, *Gender Trouble*, 67.

21. The novel was published in 1972 and Laurel is about forty. That would mean she was born in the early 1930s and would suggest her mother's birth in the century's first decade.

22. On the French feminist concept of *l'écriture*, see Ann Rosalind Jones, "Writing the Body: Toward an Understanding of L'Ecriture feminine," in *The New Feminist Criticism: Essays in Women, Literature, and Theory*, ed. Elaine Showalter (New York: Pantheon, 1985).

23. I owe this insight to Elizabeth Lawrence, my research assistant.

24. Flieger, "Growing Up Theoretical," 264.

25. See Louise Westling, *Eudora Welty*, (Totowa NJ: Barnes and Noble Books, 1989), 160, for a similar reading of the pigeon memory. It teaches "a terrible truth about human dependency," she suggests.

26. I use "regression" (rather than "progression") to indicate the difference between the negotiating subject and the "pure" subject of the linear (and progressive) plot. (Regress: an act or the privilege of going or coming back, reentry; regression: a trend or shift toward a less perfect state [*Webster's New Collegiate Dictionary*, 10th edition]).

27. Jouve, "*Ananas*/pineapple," 29 and 32.

28. Anzaldúa, "La conciencia," 431–32.

29. The passage reads, "The difference was, their song almost floated with laughter: how different from the record, which growled from the beginning, as if the Victrola were only slowly being wound up" (epigraph to "Listening," in *One Writer's Beginnings*).

30. This is María Lugones's phrase. See "Playfulness, 'World'-Travelling, and Loving Perception," in *Haciendo Caras: Making Face, Making Soul*, ed. Gloria Anzaldúa (San Francisco: Aunt Lute Press, 1990), 402.

31. Judith Butler associates masquerade with lesbian feminism. See *Gender Trouble*, 46–54.

32. "Double-cross" is a term I borrow from Elizabeth Meese. See *Crossing the Double-Cross: The Practice of Feminist Criticism* (Chapel Hill: Univ. of North Carolina Press, 1986).

33. Butler, *Gender Trouble*, 149.

5. Sifting through Bags and Bones

1. I have been assuming throughout this book that narrative is a way of knowing. Theodore O. Mason Jr. makes this point in his analysis of Morrison as novelist: "Fictions . . . have a powerful epistemological effect, acting as a method of constructing and construing the world." See "The Novelist as Conservator: Stories and Comprehension in Toni Morrison's *Song of Solomon*," *Contemporary Literature* 29 (1988): 172–73.

2. Patricia Hill Collins, "The Social Construction of Black Feminist Thought," in *Black Women in America: Social Science Perspectives*, ed. Micheline R. Malson et al. (Chicago: Univ. of Chicago Press, 1990), 309. See also Eve Tavor Bannett, "The Logic of Both/And," *Genders* 15 (winter 1992): 1–20.

3. Henderson, "Speaking in Tongues," 120. She draws on the work of Mikhail Bakhtin and Hans-Georg Gadamer, making her work a clear instance of feminist theoretical negotiations. See pp. 118–21 especially.

4. Henderson, "Speaking in Tongues," 121.

5. Collins, "The Social Construction," 323.

6. William J. Spurlin, "Theorizing Signifyin(g) and the Role of the Reader: Possible Directions for African-American Literary Criticism," *College English* 52 (1990): 739.

7. Mary E. Hawkesworth, "Knowers, Knowing, Known: Feminist Theory and Claims of Truth," *Signs* 14 (1989): 551.

8. Melissa Walker, *Down from the Mountaintop: Black Women's Novels in the Wake of the Civil Rights Movement* (New Haven: Yale Univ. Press, 1991).

9. Quoted in Bernice Johnson Reagon, "Women as Culture Carriers in the Civil Rights Movement: Fannie Lou Hamer," in *Women in the Civil Rights Movement: Trailblazers and Torchbearers in 1941–1965*, ed. Vicki L. Crawford, Jacqueline Anne Rouse, and Barbara Woods, *Black Women in United States History*, vol. 16 (Brooklyn: Carlson, 1990), 214.

10. Quoted in Mamie E. Locke, "Is This America? Fannie Lou Hamer and the Mississippi Freedom Democratic Party," in *Women in the Civil Rights Movement*, 41.

11. Quoted in Reagon, "Women as Culture Carriers," 215.

12. Quoted in Locke, "Is This America?" 32.

13. Quoted in Reagon, "Women as Culture Carriers," 214.

14. Quoted in ibid., 215.

15. Quoted in "Life in Mississippi, An Interview with Fannie Lou Hamer," *Freedomways*, second quarter (1965): 235. See Fisher Fishkin, "Interrogating 'Whiteness,' Complicating 'Blackness,'" for a recent critical survey of this idea.

16. Quoted in *Ebony* (August 1971, Special Issue: "The South Today"): 51.

17. Reagon, "Women as Culture Carriers," 212. Another civil rights worker, Ella Baker, described a role for herself that illuminates my thinking about Pilate: "The kind of role that I tried to play was to pick up pieces or put together pieces out of which I hoped organization might come." Quoted in Carol Mueller, "Ella Baker and the Origins of 'Participatory Democracy' " in *Women in the Civil Rights Movement*, 51.

18. Several essays treat Morrison's use of names in the novel. See, for example, Lucinda MacKethan's essay, "Names to Bear Witness: The Theme and Tradition of Naming in Toni Morrison's *Song of Solomon*," *CEA Critic* 49.2–4 (1986–87): 199–207. See Gerry Brenner's "*Song of Solomon*: Rejecting Rank's Monomyth and Feminism," for a reading of Pilate that is both like and different from mine. He too sees in Pilate a "culture bearer" and analyzes her wisdom not in terms of her heroic stature but in terms of her intercessions. We differ in that Brenner thinks that such a female model cannot be celebrated by feminism. My project recommends that feminist criticism relocate itself in "intercessory" spaces and knowledges. Brenner's essay appears in Nellie Y. McKay, ed., *Critical Essays on Toni Morrison* (Boston: G. K. Hall, 1988), see especially pp. 121–23.

19. It is this male/female relating that Morrison says is crucial to Pilate's ontology: she "had a dozen years of close, nurturing relationships with two males—

her father and her brother. And that intimacy and support was in her and made her fierce and loving." See Mari Evans, "The Quest for Self," *Black Women Writers: A Critical Evaluation*, ed. Mari Evans (Garden City: Anchor Doubleday Press, 1984), 344.

20. Valerie Smith, "The Quest for and Discovery of Identity in Toni Morrison's *Song of Solomon*," *Southern Review* 21.3 (summer 1985): 726. A number of essays point out Pilate's significance but few are focused on her. Gay Wilenz does call Pilate "the focal character of the novel"; see Gay Wilenz, *Binding Cultures: Black Women Writers in Africa and the Diaspora* (Bloomington: Indiana Univ. Press, 1992), 82.

21. Genevieve Fabre, "Genealogical Archeology or the Quest for Legacy in Toni Morrison's *Song of Solomon*," in *Critical Essays on Toni Morrison*, 108.

22. Toni Morrison, *Song of Solomon* (New York: Plume, 1987), 145. Further citations refer to this edition, an authorized reprint of the hardcover edition published by Alfred A. Knopf in 1977.

23. See Lata Mani's "Multiple Mediations" for a discussion of how one's geographical location intensifies certain modes of knowing. Traveling and locating suggests Pilate's knowing through geographical and cultural negotiations. *Knowing Women: Feminism and Knowledge*, ed. Helen Crowley and Susan Himmelweit (Cambridge: Polity Press, 1992), 306–22.

24. Fabre, "Geneological Archeology," 110.

25. See Friedrich Nietzsche's formulation of this perspective in *Beyond Good and Evil* (New York: Penguin, 1973). Don Palmer brought to my attention this philosophical precedent to my project.

26. Luce Irigaray, *je, tous, nous: Toward a Culture of Difference*, trans. Alison Martin (New York: Routledge, 1993), 39.

27. I know of no one, as yet, who has theorized a positive reading of a placental figure, though Emily Martin's positive rethinking about the female and maternal body is suggestive. See her *The Woman in the Body: A Cultural Analysis of Reproduction* (Boston: Beacon Press, 1992). On the whole, the placenta is imagined as agentless and discardable. Marianne Hirsch helped me consider the figurative significance of Pilate's missing umbilicus in a conversation about this chapter, 1 June 1993.

28. Reagon, "Women as Culture Carriers," 206.

29. Ibid.

30. Quoted in Madelene Sprengnether, *The Spectral Mother: Freud, Feminism, and Psychoanalysis* (Ithaca: Cornell Univ. Press, 1990), 204.

31. Henderson, "Speaking in Tongues," 131.

32. My thanks to Carolyn Denard for suggesting the significance of this detail from the "recipe" and for supplying the term "relay" to indicate the form of this practice.

33. In Evans, "The Quest for Self," 344.

34. Harry Reed makes a similar point, noticing that Morrison does not seek to dissolve the conflict between Milkman and his mother but draws Pilate in, thus triangulating the dialogue and creating more space for learning. See "Toni Morrison, *Song of Solomon* and Black Cultural Nationalism," *The Centennial Review* 32.1 (1988): 50–64; Gay Wilenz points out that Pilate possesses a "special, dis-

credited knowledge," discredited because it privileges the spiritual world and an African-American tradition. Wilenz reads the novel to connect it with African sources (see "Toni Morrison, *Song of Solomon*" in *Binding Cultures*).

35. Cornel West, *Prophetic Reflections: Notes on Race and Power in America* (Monroe: Common Courage Press, 1993), 156.

36. Quoted in Reagon, "Women as Culture Carriers," 216.

37. Patricia Sharpe, F. E. Mascia-Lees, and C. B. Cohen, "White Women and Black Men: Differential Responses to Reading Black Women's Texts," *College English* 52 (1990): 146. See also Wilfrid D. Samuels, "Liminality and the Search for Self in Toni Morrison's *Song of Solomon*," *Minority Voices* 5.1–2 (1981): 59–68.

38. Haraway's words; see *Simians, Cyborgs, and Women*, 199.

6. Negotiated Motherhood

1. Tillie Olsen, *Silences* (New York: Delta/Seymour Lawrence, 1978), 254.

2. The significance of Piercy's choice has not lessened since the novel was published in 1976. See Angela Davis's "Outcast Mothers and Surrogates: Racism and Reproductive Politics in the Nineties," in *American Feminist Thought at Century's End*, 355–66.

3. Marge Piercy, *Woman on the Edge of Time* (New York: Fawcett Crest, 1976), 140; subsequent citations in the text refer to this edition. The novel was first issued in hard cover in 1976 and was almost immediately issued in this paperback edition which includes the entire text of the original. The original paperback edition is the one widely available today.

4. When Piercy was writing, all of these technologies were being newly explored. Since her novel appeared, contraceptive technologies have been increasingly debated in feminist circles. See Michelle Stanworth, "Birth Pangs: Contraceptive Technologies and the Threat to Motherhood," in *Conflicts in Feminism*, 288–304.

5. Carmen Cramer, for example, reads the novel as presenting the classic American conflict, pitting institution against individuality. Thus the novel, in Cramer's view, breaks down into two oppositional halves. See "Anti-Automaton: Marge Piercy's Flight in *Woman on the Edge of Time*," *Critique: Studies in Modern Fiction* 27 (1986): 229–318.

6. Angelika Bammer, *Partial Visions: Feminism and Utopianism in the 1970s* (New York: Routledge, 1991), 95.

7. Carol Gilligan, *In a Different Voice: Psychological Theory and Women's Development* (Cambridge: Harvard Univ. Press, 1982).

8. See Mary Fainsod Katzenstein and David Laitin for a discussion of the receptions of Gilligan's work; in "Politics, Feminism, and the Ethics of Caring," in *Women and Moral Theory*, ed. Eva Feder Kittay and Diana T. Meyers (Savage MD: Rowman & Littlefield, 1987), 261–81.

See also Victoria Davion's "Pacifism and Care," *Hypatia* 5 (1990): 90–100, for a response to Sara Ruddick's work. Davion questions whether there are any essential connections between mothering and pacifism (as Sara Ruddick seems to suggest). The exchange between Raquel Portillo Bauman and Susan R. Suleiman, "Comment on Suleiman's 'On Maternal Splitting' " and "Reply to Bauman," *Signs*

15 (1990): 653–59, is a good example of what might be called "anxious interchange about mothering" among feminists.

9. See Carolyn Heilbrun, "Female or Human," Review of Elaine Orr, *Tillie Olsen and a Feminist Spiritual Vision, Kenyon Review* 344 (spring 1988): 127.

10. Bauman, "Comment on Suleiman's 'On Maternal Splitting,'" 653.

11. Special issue edited by Debra Pope, Naomi Quinn, Mary Wyer, "Editorial," *Signs* 15 (1990): 441.

12. Stanworth, "Birth Pangs," 296.

13. Shulamith Firestone, *The Dialectic of Sex: The Case for Feminist Revolution* (New York: William Morrow, 1970), 72.

14. Catharine A. MacKinnon, "Reflections on Sex Equality under Law," *American Feminist Thought at Century's End*, 367–424.

15. See Tillie Olsen, *Tell Me a Riddle* (New York: Dell, 1989).

16. Ruddick, *Maternal Thinking*, 129.

17. Ibid., 183.

18. Ibid., 48 and 49.

19. For extensive unfoldings of the myth, see Sandra Messinger Cypess's *La Malinche in Mexican Literature: From History to Myth* (Austin: Univ. of Texas Press, 1991). See p. 151 especially.

20. Davis, "Outcast Mothers and Surrogates." R. Radhakrishnan, "Negotiating Subject Positions in an Uneven World," in *Feminism and Institutions*, ed. Linda Kauffman (Cambridge: Basil Blackwell, 1989); 276.

21. Kathryn Pyne Addelson, *Impure Thoughts: Essays on Philosophy, Feminism, and Ethics* (Philadelphia, Temple Univ. Press, 1991), 146.

22. Radhakrishnan, "Negotiating Subject Positions," 279.

23. Luce Irigaray's phrase from "This Sex Which Is Not One," in *New French Feminisms*, ed. Elaine Marks and Isabelle de Courtivron (New York: Schocken Books, 1981), 105.

24. Gloria Anzaldúa writes her own autobiographical account of medical abuses in words very like Piercy's wording of Connie's hysterectomy: "The doctor played with his knife. La Chingada ripped open, raped with the white man's wand. My soul in one corner of the hospital ceiling, getting thinner and thinner." Gloria Anzaldúa, "La Prieta," in *This Bridge Called My Back: Writing by Radical Women of Color*, ed. Cherrie Moraga and Gloria Anzaldúa (New York: Kitchen Table Press, 1983), 203.

25. I treat both worlds of Piercy's text as fiction. I am not concerned with whether Connie's imagines the future or "really goes there." I am concerned instead with the intrusion of each world upon the other and Piercy's oscillating narrative loyalties.

26. In her present, Dolly's life of prostitution provides the narrative that makes these meanings clear. This story is privileged in MacKinnon's work, though she would not call it a story. See, for example, MacKinnon's *Only Words* (Cambridge: Harvard Univ. Press, 1993).

27. Both women's names belittle and misname the women: "Dolly" infantalizes and objectifies; "Connie" is an Anglicized nickname.

28. Norma Alarcón, "Chicana's Feminist Literature: A Revision through Malintzin/or Malintzin: Putting Flesh Back on the Object," in *This Bridge Called My Back*, 185.

29. Davis, "Outcast Mothers and Surrogates." Diana Fuss, "Interior Colonies: Frantz Fanon and the Politics of Identification," *Diacritics* 24 (1994): 21.

30. MacKinnon, "Reflections on Sex Equality," 387.

31. Alarcón, "Chicana's Feminist Literature," 184.

32. Carmen Cramer comments on Connie's "invisibility"; see "Anti-Automaton," 229.

33. Perhaps theorists "know better," but I continue to be surprised at the energy that is applied to the father/mother/son model.

34. Ruddick, *Maternal Thinking*, 254.

35. As Bauman suggests, communities exist that already practice a more corporate form of mothering. Writing about her own child, she says, "When he is in another's care there is no fear that he will love me less and no concern that his love for my sister, sister-in-law, brothers, his father, his grandparents, for any other human will affect his love for me. . . . [I have] the sense that each of these people who love my son can give him a great deal" ("Comment on Suleiman," 653–55).

36. See Walker, "In Search of Our Mothers' Gardens."

37. Haraway, *Simians, Cyborgs, and Women*, 176.

38. Marcelle Marini, "Feminism and Literary Criticism: Reflections on the Disciplinary Approach," *Woman in Culture and Politics: A Century of Change* (Bloomington: Indiana Univ. Press, 1986), 153–54.

39. I continue to use the word "trade" to imply the risk Piercy takes here.

40. Radhakrishnan, "Negotiating Subject Positions," 277.

41. Paula Gunn Allen, "Grandmother of the Sun," in *Weaving the Visions: New Patters in Feminist Spirituality*, ed. Judith Plaskow and Carol P. Christ (San Francisco: Harper & Row, 1989), 27.

42. See Elizabeth Schussler Fiorenza's *In Memory of Her: A Feminist Theological Reconstruction of Christian Origins* (New York: Crossroad, 1983).

43. My language in this paragraph is influenced by Ross Chambers; see *Room for Maneuver*.

44. Haraway, *Simians, Cyborgs, and Women*, 193.

Epilogue

1. Judy Scales-Trent, *Notes of a White Black Woman: Race, Color, Community* (University Park: Pennsylvania State Univ. Press, 1995), 115.

2. Louise Erdrich, *Tracks* (New York: Harper & Row, 1988).

3. Riparian corridors are forested patches running along rivers and streams that reconnect areas severed by deforestation. These corridors help species survive. In claiming the metaphor, I take a figure that comes to us through the poor stewardship and short-sighted politics of expansionism and retool it as a site for respectful crossings, productive negotiations. Feminism has, after all, evolved from a history of patriarchal abuse. But it is also a space for utopian thought. If riparian corridors are enlarged (whether these are actual forest corridors or the corridors of feminist academic writing), more different species will dwell here; more life with flourish; and the more we will need to negotiate.

Index

abortion, 114–16
adoption, 106–26
accommodation: and criticism, 81; and Fannie Lou Hamer, 90; and *fault*, 30; in feminist negotiation, x, 8–9; in Hurston, 46–66; and progress, 67, 93; and resistance, 6, 49, 92; in Wharton, 27–45; in women's writing, 3–4, 24
actual and possible worlds: in Hurston, 62; in Morrison, 95, 104; in Piercy, 113–26; in Welty, 71, 83; in Wharton, 29–45. *See also* this-world and other-world
Addelson, Kathryn Pyne, 111
adjudication, poetics of, 54
affirmative deconstruction, 8, 43. *See also* deconstruction
African-American: critics, 87; feminist theory, 111; history, 111; letters, 49, 59; literary negotiations, 52; women's texts, *See also* feminist criticism; women writers
age, 105
Alarcon, Norma, La Malinche myth, 116
Allen, Paula Gunn, 123
American: defined, xiii; soul, 94; studies, 47
Ammons, Elizabeth, 29
ancestress, 8
annexing: as negotiating work, 21; in Wharton 36, 38
anxiety of audience, 46–47, 65
Anzaldua, Gloria, x, xii, 3, 128; "La conciencia de la mestiza," 14, 15, 20, 81
Apollo, 53
architecture: in Wharton, 31–32
Arkansas, 20
Artemis, 53
assemblage: as negotiating work, x, 15; in Welty, 78; in Wharton, 43
assimilation/resistance binary, 86
Atlantic slave trade in 1808, 61
audience, 22; black and white female, 46–66; differences in, 46–47, 53–55; overlap, 55. *See also* differences
autobiography: author's, 16–20; Hurston's, 46–51; Welty's, 67. See also *Dust Tracks on a Road*; *One Writer's Beginnings*
Awkward, Michael, *Negotiating Differences*, xiii, 47, 65

bag: Pilate's, 93, 94, 102–4; as political and narrative trope, 22, 25, 87
balance: and movement, 100; and negotiation, ix, 29, 118; question of, 31. *See also* imbalance
Baltimore, 49
Bammer, Angelika, 107
Bauman, Raquel Portillo, 108
Bazin, Nancy Topping, 29
Beaty, Robin, 29
Berlant, Lauren, xiii
Berry, Walter, 37, 38
between, working, xi; cultures, 16–20; in feminist texts, 23–24; fields and authorities, xiii, 13; in Hurston, 46–66; plots, 106–26; positions, 67; stories, 78; values, 64; in Wharton, 31–45. *See also* in-between
Biafran War, 17
binaries: feminist use of, 70; scrambled, 119
biracial women's discourse, in Hurston, 51–66
bisexuality, 16, 21; and epistemology, 69–87; Lily's, 39, 69, 84
black: American migration, 48, 85; English, 90; female subjectivity, 54; folk experience, 15, 92; middle class, 87–88; theory, xii; women privileged in Hurston, 48, 51, 65–65
blackness: preferred by Hamer, 90; problematized in Hurston, 51, 57–58; problematized in Morrison, 100–101
blacks, as undecidable sign, 56
black/white divide, 3, 101
Boaz, Franz, 49
body: female, 41–45, 77–79, 95–97, 106–26; maternal as agent, 123
borders and boundaries, 7–8, 15, 21, 36, 77, 91; against glorifying, 128

145

Index

borrowing: and feminist criticism, 65; as negotiating strategy, 8, 63, 68, 90
both/and/yet logic, 84
bricoleur, 84, 93
bridging: as device in Hurston, 62; La Malinche as, 111; in Welty, 69, 74; in Wharton, 34–35, 37–38; words as, 107–8
broker, 58
Brontë, Charlotte, 42
"brooder," 106, 108
Butler, Judith, xiii, 76, 84

canon: female, x; in feminist criticism, 71
centers, negotiated, 63, 66, 86, 127–28
Certeau, Michael de, xii
Chicana, 107, 110
Chinese box effect, 72, 76
choice: in feminism, 3, 6, 7, 9; in negotiation, x, 88; Pilate's, 103; in Welty, 76, 78; in Wharton, 33–34, 39. *See also* friendship
Christian doctrine: turned inside out, 99
civil rights movement, 2, 68, 89–91, 86–87
Civil War, 60
class consciousness: among slaves, 61
closed negotiations, 36. *See also* negotiation
coalition: as feminist desire, 37; Lily's desire for, 39, 43; noisy, xi; in relation to difference, 47; for spacial gain, 30
Cohen, C. B., 102
Collins, Patricia Hill: "The Social Construction of Black Feminist Thought," 86, 91, 96
colonialism, 8, 23; in Nigeria, 16–20
Columbia, 49
common concerns, 88, 99–100; features of novels, 21; feminist model, 20
compromise, xii, 1–2, 13, 19; and Fannie Lou Hamer, 88, 89; and Hurston, 50, 58; and Lily, 36; question of, 67 and Wharton, 29, 43–44
consciousness raising, ix
Constitution, 88
containment: beyond, 37; as a critical, political model, xii, 1
containment/subversion binary, and overdetermination of feminist interpretation, 27–28
contracts: exchange, 34; marriage and sorority as the same, 39–40; in Wharton, 31–37. *See also* trade
contradiction: and plot, 105–26; in feminism, 8, 70, 125–26; in thinking, 97; as writing strategy, 70
corridor, 42, 53, 54, 60; riparian, 127–30; textual, 60, 121, 122. *See also* threshold
Cortez, Hernando, 110, 124

critical fictions, ix, 2
crone, 74
cross-addressing, 66. *See also* audience
crossing: and Janie, 60–66; class and race, 72; criticisms, 1, 128; disciplines, xii; of gendered fields and parental legacies, 71–87; identities, 83; loyalties, 21; metaphors, 83; and negotiation, x; plots, 106–26; resources, 24
cultural: carrier, 90–91; centers negotiated, 53, 55; signs negotiated, 60, 63–64
culture: *high* and *low*, 50; mixed context, 52
cyborg, 120–21
cynicism, question of, 20
Cypess, Sandra Messinger, 110

Daumer, Elisabeth, "Queer Ethics," 16, 20, 69
danger in negotiation, xiii, 4, 13, 17–18, 65, 112–13; for black female feminists, 47; for Lily Bart, 27, 32–33. *See also* negotiation
Davis, Angela, 116, 119; "Outcast Mothers and Surrogates," 111, 114
debate: noisy, 120, 122. *See also* coalition
debts, 21; feminist, 66, 72, 106; narrative, 107–26
Decatur High School, 18
deconstruction, 5–6, 8–9, 12, 14, 20
deconstructive feminism, 21
Democratic Convention, 88–89
Derrida, Jacques, 9, 47, 123
dialectal mix, 89–90
dialogics: and middle positions, 70–87; and negotiation, 5, 64
dialogue, 14, 89, 101, 125
difference(s): accommodated, 39; altered, 55; and commonalities, 43, 69, 86; and feminism, xi, 5, 20–21, 27; as mediated, 79; and mothering, 118–26; as negotiation, 2, 65, 71; among women, 41–45, 46–47. *See also* anxiety of audience; feminist criticism; negotiation
Dimock, Wai-Chee, 28
diplomacy, 15–16, 25. *See also* shuttle
discursive adjudication, 56
Dixon, Roslyn, 29
domestic: fiction, 33–34; legacy, 71; novelist, 28; plot, 31; slave trade, 61
domination, beyond, 64. *See also* opposition(s), beyond
doorway: bisexuality as, 69; as trope for black opportunity, 90; in Welty, 77; in Wharton, 29. *See also* corridor; threshold
doppelganger, 15, 18
double-agent, 6

Index

double alliance: as negotiating position, 15
"double crossing," 83. *See also* crossing
double stance, toward gender, 98
"double step," 10
double vision, 125
Douglass, Frederick, 49
dream motif: in Piercy, 122; in Welty, 82–83; in Wharton, 43–45
Du Bois, W. E. B., 53

Easley, South Carolina, 18
either/or dichotomy, 90, 107
Eku, Nigeria, 18
epistemology: 7–8, 24–25; and bisexuality, 69–84; black women's, 86–87, 90–91; of in-between, 78–81; and migration, 60, 64; and mothering, 106–26; Pilate Dead's, 91–104. *See also* negotiation, and epistemology
equality: as feminist goal, x; question of, 13, 78, 89, 98, 101
Erdrich, Louise, *Tracks*, 129
essential(s): feminine, 108; question of, xii, 34, 68, 81, 95, 117, 119. *See also* identity
ethical reasoning: in feminism, 8, 16. *See also* negotiation, and epistemology
experience, women's, ix, x

Fabre, Genevieve, 92
fairy tale: in Welty, 82–84. *See also* negotiation, and myths of gender
family model and criticism, 68, 79, 81
father/daughter negotiation, 74–76
"fathers" and "mothers," ix; academic and cultural, 68–84
faults, judiciously used, 43
female: agency, 120; friendship, new model in Wharton, 41–45
femininity: openness to time travel, 105–26; as resource, 83–84. *See also* danger
feminist criticism, American, xii–xiii, 51, 67–68, 70–71, 105; and *anxiety of audience*, 46–47; befriending Lily, 44; black and white women in, 46–66; Connie Ramos as emblem for, 106–126; dialogical, xiii; differences in, x, xi, 3, 5–6, 20–21, 41–45, 47; imbalance in, 47; Laurel Hand as emblem for, 71–87; likeness in method, 3, 20–21; Lily Bart as emblem for, 29–45; New Age, 105; in the 1980s, ix; Phoeby and Janie as emblems for, 46–66; Pilate Dead as emblem for, 91–104; plots of, 2, 4; stages of, ix–x, 4–5, 20, 33, 46–47, 68, 70, 128; uniqueness of, 2
feminist ethics, x, 7–8

feminist fiction, xiii; negotiating plots in, 24–25, 56. *See also* women's writing
feminist-gender criticism, 84
feminist panels, x, 65
feminist theory: and actual life, ix, 7, 8, 11, 15–16, 16–20, 47, 68, 110, 127–30; and audience, 66; rise of, x
feminist writers, 21. *See also* feminist fiction; women writers
Fetterley, Judith, *The Resisting Reader*, 2
fictive and actual worlds, 2. *See also* actual and possible worlds; this-world and other-world
Finke, Laurie, xii
Firestone, Shulamith, 109
Flieger, Jerry Aline, 3, 5, 10, 13
Florida, 62; Eatonville, 61–62
folktale, 48, 49; as mediated, 63
food/text: trope in Hurston, 49, 54, 59
forked tongue: in feminism, 21
Foucault, Michael, 48
frame narrative: in Hurston, 48–66
friendship: and difference, 43; and Hurston, 50–66; black and white female as developed in Welty, 72; as Lily's choice, 33, 36; male and female as developed in Wharton, 31–45; Wharton's, 37–38
Fuss, Diane, 114

Gates, Henry Louis, 51, 129
gender: criticism, 84; division, 30, 33–35, 38, 50–51; negotiated in Welty, 71–84; positions negotiated, 50–51, 97, 107–26
generosity, 20; and feminist negotiation, 13; in Anzaldua, 15–16; as feature of feminist fiction, 24, 25; in Hurston, 59–60; in Morrison, 91–104; in Welty, 71–72; in Wharton, 30, 37, 40
Genovese, Eugene, 61
Gilligan, Carol, *In a Different Voice*, 108–9
giving away, question of, 96
giving up, question of, 3, 8–9, 19, 24–25, 35–36, 44, 99
go-between, xii, 4, 6, 12, 13; as agent of negotiating narratives, 24, 25, 74; and bisexuality, 16; maneuvers, 20–22; Phoeby as, 57–60; subjects, 23. *See also* intermediary; negotiating, character
Goodman, Susan, 29, 44
grafting: of audiences in Hurston, 47–66; of identities and landscapes in Wharton, 27, 42, 44; as negotiating work, xii, 21, 22
Great Migration, 56, 62, 64
Greek, 17
gynocriticism, xiii, 78

147

Index

Hamer, Fannie Lou: 86, 92, 102; and negotiating logic, 87–91; and negotiating rhetoric, 89–91
Haraway, Donna, xii, 11, 120, 125
Harding, Sandra, 47
Harlem Renaissance, 49, 50
Harlem Renaissance, reception in, 52, 54
Hawkesworth, Mary, 87
hearing: in Hurston, 52–60; in Piercy, 107–26
"hearts of knowledge," 128
Hemenway, Robert, 49, 55, 72
Henderson, Mae Gwendolyn, "Speaking in Tongues," 86, 91, 96–97
heterosexuality: and homosexuality, 69; nonsexist, 31; refigured, 42. *See also* friendship
heterosexual romance, in Wharton, 28–45
hinge, as sign of negotiation, 92
home: for African-American letters, 65; and feminism, x; in personal autobiography, 16–20
hooks, bell, x, 14, 15; 68 128; negotiating theory, 47–48
Howard University, 49
Hughes, Langston, 50, 53
humor and narrative negotiation, 74–75
Hurst, Fannie, 53, 57
Hurston, John, 49
Hurston, Zora Neale, xiii, 46–66; *Dust Tracks on the Road*, 48–49; father, 50, 72; her *hearing*, 54, 57; Janie, 4, 22, 25, 46–66, 105; personal negotiations, 3, 10, 21, 25, 49–51, 56; Phoeby, 22, 25, 46–56; *Their Eyes Were Watching God*, 85
hybridity, xii, 4, 48; in Hurston, 52, 54
hyperbole: negotiating strategy in Hurston, 48; strategy in Welty, 71, 73, 76
hyphen, 64

identifications, xi; differences and similarities between, 24; negotiating, 40; overlap in Hurston, 51, 64. *See also* between
identity: and Hurston, 51, 58, 65; black, 101–2; in dialogue, 39, 89, 103, 130; contradictions in, 67; daughter's, 73, 84; feminist, xiii; future, 117–26; inessential, 81; midlife, 68–87; politics, xiii, 5, 54; questioned, 103; white, xii
images of women, x
imaginary landscape, 6–7, 11, 16. *See also* space
imbalance: between black and white (feminists), 46–66. *See also* feminist criticism
impurity and feminist negotiation, xi, xii, 10, 11, 21, 23, 70, 128–29; of colonialism, 20; and reasoning, 93. *See also* purity
in-between, 46; bid for, 129; character, 71–87; dynamics of, 76; epistemology of, 79–80; position, 70; revision of daughter as, 80; text, 55. *See also* between; negotiation, and epistemology
independence, question of, 57–58
India, 8, 9
inset narrative: in Hurston, 51–66; in Welty, 76
inside/outside, ix, xi, 2, 3, 15–16, 21, 84, 105; as condition of black feminist thought, 86; and feminist mediation, 16; in Morrison, 92–93; in Piercy, 123; in Welty, 74; in Wharton, 31–32, 36–37, 38–40, 43
"insidership," 104, 105
intercessionist, 99–100. *See also* intermediary
intermediary: La Malinche, 110; Laurel as, 72; Pilate as, 85–104. *See also* middle, woman
interpretive communities, negotiating, 87
Irigaray, Luce, 95, 97
irony, question of, 9, 12, 15, 18; in Wharton, 30, 34, 38

Jacobs, Harriet, 12
James, Henry, xiv
Jameson, Frederic, 48

Kansas, 61
Kaplan, Amy, 29, 31
King, Martin Luther, Jr., 2, 86–87, 90, 97

lady authorship, and Edith Wharton, 27, 34, 42
La Malinche, 110, 124–25
language: changed in speech, 52–66; construction in, x; mother's and father's, 78. *See also* women and language
law, not deterministic, 76
lead: female, 21–24, 67, 94; bell hooks as, 47; potential for male, 129
leaning, as figure for negotiation in Piercy, 106–26
leaving, question of, 89–90, 103–4
l'ecriture féminine, 77
Le Guin, Ursula, "The Carrier Bag Theory of Fiction," 22
lesbian, 2, 14–16, 21, 105; as opposite of heterosexual, 69
lexicon, American feminist, 70. *See also* feminist criticism

Index

liberal pluralism, and containing center, 91
liminality, 2, 39, 59, 94, 102, 124. *See also* threshold
limits: and feminist writing, 4–5, 9, 22; and negotiation, x; progress within, xiii
Lionnet, Françoise, 48, 52
listener, in narrative, 51–60. *See also* narratee
little man and little woman, 51; as secondary, 55; as shifting politics, 56, 58–59
Locke, Alain, 53

MacKinnon, Catharine, "Reflections on Sex Equality under Law," 109–12, 114–15
Malcolm X, 86–87, 97
male: birth parent, 110, 118–19; discourses, 47; feminists, 66;
male literary power, 68; theorists, xi, 8–9; values, question of, 51
Mammy, 58
margin, as a feminist model, ix, 4, 12, 68, 71
marriage, in Wharton, 30–45. *See also* heterosexual romance
Mascia-Lees, F. E., 102
masculinist strategies, use of, 63, 73, 74–75. *See also* male
Mason, Mrs. R. Osgood, 50, 53, 55–57, 63, 72
maternal: costs, 109; imagery, 31, 41–45; labor forced, 112–16; thinking, 7–8, 109–26
Mattapoisetts, 106
mediating character, 73, 74, 92; as active, 59, 81, 83, 111; of the past, 107. *See also* middle, woman
Meese, Elizabeth, x, 3, 5, 128; *(Ex)tensions: Re-figuring Feminist Criticism* 5, 6, 7, 8, 10, 11, 12, 13, 21, 65, 68
memory, 106–26
Menkel-Meadow, Carrie, xi
mestiza, 14–16, 81, 110
metaphor(s), 83, 114, 124; reopened, 118–19, 124
methodology, xiii; and feminist criticism, 46
Mexican/American, xii, 14–15
Mexico, 15
middle: and epistemology, 81; and feminism, 126–30; player, 69; position and language, 79; question of agency in, 28, 70, 72, 74, 110; woman, 68–84. *See also* intermediary; mediating character
middle passage story, 61
middle way: in black women's texts, 47; in Wharton, 28, 38, 45

midlife, 68–84, 128. *See also* middle, woman
migration: and agency, 61; black, 58, 59–60, 85; as sign of negotiation, 64; and textual production, 60–66
migratory text, 53–60
Miller, Nancy K., x, xi, 5, 6, 7, 8, 12, 23, 86
Millet, Kate, *Sexual Politics*, 68
mis en abîme, 72
Mississippi Freedom Democratic party, 88
mistakes, Pilate's, 102–3
money, 22; and Janie, 63; and Lily, 29–30
Mora, Pat: *Nepantla: Essays from the Land in the Middle*, 68
Morrison, Toni, xiii; Pilate Dead (*Song of Solomon*), 21, 22, 25, 85–104, 105
mother: as sign, 106–26
mother/daughter negotiation, 76–81
motherhood, 107
mothering, 23; biological, 106–26; debates on, 68, 106–26; forced, 109–16; language of, 106–26; Pilate on, 98–99; "play," 111; sign of care, 116–20; silenced, 112, 114
mother's: double legacy, 76–81; writing, 77–81
The Mount, 31
movement, xi, 94; and black politics, 90–91; between positions, xii, 5–6, 16–20, 30; as fictive/political device in Hurston, 52–53, 56, 60, 65; and in-between locations, 75–76; Lily Bart's, 32–44; and negotiation, xi, 12, 14; in Piercy, 121–26; Pilate's, 93, 100; in textual production, 49–66; and thinking, 86, 100; in Wharton, 28, 42, 44. *See also* migration, black; oscillation
mulatto: agency in, 63; in Hurston, 48–66; and mediation, 60
multiple attachments and commitments, 27–28, 30, 36, 37, 70, 101, 117. *See also* sides

naming, 10, 16–20, 84, 100, 130
narratee, 55
narrative and political openings, in Wharton, 36–37, 45, 69, 77. *See also* threshold
narrative relay, 12
Native American: influence in Piercy, 119–20, 129
"native" position, 19
navel, Pilate's, 95
Nazis, 9
negotiating: character, 92; history, 62–66; identities, 40; narrative, 61; plot, 107–26; positions, 107; reason, 35; subjectivity, 85; with violence, 9–10, 60–61, 106–26. *See also* negotiation

149

Index

negotiation: and autobiography, 16–20, 46–51; between black and white female feminists, 46–66; and blackness, 101–2; black political, 2, 61; dailiness of, 22, 90–91, 97; definitions of, x–xii, xiii, 3, 13–14, 16; and economics, 88–89; emergence of, xi; and epistemology, 7–8, 11, 13, 16, 24–25, 60, 69–84, 86–104; Fannie Lou Hamer as model for, 86–91; of gender and sexuality in Welty, 71–87; of gender in Morrison, 97; internal and external, xi, 7, 10, 12, 16–20, 25, 85, 94, 122–23; as interpretive model, 1–2, 8; legal, xi; moderation of, 11, 47; as movement, 6, 55; and myths of gender, 69–87; as narrative, 22–26; open-endedness of, xii, xiv, 23–24, 36, 60, 108, 121; and race, 47–66, 86–91; as sign, 46; of sorority and marriage in Wharton, 31–45; topology of, 24–26; traditional, 29, 32–36, 38; within feminism and between critical schools, 6. *See also* movement
"negotiation our text," 27, 29
"Negrotarians," 56
New Age, 106
New Woman, and social work, 30, 33, 42
New York, 30
Nietzsche, Friedrich, 9
Nigeria, 17, 18, 127; as British colony, 20

Ogbomosho, Nigeria, 16, 19
O'Grady, Lorraine, 52
Oklahoma, 61
Old Woman, 33
Olsen, Tillie, 106, 109
openness: danger in, 112–13. *See also* danger in negotiation
oppositional: model of negotiation, xi–xii; politics, 1. *See also* opposition(s)
opposition(s): beyond, 3, 14–15, 21, 33, 44, 46, 59; as determinative in feminist criticism, 28–29; indifference of, 31, 35; in narrative, 23; productive relations with, 2, 37, 44, 67, 71, 85, 91, 93
optimism, xii; in feminist criticism, 87, 127–28; in Welty, 75–87
oral transmission, 46–66, 96
originality, ideology of, 58
oscillation, 8, 14, 15; authorial, 25; feminist critics', 68; and Lily Bart, 32–33, 38; as plotting device, 24, 28, 64, 76; as politics, 49, 89; and reason, 99; as swapping, 64. *See also* movement; negotiation
Ostriker, Alicia, 2
othering, xi, 70; question of, 63

otherness within, 12, 16, 18–20, 43, 51, 86. *See also* difference
other(s): 47, 81, 89–90; Americans, 89; audiences, 54, 64, 96, 102, 104; women, 10, 24, 106; women's labor, 78–79, 111
overlap: as constituting fictive and critical negotiations, 21, 28, 31, 62, 123–26; in feminist theory, 111; umbilicus as figure of, 95–96

Parker, Alice, 65
"peculiar affirmation," 75
"per," 117
peripatetic characters, 28, 37, 38, 52, 55, 60, 75, 80
Persephone, 74
personal and political, in feminism, 8
Phoenicians, 53
Piercy, Marge, 10; "leads," 21; Connie Ramos (*Woman on the Edge of Time*), 23, 25, 125–26
placenta, textual, 95–96. *See also* navel; umbilicus
plot: domestic and resistant, 31; female, 35, 45; lateral and oscillating rather than vertical and linear, 24, 28, 64; marriage, 38; Piercy's, 105–26. *See also* oscillation; movement
porch: and narrative desire, 64; as negotiating space, 48–66
possible past, 107, 121
postcolonial, 21
postmodernism, xiii, 14, 52
poststructuralism, 10, 118
power, transformative, 120–26
power relations, xi, 9, 68; and Fannie Lou Hamer, 89–91; in Hurston, 55–56, 59, 62, 63; negotiated in Welty, 76–77; in Piercy, 114; shifting, 4, 12, 14–15, 24, 42, 119; in Wharton 33, 42
private ownership, 119; of identity, 102
privilege and negotiation, 8–9, 16–20
production of (female) self, 16, 46, 60. *See also* self-making
purity, 4, 44, 52, 54, 65, 81, 91; Hamer's argument against, 90. *See also* impurity

queer, 14–15, 19–20
Queer Theory, xiii

race: against essentializing, 65; revised, 119
race, class, gender, 5
racialized subjectivity, 47
Radhakrishnan, R., 111

150

Index

Reagon, Bernice Johnson, 90, 96
realism: literary, 110; and romanticism negotiated in Wharton, 39–45
Reconstruction, 62, 85
recycling, 13, 59, 92, 118, 119–20; narrative in Welty, 71. *See also* revision
relay, critical, 60, 104; as figure for negotiation, 94, 98
reproduction, 107
resistance, x–xi; and accommodation or connection, 21, 31, 92. *See also* accommodation
"resting" and negotiation, 9
revision: in Welty, 71, 82; in Wharton, 43–45
rice, mulatto: in Hurston, 54–60
Rich, Adrienne, 3; "Negotiation the Metalogic," 5, 8, 21
Rouch, Helene, 95
Ruddick, Sara, 7, 109–11, 116–17
Russ, Joanna, *The Female Man*, 107

Said, Edward, 48, 68
sameness: among feminist critics and women, 44; within, 86, 97, 103
Scales-Trent, Judy, *Notes of a White Black Woman*, 127–28
scenes of power, x–xi, 13, 16, 24, 27
self-consciousness, x, 5, 10; liabilities of, 47; need for, 78–79; 63
self-effacement: in Morrison, 98; as negotiating device in Hurston, 58–60; in Welty, 69–70, 83. *See also* feminine
self-making, 20–21, 28–29, and Hurston, 48–51. *See also* production of (female) self
self-reflexivity, 12; in Hurston, 51, 54. *See also* self-consciousness
separatism: beyond, 38, 39, 54, 55, 58, 121; as a feminist model, x, 2, 4, 11, 13, 21–22
setting aside, 9, 13, 100
sexual accomplice, 6
sharecroppers, 88. *See also* tenant farmers
Showalter, Elaine, 2, 28, 68
shuttle, 6, 12–13; as feature of feminist fiction, 25, 56, 76, 80–81
sides, ix; in Hurston, 59; multiple, 47; in negotiation, xii, 7, 12, 13, 16; in Piercy, 107–26; in Pilate's knowledge, 95, 100; in Welty, 70, 75, 76, 83; in Wharton 37, 44
sieve, as negotiating tool, 81, 128
silence and negotiation, 1–2, 3, 10–11, 79. *See also* negotiation
Sleeping Beauty, 83
Smith-Rosenberg, Carroll, 33

Snitow, Ann, 5; "A Gender Diary," 6, 7, 8, 10, 11
solidarity and exchange, 48
sorority: refigured, 42; in Wharton, 28–45. *See also* friendship
sourcebook, 104
Southern Baptist, 16
space: between, 64; for change, 13; for complex audience, 64–66; for debate in Piercy, 107–26; for the daughter, 79; enlarged, 95; interval, 52, 64; and knowledge, 94–95; lack of, 113–14; middle, 44–45; negotiated in Hurston and Welty, 70; negotiated in Wharton, 31–45; to reason, 99; shared, 20; for women and feminists, 12, 15–16, 24, 30, 36, 46
spiritual guide, 93
Spivak, Gayatri, 5, 112, 128; "Feminism and Deconstruction," 8, 9, 10, 11, 13, 43, 75; "peculiar affirmation," 75, 88
sponsorship: male, 38; white, 50, 56, 65
Spurlin, William, "Theorizing Signifyin(g) and the Role of the Reader," 87
Stanworth, Michelle, 108–9
subaltern, female, 8–9, 88, 112
"subject to negotiation," 23
subversion: challenge to: 29, 39, 49, 51, 54, 60, 73, 78; as a feminist model, ix, x, xi, 1, 2, 4, 11, 21–22, 26; pure rhetoric of, 23
Suleiman, Susan R., 108
surrogacy, forced, 111, 114
swapping, as sign of negotiation, 59–60, 64–66
sympathy and criticism, 33, 37–38, 94, 100

technology, negotiating, 65, 106–26
tenant farming, 62
"third character": in Morrison, 92, 100; in Welty, 69–87. *See also* intermediary; middle, woman
Third World, 13
this-world, and other- or better-world, xii, 11, 16, 106; elements of negotiating narratives, 22–23; with Phoeby and Janie, 22. *See also* utopian
threshold: in Morrison, 94; in Welty, 73; in Wharton, 30–45. *See also* doorway; liminality
time travel, 25, 106–26
Tompkins, Jane, x
trade: against, 34, 37–38, 42, 44, 127; in Piercy's narration, 123; in women, 29, 32, 35, 110

151

Index

Uhrobo, 18, 19
umbilicus, 106; Pilate's, 95. *See also* placenta
Underground Railroad, 61
unequal positions, 6, 15
"up from slavery," 60
utopian: edge, 15; fiction, 107, 110; figure, 22; link, 120; outposts, xii; program, 15; visions, 4

violence: negotiating with, 98–101; past of, 104
vision, loss of, 72
voice, 22, 25

Walker, Alice, 13, 50–51; "female artistic genealogy," 78, 120; *In Search of Our Mothers' Gardens*, 68
Walker, Melissa, 87
Wallace, Michael, 47
Warner, Michael, xiii
Washington, Mary Helen, 50
Welty, Eudora: 21, 26, 65; as feminist, 77, 80; Laurel Hand, 4, 25, 67–84; 105; *One Writer's Beginnings*, 69, 72, 78, 82; *The Optimist's Daughter*, 103; "Writing and Analyzing a Story," 69
West, Cornel, 101, 129
Wharton, Edith, xii, 3, 25, 48; 65; *The Decoration of Houses*, 31; *The House of Mirth*, Lily Bart, xii, 4, 21, 23, 24, 25, 27–45, 103, 105; personal negotiations, 28, 29, 34, 37–38
white: American feminism, 96; critics and theorists, 47–48; feminism negotiated, 48;
identity, 90; middle-class women, 108; privilege, 65; sponsor, 56; violence, 60; women authors, 65
whiteness, 16–20, 47, 63; blackness in, 90
Whitman, Walt, "Song of Myself," 90
woman, ix; as undecidable sign, 56; Derrida's, 9, 107
woman: as object, against, 39, 43, 113, 116; new definition, 44
womanist, 13–14, 45, 66, 85
women, black and white: complexity between, 62–63; in Hurston's fiction, 60–66; market in, critiqued, 42
women and language, Welty's story of, 77–81
women's fiction, xiii; American, 3, 105; and audience, 46–66; plots in, 56. *See also* women's writing
women's voice, 4
women's writing, xiii, 23, 26; agency, 46; differences in, x; twentieth century American, xii–xiii; working class, 43. *See also* feminist criticism; women's fiction
word(s): leverage with, 117; matter, 116; migratory, 55, 59–60
working class, 30, 43, 64, 105; mothers, 106
Working Girls' Clubs, 35
"world-travelling," 83
Wright, Richard, 3, 51

Yoruba, 16, 17, 18, 19

zero-sum negotiation, 101, 124

Feminist Issues: Practice, Politics, Theory

CAROL SIEGEL
*Lawrence among the Women: Wavering Boundaries
in Women's Literary Tradition*

HARRIET BLODGETT, ED.
*Capacious Hold-All: An Anthology of
Englishwomen's Diary Writings*

JOY WILTENBURG
*Disorderly Women and Female Power in the Street Literature
of Early Modern England and Germany*

DIANE P. FREEDMAN
*An Alchemy of Genres: Cross-Genre Writing by
American Feminist Poet-Critics*

JEAN O'BARR AND MARY WYER, EDS.
Engaging Feminism: Students Speak Up and Speak Out

KARI WEIL
Androgyny and the Denial of Difference

ANNE FIROR SCOTT, ED.
Unheard Voices: The First Historians of Southern Women

ALISON BOOTH, ED.
Famous Last Words: Changes in Gender and Narrative Closure

MARILYN MAY LOMBARDI, ED.
Elizabeth Bishop: The Geography of Gender

HEIDI HUTNER, ED.
Rereading Aphra Behn: History, Theory, and Criticism

PETER BURGARD, ED.
Nietzsche and the Feminine

FRANCES GRAY
Women and Laughter

NITA KUMAR, ED.
Women as Subjects: South Asian Histories

ELIZABETH A. SCARLETT
Under Construction: The Body in Spanish Novels

PAMELA R. MATTHEWS
Ellen Glasgow and a Woman's Traditions

MAHNAZ AFKHAMI
Women in Exile

DEIRDRE LASHGARI, ED.
Violence, Silence, and Anger: Women's Writing as Transgression

CATHERINE HOBBS, ED.
Nineteenth-Century Women Learn to Write

PATRICIA MORAN
*Word of Mouth: Body Language in
Katherine Mansfield and Virginia Woolf*

ELAINE NEIL ORR
*Subject to Negotiation: Reading Feminist Criticism and
American Women's Fictions*